# SHARPER

*Bringing It All Back Home*
*Part Two: 1980-2013*

THE BIOGRAPHY OF
MARTIN SHARP AS TOLD TO
LOWELL TARLING

**ETT IMPRINT**
EXILE BAY

First published by ETT Imprint, Exile Bay 2017

This book is copyright. Apart from any fair dealing for the purposes of private study, research, criticism or review, as permitted under the Copyright Act, no part may be reproduced by any process without written permission. Inquiries should be addressed to the publishers.

ETT IMPRINT
PO Box R1906
Royal Exchange NSW 1225
Australia

Copyright © Lowell Tarling 2017
Photographs copyright © photographers as noted within
All OZ and Sharp covers courtesy of University of Wollongong
ISBN 978-0-925706-16-1 (paper)
ISBN 978-0-925706-17-8 (ebook)

Design by Hanna Gotlieb

*Synchronicity is an ever present reality for those who have eyes to see.*

*Carl Jung*

# THANKS

The first and greatest thanks to Martin.

Secondly, I would like to thank my family: Amber, Joel and Zoë, and especially my wife Robbie who urged me to transcribe all my taped interviews, pushed me to write this biography, listened to every draft chapter and made innumerable suggestions.

*Roger Foley and Tim Lewis read the entire manuscript and made suggestions and corrections. Other individual chapters were read and corrected by Tony Bond, Mic Conway, Peter Draffin, Sam Marshall, Michael Organ, Dave Rowe, Peter Royles, Robert Tilley, Greg Weight, Robert Wolfgramm.*

Thanks to Tom Thompson who made this production possible.

And to all who I have not mentioned by name, who spoke with me and emaied me, whose words and ideas I have used, my heartfelt thanks.

# TABLE OF CONTENTS

1. The Funfair & the Nightmare
2. Wirian
3. Hokusai, Elvis and the Dingo
4. Unpicking the Code
5. Devil in the Detail
6. Tidying Up
7. The Brighton Cut
8. This is Not the Yellow House
9. Courage My Friend
10. Tiny Tiptoes Off-Stage
11. Gospel According to Martin
12. Greatest Editor
13. Telford, Travel and the Tiny Tim Show
14. Changing Dimension
15. Hippie Hippie Shock
16. Poverty Delux
17. Stayin' Alive
18. Why Martin Matters

Notes
Bibliography
Index

# 1.
# THE FUNFAIR AND THE NIGHTMARE

*I heard bikies talking about kerosene and matches in the Ghost Train.
Because of their attitude I gathered that they had lit the fire.*
Leslie Dowd

Luna Park was closed immediately after the fire and a Federal Inquest was held into its cause. Coroner Kevin Anderson resolved nothing in declaring, 'The cause of the fire cannot conclusively be stated', adding somewhat gratuitously, 'a statement made to Police soon after the fire indicated that it had been deliberately started, that statement had been shown to be false and mischievous'. [1] False and mischievous! *He doth protest too much* - is what Martin reckoned.

Witness Tina Shakeshaft testified that she overheard someone in a group say, 'You shouldn't have done that' followed by talk of kerosene and matches. (2) Her companion, Trevor Dinsmore backed her account. [3] By-stander Robert Baikie said, 'I heard someone mention a jet of flame. I thought, well, how on earth can an electrical fire start a jet of flame?' [4] And Leslie Dowd added, 'I heard one or two bikies talking about kerosene and matches in the Ghost Train...because of their attitude I gathered that they had lit the fire'. [5]

The Park owners were found not guilty of criminal negligence and so – to general relief – they avoided criminal prosecution but didn't get off unscathed. The Inquest publicly criticised their 'reluctance' to implement full and proper fire precaution measures. [6] Management took it hard. As the sorry tale seeped out, many people felt guilty. Leon Fink 'did a lot of weeping,' said Martin, adding, 'He did confess to me one night that he felt one eighth responsible'. [7] Summing up the artists' feelings Peter Kingston (Kingo) admitted, 'We were all culpable'. [8] Martin also carried that weight, 'There are some who are consciously responsible but a lot of people are unconsciously responsible. We (the artists) made it look safe.' (9)

Martin came to believe the fire was the collective negligence of the entire City of Sydney. But the cause, Martin believed, was a deliberate criminal act. He was convinced that Abe Saffron had hired a bikie gang to torch the park to make way for future developments. Said Martin, 'Juanita Nielson disappeared from the Carousel Club at the Cross - that was the connecting bond between her and Abe Saffron. (Plus you get the same fairground imagery – the Carousel, right?) He's also the secret figure behind Luna Park'. (10)

Abraham (Abe) Gilbert Saffron was third generation Australian Russian-Jewish stock, born in inner-Sydney Annandale (1919). He attended Fort Street High School. His mother wanted him to study medicine but Abe was too street-smart for that. By the age of 8 he was dealing in cigarettes, selling them to his father's card-playing kitchen-table friends. Abe quit school at 15 to pursue a career in the family drapery business Saffron & Sons. His extra-curricular business activities got him into trouble.

Shortly before World War 2 Abe was caught being a runner for an SP bookie. His second brush with the law came in 1940 when he was caught selling six 'hot' car radios. Author Duncan McNab wrote, 'The magistrate took a rather dim view of his enterprises and gave him six months' imprisonment for shock value, then suspended the sentence on the proviso that Abe was of good behaviour. He went back to the family business.'

In January 1942 (a fortnight before Martin was born) Abe started two-years service as an enlisted soldier. After his discharge, Abe signed up for a stint in the merchant navy where he ran into an old friend, Hilton Kincaid who treated wartime rationing like six years of opportunity. Caught with 60 bottles of whisky, Kincaid was suspended from duty for three months and not deemed an appropriate person to hold a Hotelier's License. This is why he needed Abe to partner his future operations after they both left the navy in July 1944.

These were the days of the '6 o'clock swill' where all pubs were legally required to close at 6.00pm, so there was a lively market for sly grog. Abe Saffron & Hilton Kincaid's first pub was in Kurri Kurri, then Hotel Newcastle, West End Hotel Balmain, Gladstone Hotel Darlinghurst, also pubs in Bankstown, Mortdale, North Sydney and the Civic, corner of Goulburn and Pitt Streets Sydney. Every deal was a partnership, sometimes involving Abe's brother Henry. These acquisitions gave them the leverage to buy the Roosevelt nightclub in Orwell Street Kings Cross, in 1947, the jewel in their crown.

The Roosevelt was the toast of Sydney society and the second home of American commissioned officers. It was a top glamour spot for senior police with their demoiselles and sometimes their wives. The Roosevelt comprised restaurant facilities, singers, musicians, dancers, baccarat, sly grog, burlesque and (later) topless showgirls who – like London's better known *Windmill Theatre* – were permitted to bare their breasts if they didn't move, like a tableaux. Women wore evening gowns and gloves. Men wore suits and silk ties. Abe gave plenty of money to charities, treated his staff like family and was regarded as one of the outstanding young men of Sydney's business community.

However, in 1951 Abe was required to give evidence at a Royal Commission into the amount of alcohol being consumed outside the legal trading hours. The proceedings exposed Abe's network of silent partnerships, revealing that he owned many more slices of the pie than anybody had previously thought. Five years later the press trashed his reputation. For someone who eschewed publicity, Abe must have found the hypocrisy disturbing – (Protestant revenge on an up-jumped Jew?). The Vice Squad raided his Macleay Street office and found a feather duster, an electric vibrator, (deemed 'obscene'), a copy of Marquis de Sade's *120 Days of Sodom* (on the banned list) and other paraphernalia - like a camera. It was an exciting court case being the only way Sydney-siders ever saw words like 'sodomy', 'vibrator' and 'penis-like fertility symbol' in print. The case was eventually dropped but Saffron emerged with a sleazy reputation. The Roosevelt and other Saffron establishments suffered a downturn. [11]

Towards the close of the 50s Abe teamed up with another old friend, entertainment entrepreneur Lee Gordon, an American living in Australia. Lee had contacts and Abe had collateral. They brought Frank Sinatra to Sydney, which made them plenty of money. Author Duncan McNab, surmises that meeting Sinatra in Las Vegas may have been Abe's first brush with organised crime. The success of the Sinatra show spurred them to bring out Top 40 acts that Martin and his art school friends faithfully attended at Sydney Stadium: Nat King Cole, Harry Belafonte Johnny Cash, Crash Craddock, Chubby Checker, Bobby Rydell,. Roy Orbison - 'everybody'. [12]

By the 1960s, Abe had interests along the Dirty Half Mile between El Alamein Fountain to the Coca Cola sign at the Darlinghurst Road and William Street intersection. Clubs included the Pink Panther, Persian Room, Venus Room, Crazy Horse, Les Girls and the Pink Pussycat. By now Abe was acquainted with heavies like Lennie McPherson, Big Jim Anderson, Last Card Louie and the Black Prince.

Family was one thing – business another. Abe's wife Doreen persuaded her husband to purchase a smart 3-storey residence in Hopetown Avenue Vaucluse, which became the Saffron family home. In 1969 Abe moved office from 44 Macleay Street (across the road from Clune Gallery) to Lodge 44, 44 New South Head Road. About the time Abe moved out of Macleay Street, Martin and the Yellow House team moved in. The Yellow House was almost opposite Abe's former Macleay Street office.

The police certainly noticed the Yellow House. Sex and drugs were associated with the premises, so they dropped in hoping for a payoff. They had no idea what Hippies were about and were disappointed to find an art place not a bordello. Roger Foley (Ellis D Fogg) recalled, 'I was there when the police came around.

They knew there were a lot of women in the Yellow House. They thought it was some kind of brothel. They never actually asked for money but implied that something could be arranged. There was a lot of sex going on in the place - but it was free. That's when they lost interest.' [13]

Roger's girlfriend performed at Sandra Nelson's club (not a Saffron club). Gretel Pinniger, known as Madam Lash, took part in a televised discussion panel in which she openly spoke about corruption in the Kings Cross Vice Squad. According to her biographer, Abe wanted her rubbed out! Fortunately for Gretel, one of her suitors Lennie McPherson stepped in and calmed the waters. [14]

Like all Yellow House residents, Jonny Lewis had to deal with underworld characters whose aggression might turn on a whim. Jonny described one encounter, 'Peter Wright and I were in the bar at *Juillet's*. Jimmy Sweeten was there. He pulled a gun out, put it in my tummy and clicked the chambers click-click-click-click. I was that stoned I don't think I responded the way he wanted me to - I just ordered my drink.' [15]

David Litvinoff had genuine underworld connections, as he did in London. Sometimes he bought heroin and kept it secret. The Yellow House tribe were acid-eaters and stoners, they had no interest in smack. As the 70s progressed, Martin would see *'the needle and the damage done'* when heroin ravaged some of his closest friends and associates, so he grew to hate the stuff.

By the mid-70s Abe's business arrangements had become increasingly complex. Although his name doesn't appear on the documents, he had a piece of the action in most fringe entertainment venues on that Dirty Half Mile. One example - in 1977 Togima Leasing P/L acquired a lease where Kings Cross Station now stands. The Saffron name was absent even though Togima was a Saffron corporate entity. The premises were retail sex downstairs and gambling upstairs. Although his name is not on the documents, in like manner, Saffron certainly had a business interest in Luna Park, especially in the gaming machines. [16]

Martin continued, 'Anyway - skip 18 months or so – I'm at Wirian, cutting the film, Haydn Keenan's working with me and some friends of his came over who were drunk and mandied. A really heavy-looking chick had black hair and a white face. She was beautiful in a sinister way and very out of it. She gets bored with the film, comes out and says, "I used to work at the Park". I said, "Oh, really?" She said, "I used to work in the Magic Shop". And I said, "Oh?" (*Bang-Bang-Click-Click.*) She said, "Yeah, Abe got me the job there. He runs it with two Sydney businessmen". So Abe was involved back then! Abe had the Magic Shop and all these bloody spooky monster images were radiating out. That was the beachhead he took the place from.' [17]

Martin embarked on an intense study of spiritual significators pointing to aspects of the Luna Park story. Police and Inquest statements were just the beginning. Martin kept press clippings, photographs, extracts from occult encyclopedias, metaphysical indicators, symbolic evidence and Biblical verification.

Examples: (1) the name 'God-son', (2) $13 price tags at the Magic Shop, (3) the Pope on a train to Auschwitz for the first time ever, (4) Bob Dylan recording his *Slow Train Coming* album, and (5) Saffron's Jewish connection, 'Behold, I will make them of the synagogue of Satan, who say they are Jews and are not' Revelation 3:9. Martin made a point of following the imagery – masks, skeletons, clocks – and if couldn't figure what it all meant, he was damn sure it meant something!

Tenders for the use of the park site were called on 31 July 1979. These were hastily withdrawn and responsibility shunted from the Department of Lands and Services to the Premier's Department. That switch meant that as prime real estate, Luna Park could be bulldozed and turned into a casino, a World Trade Centre, high-rise apartments or anything else. This sparked an urgent call to action. Martin, Kingo, Richard Liney and Tim Lewis started an affirmative action group known as *Friends of Luna Park*. Towards the close of 1979 they staged three exhibitions of toys and memorabilia as part of their strategy for generating wider public concern.

When State Government regrouped for discussion, it decided to stay with a theme park concept - modernised where necessary - in line with what was happening to such parks all over the world. The government called for a second round of tenders. After considering them all, it concluded that none satisfactorily met the requirement to provide amenities similar to those available before. A third round of tenders was called in March 1980.

One of the Friends of Luna Park, Sam Marshall, witnessed the next development. He wrote, 'Realising the gravity of the situation, the artists who made up Friends of Luna Park were joined by people of all backgrounds, professions, ages and municipalities to preserve Luna Park.

While the tenders were being considered, Friends of Luna Park staged a "Save Luna Park Day" on 28 June 1980. Support for the traditional Luna Park was demonstrated by a protest march from the Opera House over the Bridge to the Face where a free concert appropriately headlined by rock group Mental As Anything included a play by Bundenna school children – "Luna's Longest Laugh". Friends of Luna Park was concerned that one of the world's last traditional amusement parks would become a casino or an American-style theme park. At the rally it was announced that, at the Friends request, the National Trust had classified the face and towers as items of national heritage, and given the rest of the Park a "recorded" classification.' [18]

As well as contributing artwork and other resources, Martin arranged for these events to be filmed and spliced into his film about Tiny. He thanked Friends of Luna Park in his film credits.

Following their success, Friends of Luna Park held a well-attended public meeting in the Lower Sydney Town Hall in mid-July. Three months later the Department of Public Works commissioned the group to prepare a formal report – known as *The Luna Park Report* - in which they would make recommendations for the individual rides and the future of the whole park. For the next five years, a bound copy of this A3-document had a permanent place somewhere on the long table in Martin's Inner Sanctum studio. [19]

On 23 September 1980 the lease was granted to Australian Amusements Associates (later known as Harbourside Amusements). Harbourside Amusement Park Pty Ltd comprised: Sir Arthur George, brothers Harold and Colman Goldstein, Brian Treasure, Michael Edgley – all co-directors, and David Baffsky as solicitor. [20]

'It looked like a very solid sort of thing,' said Martin. 'The public get given what looks like a strong show business team. Suddenly it falls apart, Edgley drops out.' [21] Leaving, Brian Treasure who had a business connection with Saffron, Harold and Colman (Col) Goldstein his first cousins once removed, David Baffsky was Saffron's lawyer. And a Saffron-controlled company Arcadia Amusements & Vending hired its machines to Harbourside Amusements.

Martin said, 'I go along to a party. I see Marcia (Premier Wran's first wife). She says, "What's happening at Luna Park?" I say, "Col Goldstein has got it". She says, "Col Goldstein! Abe's always wanted that". I can't believe it! She said, "Abe's always wanted the Park!" Col Goldstein is Abe Saffron's cousin! And the whole thing went snap - one step further into place.' [22]

In a taped statement made to Russell Sharp, Maurice Spatt confirmed what was said, 'The winners of the tender have screwed the government. You know who you are dealing with? Abe Saffron. You know who's behind this? Sir Arthur George, Col Goldstein and his brother, and it's Abe Saffron. Hal Goldstein told someone who I know very well, who told me to my face that Abe Saffron is in it with them. That's who you are dealing with. They want the place to peddle drugs to the children, they don't give a fuck about Luna Park'. [23]

Sam Marshall summarised the next development. He wrote, 'On a rainy 31 May and 1 June 1981, an auction was held within Luna Park to sell anything detachable. Larry Freels, a collector from San Francisco, paid $140,000 for the Carousel and $20,000 for the Gebruder organ. The carousel animals were shipped back to America…Friends of Luna Park bought the Barrels of Fun, Turkey Trot and Joy Wheel for $9200 to keep them in the Park. In these two days, Luna Park, including the name, was dismembered and scattered about Sydney'. [24]

Many of the original rides, placards, games, effects and murals were auctioned off by Geoff K Gray Auctioneer. [25] With a view of some day bringing it all back, the Friends of Luna Park bought as much as they could. After the auction, Martin and friends followed a truck to the tip, grabbed what was salvageable and stashed in Wirian for safekeeping. Visitors were now greeted at the front door with a display of vintage fairground art.

Said Martin, 'After the fire came the auction. We saved some Arthur Barton's paintings from being thrown out and others we recommended be saved – which they were. We brought some over here and we've been restoring them. I wasn't strong enough to hold it all. You can only hold so much. Some were too damaged and old.' [26]

'The Mystic East had a real Buddha - a real religious figure in a world of plaster and fantasy - as part of that fantasy. Sitting on an endless river - Buddha, beautiful, marble, it was the heaviest thing in the Park. It was sold at the Auction, sitting with a number on its wrist and bought by this guy from Sunshine Advertising Agency. They had to pillage the place to get this enormous marble statue. They needed cranes to get it out. It was taken on the back of the truck, chained like a prisoner. Its expression of course was bliss. It was like a lynchpin in the place. After it went, they should have destroyed the Park.' [27]

Demolition began two days after the auction. Along with the Big Dipper and Davy Jones Locker, the River Caves were bulldozed. The Wild Cat and the Carousel were dismantled and removed. Kingo said, 'There was a lot of art at Luna Park, which disgracefully got sold at the auction. It should have all been "not for sale". A lot of it got dispersed, such as the Buddha. The whole of the River Caves was taken as landfill.' [28]

Friends of Luna Park - Martin, Kingo and others - compiled the bulk of the text for *The Luna Park Report*. From his Developing Room underneath Wirian, Jonny reconstructed old photographs taken by the Park's former electrical engineer, manager and (later) owner, Ted Hopkins. Jonny says, 'All those photos in the Report, they were Hoppy's photographs. What I did was "liberate" all the old negatives from the Luna darkroom - and I'd print them.' [29]

Around this time, photography student Michael Barker called on Martin. Said Martin, 'Michael comes around and says, "I'm interested in your work, I'm doing a project on you, I'd like to come to Luna Park". I was very impressed with his demeanour, enthusiasm, personality and everything. I said, "I can only let a certain number of people in and the place is full up".

'But Jonny Lewis dropped out of being the photographer so I asked Michael to replace him and he agreed, he was thrilled. I feel in a way it was fated, that I was destined to meet him somehow. Luna Park was very heavy to go into at that time. It was dark and rainy, the place looked like a misery. We hadn't been in since the fire. I did wonder whether it was too heavy for Michael, but he seemed such a fantastically optimistic person, enthusiastic, tremendously helpful and he took some absolutely fantastic pictures. He was a lovely young guy very balanced, very together.

'We were preparing the *Report*. I'd always had the feeling that there were to be eight people to die in relationship with the fire, before that thing had passed its passage. The tension was incredible – someone – something - has got to go. We just had to ride it out somehow.'

Martin had three strong premonitions. The first was Greg's photograph of the Ghost Train exterior where seven clocks are apparent but an eighth clock was hidden by a carpenter (or someone like that). Martin's second premonition was a photograph of the North Sydney Olympic Pool, with the Luna Park Face in the background. It revealed eight 'crosses' marking the eight lanes. The third was the arrival of a sacred blue kingfisher – symbol of peace and prosperity - that would later appear in Martin's *Tapestry* (1990) and other pictures. Michael Barker was in an upstairs building in the Park when a blue kingfisher flew onto the paving then onto his finger, as Michael showed Martin. A blue kingfisher in the city of Sydney was a rare sight indeed. A wild bird, hopping on Michael's finger and remaining there was truly extraordinary!

Martin continued, 'the Report was finished and Michael went back to art school. We then got the proof copy and Michael came over to look at it. He asked if he could take a photograph of himself standing on the Big Dipper looking towards the Harbour Bridge then he headed off to a class party at Paddington Town Hall.

'It was a full Moon, Kiss was giving a concert in town. (I mentioned the Kiss concert because the crowd was a strange manifestation of the Ghost Train thing.) Michael was riding his motorcycle home from the end-of- year party where he had completed the second-last year of his photography course. He was driving along Tara Street and came up to the Ocean Street intersection. A car ran into the back of him, pushed him into a stream of traffic, he was hit by a car and killed. We dedicated the Report to him.' [30]

Michael Barker died on 21 November 1980, aged 21. Martin expressed deep sorrow to the Barker family. In response, Michael's brother John started calling on Wirian. He became involved in filming Luna Park, which Martin found incredibly courageous. Their mother wrote Martin a long letter of thanks. Martin treasured it. [31]

Most of Martin's friends date his conversion to Christianity to the time of the Ghost Train fire. There were other influences too. 'Vicki Cobden got religion in a pretty bad way', said former Yellow House resident, Mal Ramage. 'Vicki Cobden was important in the matrix of Martin's behavior.' [32]

Vicki wasn't the only one. Susan Jensen too, 'I became a Christian in 1981 and clearly remember a conversation with Mart soon after when he said to me "I wish I had your faith". I said, "you can, it's just a choice like any other choice". I think he already did believe at the time - the fire was his spiritual wake up call. I agreed with Martin that the fire was arson and the work of the Devil. I hope it was comforting to him to know that not just I, but others also, recognised that real evil was clearly active in that event and we didn't think Martin was overreacting or imagining things.' [33]

Former owner of the Yellow House building Ian Reid, who married Martin's cousin Kate, occasionally called on Martin. Unimpressed by his religious direction, he said, 'I studied with different eastern masters and that became my orientation. Martin was his own authority and was immersed in the Bible, Christianity, revelations and magical thinking which I didn't want any part of.' [34]

Martin actually dated his interest in Christianity five years earlier, back to 1974 when watching Tiny on stage in a Newcastle Leagues Club, 'like a prophet' ad-libbing *Heaven Is My Home*. [35] Much later in life, sensing his unworthiness, Martin said, 'I still wouldn't call myself a Christian' although Richard Neville certainly did. In one of his newspaper columns he announced, 'Martin is a Christian. He has been known to pace up and down his old family mansion reading out favourite verses from the New Testament to startled young girls'. [36]

Martin's concern was the fate of Luna Park, which connected with his thoughts on collective guilt, action and redemption. When uncertain how to proceed he said, 'I got my instructions for Luna Park from an eight-year old girl playing ping-pong on the terrace. Kids can be totally freaked out by fire. If they didn't want the Park any more, I could understand that. It was up to them because they were the ones who'd been sacrificed. If the kids didn't want it, what was the point? I wanted to find out. The people who were running the Park didn't run it in the right way - they didn't clear the soul of the place. Tiny sang, "Every time I look into the Holy Book I want to tremble, when I read about the part where the carpenter cleared the temple..." and Luna Park was the temple. "And the buyers and the sellers are no different fellas than what I profess to be" that was when Tiny marked the turf!' [37] And Michael Barker with the iridescent blue kingfisher on his finger was 'like a young St Francis'. [38] Such references were being peppered throughout Martin's works, especially the film.

In May 1981, Martin hired Michael Edols and crew to film Tiny in his home town. The New York footage starts with a trip down memory lane, sites from Tiny's old neighbourhood. His mother Tillie, showed the film crew Tiny's bedroom with 'Jesus Saves' in his youthful scrawl still visible on the peeling wall.

Notwithstanding his strict Christian ethic ('you can look but you mustn't touch') one evening, Tiny told Edols to bring his film crew to his hotel room. There they found an alcohol-affected Tiny in the company of Pleasure Aims, a performer from *Melody Burlesque*. For the benefit of the camera, Tiny declared the wonders of champagne and Ms Aims bared her breasts. [39]

Back in Australia, Martin included the Pleasure Aims segment in the film, which he screened for Tiny's management when he visited New York later in the year. 'They were horrified!' said Martin. [40]

Adding to this, Martin spliced News footage of the Ghost Train fire with songs from the marathon. Some was quite subtle, Tiny blowing a kiss became the Judas Kiss in the Garden of Gethsemane, ('...and if I kiss you in the garden...'). Martin explained this at length to all his assistants. [41]

There were also practical aspects to consider, and complications concerning song copyrights, each needing to be cleared by their respective estates. That was one of Marilyn's jobs – first to locate, then contact, representatives of each estate and come to a financial agreement for inclusion of their song in the marathon, which spanned 139 songs. Martin explained, 'A song that is crucial might cost $50,000 for 30 seconds and not $150 like most of them'.

Cutting and pasting on his editing machine, created a film that seemed more like a collage rather than a tightly scripted plot. Martin had hopes of success, 'People will be forever trying to make a cult film – or another Rocky Horror. You can't manipulate or predict things like that. People will see the film on Tiny and they'll go see it again and again. They'll sing along with it, they'll really get into it!' [42]

Briefly, there was some talk of releasing the entire Marathon in cassette format [43] but other Tiny Tim music – tighter projects - took priority. The first was a 45rpm single to commemorate Luna Park. Tiny sang the 1930 Rudy Vallee song, Wind in the Willows, on one side, the other was their own Luna Park Song. Martin got Al Jones and his friend Mic Conway to write and perform it. Al had a solid background in Pop/Rock/Country music. Being a member of Slim Dusty's Travellin' Band, 10 of Al's songs had appeared on various Slim Dusty LPs. And Mic had co-written hits for the Captain Matchbox Whoopee Band. Coming from a Vaudeville/jug band background, Mic had always admired Tiny. 'When I was at school, a lot of people worshipped Sgt Pepper. Well, Tiny Tim's God Bless LP was my Sgt Pepper!' Mic affirmed. [44] Al and Mic co-wrote the *The Luna Park Song* though Al recorded the song without Mic because he was on tour. Street of Dreams Production released the two sides as a 45rpm single. Martin's cover artwork was in the same vein as his *Friends of Luna Park* letterhead and the *Save Luna Park* poster.

Martin did lots of other work too. He wasn't painting much on canvas but he was certainly creating posters. He did one for another kind of OZ – *Circus* OZ. In 1978 the Soapbox Circus and New Ensemble Circus amalgamated to create Circus OZ with Mic as front man. Martin also designed the Al Jones Late Show poster for the Stables Theatre where Al worked with actor Lex Marinos. [45] He also did the poster for Jeannie Lewis' cabaret show. She said, 'At the end of 1979 we did *Krazy 4 You*. Martin did the poster for that. And then I did *Piaf*.' [46]

Martin also created several other black and white (or black, white and red) posters in this period - for the Patrick White play *Signal Driver* and the Louis Nowra play *Visions*. Also - Finks Circus, Circus Animals (for Cold Chisel), as well as the prints, *Ignatz Paints His World* and *Ginger Meggs in Japan*, the later of which – in time – Martin and Tim would repaint together on canvas. Another new piece was *Couples*, (bought by Patrick White) a collage worked with scissors and glue. [47]

While Martin was busy being prolific, his Face of Luna Park was being refaced. A cast was taken so a replica could be made. In mid-1981 the largest piece of Pop Art in the Southern Hemisphere was defaced, dismantled and dumped on the ground in front of the Park's twin towers, awaiting a couple of surfboard makers to make a fiberglass mould.

Writes Sam Marshall, 'Surfboard makers Darryl Holmes and Stephen Johnson grappled with the difficult task of working with facial features on such a huge scale.

They repaired the face then made a fibreglass mould and demolished the original face. The mould was reinforced and reinstated but it was a poor copy of Martin Sharp's clown face with a lumpy forehead, bloodshot eyeballs and pupils that were at the centre of the eye opening – the position of the eye when terrified.' (48)

# 2.
# WIRIAN

*Wirian is an internal Yellow House rather than an external one.*
Martin Sharp

**Pre-AIDs Sydney 1980s:** Taylor Square, Imperial Hotel, Kinselas, Sylvia and the Synthetics, Jimmy & the Boys, Mad Max, Brett Whiteley's *Lavender Bay* series, Hogarth Gallery, *Billy Blue* magazine, Wild & Woolley, Patrick White & Manoly Lascaris, the 4th Sydney Festival, Oxford Street shops, The Rocks, Nimrod Theatre, Australian Film Commission, Lord Dudley Hotel, Regular Records, Singo, the Madam Lash shop 'Gay Birds', Vittorio Bianchi's Piccolo Bar, Double J Radio, the Elton John tour, the Gay Mardi Gras after-party, amyl nitrate, Flamingo Park. Sex joints, soirees and excess.

Martin entered the 80s with a partly shot film, an inheritance not properly under his control, a rickety love life and the cause of the Ghost Train fire an unsolved mystery. Although the media still portrayed him as one of the naughty wizards of OZ magazine, he wanted to be remembered for other things. He wasn't all about Artoons and OZ. Although Martin didn't paint much, he created posters, edited film, produced records, organized Tiny Tim concerts and deciphered religious and quasi-religious imagery gleaned from the general media. He videotaped pertinent news stories and collated press clippings into A4 plastic folders, which he referenced for synchronicity and symbolism. 'I'm just trying to make dilettantism into an art,' he quipped. [1]

In fad-conscious Sydney, the new kid on the Art block was Ken Done. Done walked out of corporate life as Creative Director at the influential J Walter Thompson advertising agency. He started his own business selling hand-painted Sydney

Harbour t-shirts from his house in Ridge Street North Sydney and quickly became Sydney's most accessible artist. He held his first exhibition in 1980 at Holdsworth Gallery. Soon after, he and his wife Judy opened a shop in The Rocks and sold fabrics, designs and prints. He produced postcards, magazine covers, t-shirts, posters, sheets, pillowcases, calendars, books and even paintings. Done's blatant commercialism annoyed fine art critics but he didn't care. Done Art had tourist appeal. Sydneysiders wanted Ken Done sheets and Martin Sharp posters. Done's exuberant beachscapes were inescapable as t-shirts and Martin was commissioned to create the 1981 City of Sydney festival poster.

'I always accepted that I was selling something,' said Ken, 'some artists pretend they don't but there are no artists who don't want to sell their work. I work on that principle'. [2]

Martin's colleagues were no longer the frontline provocateurs they were in the 60s. By the 80s, each of the OZ Trio (for different reasons) loathed the unprincipled hedonism that they were credited having unleashed. Martin had always been kinda cosmic. Richie Walsh had always been kind of sensible. Richard Neville was the puzzle. Along with Germaine Greer, he had been a judge at Amsterdam's art and pornfest, the 1970 Wet Dream Film Festival - how could this same Richard loathe the New Hedonism? Well, he did. They all did.

Now married, Richie Walsh edited and managed *Nation Review* until its sale in 1979. He then moved into the corporate side of publishing. Whenever he and Richard got together they bounced ideas, puns and jokes off each other. The two Richards were a great two-person act when they shared the media 'I talk without full stops' is how Richie Walsh described himself. [3] And of course, Richard Neville was a self-confessed motor-mouth dating back to university days.

Writer and journalist Julie Clarke knew Martin from the Yellow House and he introduced her to Richard. Richard and Julie became a couple and co-authored an unlikely biography, *The Life and Crimes of Charles Sobhraj*. Many were shocked that the Eternal Groover who had idealised the counterculture, would give any credence to a Hippie killer. That Richard found the experience harrowing was a bit of a relief. [4]

Richard and Julie married in December 1980 and bought a property in Blackheath NSW. He took on the improbable role of presenter on Channel Nine's *Mike Walsh Show*, a sort-of TV Housewives Choice. Core material was whatever was faddish in popular culture: Hippies, Yuppies, Greenies, eco-tourists, mystics, lifestylers, the New Age, the lot. This laid the groundwork for Richard's next incarnation as a Futurist. [5]

Richard and Julie's 45-acre *Happy Daze* property was 4k out of Blackheath on the fork of Pulpit Rock and Hat Hill Road. (Jenny Kee would soon buy 5-acres also on Hat Hill Road.) Richard and Julie both had family connections in the upper Blue Mountains. Richard's grandparents owned *Upalong*, a fine house in Mount Victoria beyond Katoomba. And Julie's brother Rolley lived in Mount

Victoria and was a handy carpenter. Over the years the out-of-the-way location of Happy Daze provided a haven for Sallie-Anne Huckstepp, Martin and even – at one stage – Salmon Rushdie.

With the Rolley's assistance and Richard's nephew Michael Braund, Richard and Julie added two studios, improved the gardens and extended the house to maximise their breathtaking views of the Grose Valley. In time, they made Happy Daze spacious and attractive. Before Richard and Julie fixed it up, it was a derelict party house where young people gathered on weekends to drop acid and party. It didn't even have electricity. Having fantasised about buying it himself, local resident, Max Skeen recalled the selling price being $50,000 ('A lot of money back then') but added, 'Richard bought it cheaper than that'. [6]

Back in Bellevue Hill, Wirian housed Russell Sharp, Martin's cousin and personal assistant. Also at Wirian were society photographer - William Yang, slightly world-weary jack-of-all-musical-trades - Al Jones, assistant film editor and advisor - Marilyn Karet who a guest described as 'the only Wirian-person who was patently sane'. Albert Peck ran the house. There were many other assistants, helpers and advisers too, including Nathan Waks, Paul Healy, Chris Cordeaux, Sally Fitzgerald, Peter Kingston and sometimes drop-in guests who no one had ever heard of - like 'Robert' the Jehovah's Witness who rapped on the front door and was surprised to be invited inside for coffee and a welcome discussion about the Apocalypse. He gave Martin a Watchtower magazine that Martin kept on display for ages, next to the cardboard figures of Charles & Di waving.

In the 14-year interim since Martin and Richard went to London most of the OZ and Yellow House people had traveled overseas too. Some never came back. Germaine Greer and Barry Humphries remained in England. Robert Hughes and Little Nell moved to in New York and Jim Anderson vanished to Bolinas California where he stayed for years. Jim flashed back to Sydney in 1981, held a show at Hogarth Gallery, caught up with a few friends including Martin and Richard, who he met in a pub in Paddington. Jim then returned to Bolinas where he re-mained until the mid-90s. [7]

After the success of his film about bushranger *Mad Dog Morgan*, Philippe Mora moved to Los Angeles where, in 1980, he married Pamela and laid the groundwork for his next film, *The Beast Within*. Philippe's painting *Da Corner* was permanently parked in the Wirian hall beside remnants of Luna Park. It was among the first things visitors saw when they walked in. [8]

The old team was well and truly scattered. Garry Shead was in Budapest where he had met his future wife, artist Judit Englert. Brett Whiteley and his family lived in Fiji before returning to Lavender Bay where Kingo and John Firth-Smith also lived. Mick Glasheen moved to Sydney's northern beaches. John Bell journeyed from Northern Australia to Papua New Guinea. George Gittoes and Gabrielle Dalton moved south to Bundeena. Tim Lewis, Albie Thoms and Jonny Lewis traveled extensively throughout America, Europe, Asia and the Middle East. Greg and Sue Weight bought an acreage near Glenorie, 44k north-west of Sydney and Roger Foley-Fogg stayed in Sydney and worked with designer Maggie Tabberer. [9]

Martin was still childless but the first wave of children was born to many of his friends: Arkie Whiteley, Claudia Karvan, Christabel Draffin, Tilly Lewis, Gria Shead, Naomi Gittoes, Alex Weight, Osha and Minyo Weight. In their own way they were all fascinated by the Dream Museum and its toys. Little Sky McCreadie from next door was another regular.

Amber Tarling was one of the Dream Museum kids. 'That Dream Museum!' she reminisced. 'There were certain things you couldn't touch. There was a respect, there was an order and we always had to pack it up after playing. George Gittoes' daughter said to me that Martin was like an uncle. It's a shame he didn't have children. He would have been a great Dad.' Her sister Zoë's childhood perspective was, 'Martin's home was focused on creative play - drawing or painting.' [10]

Over the years, Wirian inspired lots of kids. Martin welcomed student projects and happily cooperated. Mart's art was the subject of many school activities. Roger's daughter Electra did her Year 9 assignment about one of Martin's paintings. [11]

Wirian was gradually becoming an extension of Martin's fascinations. Almost every scene that follows will happen somewhere in Wirian. When Tiny came to Australia, he always spent a lot of time at Martin's house. The Anglican Archbishop of Sydney visited Wirian. The Governor of New South Wales did too. Princess Eugenie showed up in beachwear. Bob Geldof, Russell Crowe, Keith Haring, Peter Allen, Jimmy Barnes, Reg Mombassa, Jack Thompson, David Gulpilil, Zandra Rhodes, Eric Clapton, Marianne Faithfull, Lin Utzon and many other distinguished guests have dropped in over the years, as did Tiny Tim's cousin Hal and his wife Sherry. [12]

Martin's pictures and posters were all created on the premises, either in the hall, the Dream Museum, his bedroom studio and his Inner Sanctum. Some, like the restoration of Arthur Barton's 1935 *The Building of Loona Park* (4.25 x 3.5 m), demanded the kind of space only a big hallway could provide. The size of Wirian made all this possible.

From a family residence, under Martin's governance, Wirian slowly but irrevocably evolved into an artist's studio and storage space. Wirian is prime Sydney real estate in up-market Bellevue Hill across the road from the Fairfax mansion and next door to the Cranbrook School. Built for the wife of a grazier in 1923, Stuart and Vee Ritchie bought it in 1937. [13] Designed by Halligan & Wilton architects, Wirian has a *porte cochère*, formal lounge room, smoking room, ballroom, butler's pantry, four majestic upstairs bedrooms, servants' bedrooms, two (later three) upstairs bathrooms, an upstairs bow window with leadlight glazing, a room under the house where boarders have lived over the years and a kitchen with its still-working Kooka stove. Before Martin settled his probate debt by selling part of the land to Cranbrook School, Wirian also had a garage with chauffeur's accommodation, tennis court and turning circle-cum-parking area at the end of the driveway on the Cranbrook side of the property. (14)

Wirian had a history of hosting grand social events, that Stuart and Vega Ritchie continued. While Martin's father and uncles endured the horrors of World War II overseas, their womenfolk were attending lovely soireés, dances and cocktail parties in Wirian's grand rooms. Guests included industrialists, celebrities, Governors-General and many other illustrious guests. Martin and his mother lived there for the first four years of his life. They moved into their own house in Cranbrook Lane after his father was demobilised from the Army.

Martin inherited Wirian when he was in his mid-30s. It took a while, but he eventually moved into his grandmother's quarters. Her enclosed bedroom verandah became Martin's second studio (the first being the grand dining room which Martin's guests dubbed the Inner Sanctum).

Martin did not nest easily in the mid-70s, he was too used to moving around. He came-and-went between Sydney, London, Paris and New York usually leaving Tim Lewis back home to 'hold the fort' (as Martin called it).

He encountered Andy Warhol in New York. In the 60s, Warhol's New York City studio, The Factory, was a model for open-door art houses. By the end of the decade, things got too crazy. Valerie Solanas shot Warhol on behalf of the Society for Cutting Up Men (SCUM), of which she was president, secretary and its total membership. The shooting had a profound effect on Warhol. He retained his most trusted art-workers, shut the door on the rest and entered his entrepreneurial phase.

Martin recalled Warhol's calm manner of handling public pressure, 'I was in New York visiting Tiny and Nell took me to an opening of an exhibition,' Martin recalled. 'It was all going on inside and he was sitting outside on a little table being very quiet, just taking photographs of people every now and then. He was being so polite, being very kind to everyone who came up to him - and he had a lot of people. I noticed he was making an incredible effort and he was actually shaking a little bit under the table.

'There was something about his poise and I said, "Do you go to church?" He said, "Yes I go to Mass every Sunday". I thought that was incredibly interesting. I didn't know why I asked that particular question, just that he was being so kind to people. He was giving himself to an extreme degree and I could see under the table, at a considerable cost to himself.' (15)

But Martin had no idea how to run a grand residence. He turned Wirian into part museum and part artists' colony then mortgaged it to finance his film. (16) Artists and musicians came and went. In his absence, Tim Lewis and Richard and Sharon Liney were great at fanning Wirian's bohemian vibe. Then Martin came back and it became Tim's turn to go overseas so Martin and Richard Liney created the 1978 Dream Museum Exhibition for the Art Gallery of New South

Wales. Shortly afterwards, the Lineys left, which left a vacancy in the guardianship of Wirian.

Martin invited his grandfather's former servant/gardener to move in and Albert Peck monitored everything. He charged each tenant $25pw rent and ensconced himself in Martin's grandfather's upstairs bedroom.

Said Martin, 'I thought it went really well for a number of years. I liked him. I thought he was teaching me how to run the place. He was quite good with money. There was a bit of a crisis though…' [17]

The new Wirianites (not all at the same time) were Melody Cooper, Stephen Teather, Susan Jensen, Richard Neville, Julie Clarke, William Yang, Victoria Cobden, Al Jones, Victor Rubin, Marilyn Karet and Cressida Campbell. [18]

The house was beginning to shape into Martin's personality. The dining room became his Inner Sanctum studio, the ballroom became the Dream Museum, the Smoking Room became the film editing room and every room was a smoking room. There was a blur of people coming by day and staying overnight or a bit longer - like Salami Sisters, Kathy Lette and Gabrielle Carey. Lette wrote about it: 'We lived under Martin Sharp's dining room table for a while. Martin had a huge empty mansion, full of ghosts, but he was only supposed to live in the back bit, the servant's quarters under a weird will; then as he got older he could move into other areas. The house was full of artists and musicians.' [19]

Informed that Sallie-Anne Huckstepp was on the run from the underworld, Richard rescued her and housed her in the privacy of *Happy Daze* in Blackheath. After a time, he asked Martin if he could move her into Wirian. Martin said okay. Sallie-Anne arrived spaced out on Mandrax and slurring her words. She lived there but had little to do with Martin who told her biographer John Dale, 'She had a broken leg when she came, she was on crutches, Richard told me she'd had a miscarriage. It wasn't a blessing to have her but there was enough room. She had a little daughter. Some guy used to come and visit her, quite a tough guy on a very expensive motorbike.' [20]

Photographer, William Yang moved in too. He said, 'In September 1979 I had hepatitis, so I decided I'd come from Brisbane to Sydney in the Spring. Melody and Steven were the two lodgers and Albert was a retainer. Richard and Julie lived there. It's a large house and people find their own way, where they fit it. Nothing is defined. It's totally intuitive. Albert assumed that Martin was incapable of looking after his own finances. He paid all the bills, collected the rent and had all the keys, so he had a considerable position of power in this place. If you wanted to gain admission to this place you had to be screened by Albert. If Albert didn't like you he could make life hell. He spent a lifetime tyranising the lodgers. Albert put a price on everything. People would borrow objects but with Albert there was always a fee. Albert regarded Martin as profligate with money. And for an ordered mind it was almost an unbearable situation for Albert to be in, to look after the books - yet Martin would spend money like he usually did.' [21]

Albert had the territorial imperative over the house. To prohibit houseguests from watching 'too much' television, he kept the TV set in his room. As punishment for being untidy, Albert confiscated all cigarettes and alcohol lying around from the previous night. These he stashed in his room and – like the 8-year old Abe Saffron - sold them back to visitors when they ran out. Friends urged Martin to get rid of Albert but he wouldn't. Then, it came to a head. Said Martin, 'That whole thing had a very strong rich metaphysic to it. There was a big Luna Park meeting and Peter Royles came from the bush and stayed.' [22]

Late one evening, while sitting around chatting, Richard Neville said, 'I'd like a drink'. Albert replied, 'I've got some scotch'. So Richard bought himself a nip or three. Next day Richard was talking and let slip the sentence, 'Albert sold me whisky' which caught Martin's attention because he felt the whisky was the property of Toto Renshaw, another visitor. So Martin fronted Albert, 'Did you see any whisky?' And Albert said no. 'It was the wrong answer for Martin,' said William, 'that was the beginning of the end.' [23]

'I thought Toto would come back for his whisky,' Martin explained, 'Everything was in a state of flux. I was with Cress (Cressida Campbell) at the time and I'd given up smoking, so I was putting myself through quite a bit. Melody asked to have a party and use the end room. The last thing I needed was a party around the place. I was totally cloistered in my room, keeping very quiet. There was a lot of ping-pong being played on the balcony and I was trying to be peaceful. I couldn't get to sleep.

'I came downstairs and told Melody and Steve it was time to move along. Certainly there was a loss of temper, that's for sure. Sometimes I've gone right off and thrown things everywhere. Sometimes just one thing - well aimed. It only happens under rare circumstances. Paranoia builds up and everything you've been holding back comes out. You've lost communication with people. I felt I'd been pushed into a situation where you just explode. I didn't want things to happen the way they did.' [24]

Melody helped Albert move out. She and Stephen left as well. Says Melody, 'Albert left at the same time that Stephen and I left. Mart had given up smoking, told no one he was doing it, but gave permission for me to have a party. It was for the end of a season of a play I had done at Sydney Uni for Rex Cramphorn. During the party, where we of course were smoking joints, Mart lost the plot and threw us all out. He apologised the next day and wanted us to stay but the damage had been done. Stephen and I helped Albert take all his stuff to his sister's house, and I never saw Albert again.' [25] Albert's demise left another vacancy. William explains, 'The physical world doesn't touch Martin much and so there's always a role here for the physical protector of the house.' [26]

Admitted to the bar in 1977, Anthony (Toto) Renshaw was a barrister working from Clive Evatt's Wardell Chambers and - like Jonny Lewis – he was the son of a former Premier of New South Wales. Although his father Jack Renshaw was a

Labor premier, Toto had upper class affectations. He was a first-rate Go player, collected samurai swords, drank Johnny Walker scotch, played Japanese Gagaku music, thought nothing of calling people 'fools' to their faces if necessary and dressed awfully well. Some people found him frightening.

Said Martin, 'It was just after the second mortgage had been taken out, the second hump of the Tiny film. A friend of Andrew Sharp, my cousin, brought Toto around. I was pretty amazed by Toto. I was pretty wary of him as well. I saw the performer in him immediately and his fantastic brain (not really being used in the right way somehow). His clothes, the look, the pose, the whole thing was like Old Wirian, as it would have been in my grandfather's days. Toto knew the city as a commercial centre with a hierarchy in a sort-of sense. He knew some of people from the other side - Arthur George, the Masonic stuff and the behind-the-scenes political maneuvering. It was the time of the Luna Park business and Toto brought the whole of that world into visibility.' [27]

For a brief time, Toto might have moved in to take up Albert's former role. Cousin Russell Sharp took that role instead. Russell was the younger son of Dr Frank Sharp. After an idyllic childhood, his mother died in 1972. His father died two years later. His childhood home in Longueville was sold and 25-year old Russell was shaken to the core. He tried working in sales, selling cookware, water reticulation systems and real estate but he didn't enjoy the work. One day he ran into Martin at the Piccolo Bar in Kings Cross. Martin suggested he move into Wirian. Russell agreed and fell straight into the role of getting Martin's affairs in order. Russell put the film and recording company *Street of Dreams Productions* onto a business footing. Also - working with Don McGregor (of McGregor Screenprints) - an attempt was made to sell Martin's posters commercially. Melody explained, 'Russell helped with posters and the business side of the Noive & Voive record label.' [28]

Russell said, 'I moved in after Albert had moved out. I was just a gofer. I did what I could. I organized quite a lot of posters, especially the ones done by Mambo and the McGregor Prints. The Nimrod posters - I sold those, I remember at the time Martin took possession of a lot of them and he was selling them. Some were $300. Then we did a whole series of other posters. Stephen (Lawson) printed an edition of about 100 and I sold them, it was a 3-way split.' [29]

Back from overseas, Roslyn Sharp made a point of visiting Wirian. Over the years she got involved with Martin more and more, but at this stage Russell was her main concern. She said, 'I'd go there mainly to see Russell. After our parents died, Russell suffered a lot and Martin was very kind to him.' [30]

'I was there for two and a half years,' said Russell. 'I was devoted. Cressida Campbell was there for a little while. She was going out with Martin. Willy (William Yang) was there. Jonny Lewis had his studio there. Alistair was there. We had *Noive and Voive* Records. That was our little record label. I incorporated *Street of Dreams* and we also created the *Chameleon* record covers.' [31]

Returning to Australia in 1980, Tiny – now with mulberry-coloured hair - completed the remaining tracks for the Chameleon LP. They were Deep Night, Song Without A Name, My Song, Dietetic Baby and Tiny Bubbles (the last two were not included on the release). St Louis Blues and Dancing in the Street were held over until 2006. They also reworked Stayin' Alive with Australian actor/musician David Gulpilil on didgeridoo (which somehow got lost in the mix when released to LP). Added to these were the masters for a song titled Country Queen recorded by Tiny on the day of Elvis' death in 1977 but not released. It was added to the LP record. Eight hundred copies of the album were released. Martin gave most of them away to friends. The few that were sold did little to recoup costs. [32]

When it came to Arts Grants, the 1970s was a most generous decade, especially for someone as established as Martin. Financial support may have been forthcoming had 'Tiny Tim' not been associated with Martin's project. After some negotiations, the Australian Film Commission (AFC) agreed to support the project with a small grant. Martin was surprised, 'Haydn Keenan helped a lot. When we showed the first compilation I didn't expect them to be interested.' [33]

Other than that $20,000 contribution from AFC, Martin carried all the production costs that he had hoped to share. In order to finish the film, produce records and keep running concerts, Martin re-mortgaged Wirian. Tiny must have been pleased to know that from this time onwards, and for the rest of his life, somewhere in the Antipodes was a small outpost constantly working on his music, taped conversations, film and visual images, the first-fruits of which proved excellent.

Artistically, things were going well for Martin and his ragtag crew, but privately there was some sadness. Martin had a very candid and close relationship with his mother. They shared things that most young people keep secret from parents. Martin discussed all aspects of his love life with his Mum, including pregnancy terminations. For all his achievements, Martin only had to do one more thing to impress her - father a child.

Said William Yang to Martin, 'Jo said to me "There's only one wish I ever wanted".

'And that is what?' he replied.

'The child – the child isn't it?'

Said Martin, 'I guess so, yes.' [34]

Martin's girlfriends were generally okay about the tight mother/son bond but unimpressed with Tiny's commentary on their relationship. In his lengthy phone conversations with Martin, Tiny expressed strict views on birth control and abortion, which Martin seemed to accept. 'I don't believe in birth control. I don't believe in rhythm. I don't believe in abortions,' Tiny effused, 'I believe according to the Scriptures man's duty is to be fruitful and multiply!' Was Tiny over-moralising as a form of satire? Martin didn't think so. [35]

Faced with another pregnancy termination, Martin fell to pieces, 'Tiny showed me the wrongness of it. I felt the real physical and spiritual effect of the whole thing. I was always disappointed. Things were going awfully wrong. I'd taken an awful lot of risks I guess. At that time I was really self-aware. I don't know if that was prayer or whatever but I was on the edge of hysteria. Sobbing. It was the worst sort of agony I've had.' [36]

Martin had a mini-breakdown. In an act of contrition, he burned off his hair. [37]

# 3.
# HOKUSAI, ELVIS AND THAT DINGO

*Two guys are looked upon as having the same talent, going back 10 years – Brett Whiteley and Martin Sharp. Brett Whiteley is an independently wealthy man. Martin Sharp is independently bloody unwealthy, unhealthy and his paintings are very hard to buy.*
John Singleton

Martin was trying to get organised. He had a stack of A4 folders into which he filed news stories. The latest was that Harbourside Amusement planned to reopen Luna Park at the end of April (1982). In another group of folders, Martin stored Tiny Tim clippings from the 60s to the present. He kept historical pieces like 'The Great Crooners' Tiny's 1969 *Playboy* magazine article, Miss Vicki's 1975 nudie spread in *Oui* magazine - up to the latest from the Sydney Morning Herald's *TV Guide*: 'Don't be fooled by the unusual appearance of Tiny Tim, underneath is a very talented man'. Plus the sheet music for *Tiptoe Through the Tulips* and whatever the American press was writing about Tiny. Martin kept adding to those folders until they needed shelves. Then he added to the shelves until they needed a room. The room was the original Butler's pantry, easy access from the Inner Sanctum.

There, assistants catalogued Martin's taped conversations with Tiny, which comprised a library of 200 cassettes that kept growing. Tiny often phoned Martin from anywhere in America, sometimes anywhere in the world, and they'd talk for an hour or more, which resulted in at least one more tape to label, date and file. Martin said, 'Tiny is a difficult person to understand. I've been given a particular insight, especially by seeing the Albert Hall concert, so there was never any need to convince myself. I need re-convincing every now and then, which the tapes help do because I listen to them. I've got some friends who've hated Tiny. Some people I've been very close to haven't understood the interest. It puts a lot of pressure on those particular relationships because it means the best part of oneself one cannot share with them. People say, why don't you do more cartoons? Why don't you do some paintings? A lot of people are more sentimental about me returning to those areas. Maybe I'll do some again. I see no difference between doing a poster, a painting or a Tiny Tim show. I don't discriminate between what the medium is, I'm only following the spirit of the thing in understanding as best I can how to respond.' [1]

With a push from Russell and following the successful process of the Al Jones/Mic Conway *Luna Park Song* single, Street of Dreams Productions released Tiny's *Chameleon* and *Wonderful World of Romance* LPs.

Then a Nimrod Theatre employee found a stack of Martin's original Nimrod posters stashed under a staircase: Kaspar (1973), Ginge's Last Stand (1975), Young Mo (1977), Kold Komfort Kaffee (1978), Sideshow in Burlesco (1979) and Venetian Twins (1979). Street of Dreams Productions (ie. Russell) bought the lot for re-sale. The timing coincided with Nimrod commissioning Martin to mark the 10th anniversary of the theatre with another poster. Russell arranged for a new edition of 1000 to be produced on better quality paper and sold in sets of seven as a fundraiser for the theatre. Martin's Nimrod Series generated a lot of interest. The Mo poster was made into a keyring and Nimrod 10 became made a badge. [2]

Other poster commissions followed, not all as successfully. Against his better judgment, the Nuclear Disarmament Party talked Martin into doing their poster. Despite their best persuasive efforts, in the end they wouldn't use his 'Drop the Bomb' motif. 'That's the whole point,' Martin exclaimed, 'Nobody would drop the bomb!'

One evening Martin ran into former Labor PM Gough Whitlam at a party. In chatting, Gough told Martin that his antecedent, William Sharp (1844-1929) was a great Labor man. Martin hadn't given Great-Grandfather Sharp much thought. He was feeling slightly estranged from his father's side at the time. Said Martin, 'I found out my great-grandfather was the Labor Member for Redfern, Gough told me that. My family never told me that, never! They were all Liberals.' [3] Seizing the moment, Whitlam asked Martin for a poster for the International Socialist Congress. Martin explained, 'I normally don't do posters for the Socialist Congress but when Gough Whitlam rings up you don't really say no, do you? (Well… sometimes I do.)' [4]

So Martin did the poster and – like the Nuclear Disarmament Party - they didn't use it. The problem was that Martin expressed what he wanted to express, which was not necessarily in sync with the person doing the asking. Over the years, Martin's (later) assistant Dave Rowe saw him struggle with many commissions, 'With Circus OZ he was comfortable. He'd name his figure and they were happy. If it was someone like Cold Chisel, he was happy. He'd name the figure and do the poster. But when it was an outside source - Martin wasn't any good at deals.' [5]

Martin said, 'The ingredients they gave me were the fist clutching the rose, the Australian flag and the world in crisis. So I ask – "name me a time in history when it hasn't been in crisis?" In the end, the Socialist Congress' sub-committee declined to use the poster. I don't mind if people don't like it but I wish they hadn't asked me in the first place because all I did was give them what I thought was a good poster. That's why I don't like dealing with committees. Usually when I do a poster I say: if you want a poster sometime, let me know. Gough was a bit embarrassed, I don't think he was quite embarrassed enough!' [6]

Yes, Martin disliked committees but enjoyed creating posters for Circus OZ, Cold Chisel and friends. He'd volunteer his services, as he did for Mic and Jim Conway's *Vaude Villains* show and Jeannie Lewis' new *So You Want Blood* show that accompanied her new album of the same name. Jeannie was also involved in a fund raising concert at Paddington Town Hall, the *Apmira Art Sale for Land Rights* held at the same venue. Martin did their poster too.

In 1983, the State Government of New South Wales was moving towards passing the Aboriginal Land Rights Act in line with other States. 'Apmira' is the Arunta word for 'land'. Jeannie had been involved in the Land Rights movement since the early-60s. Gary Shearston too. He set Kath Walker's (Oodgeroo Noonuccal) *Aboriginal Charter of Rights* poem to music and wrote the song *Dingo*, which Martin began listening to intently because it linked to current news events. [7]

Martin revisited the guilt he felt over losing the Abalone Diver print. He was convinced it was a 'lost' Hokusai print of his daughter diving for abalone. Martin worried about it, wrote about it, and went over and over it in his mind. He checked with foremost Hokusai scholar Joseph Hillier, who concluded it was not bona fide. He didn't convince Martin. A woman who ran a Japanese shop in Double Bay told Martin that she knew some experts on Japanese master painters and Martin let her take it to Japan. He said, 'I got a letter from the woman saying, "Bad news, I've lost it at the airport." I was completely shattered because (a) I'd lost something very valuable and (b) because it was probably one of Hokusai's last and major works as a print. I felt I'd let him down – I had discovered it and I'd lost it.'

Uneasy about the loss, Martin wanted to preserve the image, it was the least he could do. Martin and printmaker Kristin Coburn recreated a print from a photograph taken by William. Martin and Kristin reproduced it faithfully, without commentary. 'I was so ashamed for having lost it,' said Martin, 'this way, I could at least to keep it alive.' [8]

Ever one to write letters, Martin corresponded off-and-on with the producer of Tiny's hit albums God Bless Tiny Tim and Tiny Tim's Second Album. Richard Perry had gone on to produce some seriously big names, like Ray Charles, Ringo Starr, Captain Beefheart, Rod Stewart, Pointer Sisters and many others. Perry had a soft spot for Tiny, whose first album literally launched his career. He appreciated Martin's efforts and - as musical director of the brilliant 1968 concert at the Royal Albert Hall - Perry held the original 4-track master tapes of the night. He copied them to cassette for Martin who now shared his Damascus Road epiphany with friends. The shattering version of I Got You Babe usually quelled any detractors. [9]

Known for his biographies of Lenny Bruce and Elvis Presley, Martin read Albert Goldman's sympathetic treatment of Tiny in his biography of Lenny Bruce. Goldman reckoned that Tiny had a unique understanding of the language of popular song. In 1968 he wrote, '…a dream theater that echoes beguilingly with all the voices of Tiny Tim. To say that these are the most perfect impersonations of old singers ever heard would hardly do justice to the art that has re-embodied these entertainers in electronic avatars, summoning them up out of the past to caper again before a strobe-lit oleo.'

Martin was miffed that someone as insightful as Goldman could be so hard on Elvis. In his final concert, Martin was awed by Elvis' rendition of My Way whereas Goldman found it embarrassing. How could a perceptive writer like Goldman not see what Martin saw? [10]

So Martin wrote him and included a cassette copy of Tiny's Royal Albert Hall concert. Although he failed to change his mind about Elvis, Martin reactivated Goldman's interest in Tiny. Goldman wrote back, 'Dear Martin Sharp, I appreciate your suggestions for Elvis though I must confess that I am not as impressed by the evidence of what used to be called "second sight" as you are. Elvis had been singing My Way, an absurdly inappropriate song, for some time prior to the last show. I suspect his problem with the words owes more to what is called a mental block than a sign of deathly weakness. I forbear to go further'. [11]

About Tiny he enthused, 'I had never heard him with a big orchestra in a large hall. Tiny Tim remains a unique and remarkable performer with an astounding sense of the history of popular song'. In return he sent Martin a signed copy of his book, Ladies and Gentleman Lenny Bruce!! with references to Tiny underscored. [12]

Negotiations were underway to bring Tiny back to Australia in September. Notwithstanding that he had completely run out of money, Martin decided that this time Tiny should play the best available venue in town – the Concert Hall at Sydney Opera House.

Martin worked on the poster with enthusiasm, shaping Tiny's face into the vaulted Opera House roof with the Harbour Bridge with Luna Park aglow in the background. Red, white, yellow, light blue and dark blue. Martin believed this poster was as memorable as anything he'd ever done. When asked, 'What do you think will be remembered of Martin Sharp?' he pointed to the Tiny Tim/Sydney Opera House screen print and said, 'That one – certainly!' [13]

Tiny's September tour set the template for all future ones. An entrepreneur (this time Peter Conyngham) brought Tiny out. He checked the Eternal Troubadour and his manager into the Cosmopolitan Hotel not far from Wirian and booked him into shopping centres, RSL Clubs and other ordinary venues. Sometimes it was tough going. 'Tiny Tim for tiny prices!' yelled a Grace Brothers spruiker, 'Underpants reduced to only 99c while Tiny Tim is in the store!' [14] After the completion of those tedious bread-and-butter commitments, Martin kept Tiny in the country, took over the costs, ran a concert at a prominent venue and whisked Tiny into recording studios. All subsequent visits to Australia would follow this pattern.

In August, Tiny arrived at Sydney's Mascot Airport accompanied by his US manager Bill Hollander. Representing Martin's interests, Russell was Australian tour manager. One of the first things Tiny did was to sit with Martin and look at footage of the film, which he enjoyed. Tiny teased the press. 'It took Mr Sharp years to get it together, editing. He's got so much film. He took the film to New York. There were some scenes with...er ...you know...er...naked women in it.' [15]

He spent the next day discussing various booking arrangements with Conyngham, then back with Martin for recording and concert ideas. Tiny appeared at a Beauty Show at the Chevron Hotel, performed the Bexley North RSL Club, performed at the Campbelltown RSL Club, did radio interviews with Jonathon Coleman, John Singleton and Lex Marinos. He then met Mic and Jim Conway with whom he would be performing at the Paddington Town Hall. The following day, Tiny did an interview with Roger Crosthwaite from the Daily Telegraph followed by the interview with Southern Flyer - which is how I met him - on the deck, in the sunshine, at the Cosmopolitan Hotel Double Bay. [16]

The 1982 tour comprised a series of club gigs, press interviews and department store appearances, not all well attended. Martin took it all on the chin. He described one venue, 'Six people at Sylvania Heights. There's this huge empty room, they've stayed away in droves! And Tiny did another powerhouse performance. He said, "Whenever there's more than two, it's a show" (a reiteration of Matthew 18:20 - "Whenever two or three are gathered together in my name...") and an amazing show I guess. They're all joking at first and digging each other in the ribs. He'll wear them out. He'll wear out all their resistance until they're up there on the floor dancing. He'll amaze them and they won't even remember it because they won't even want to say he was amazing!' [17]

The Opera House Concert was the big one. It was the place to be if you were in town that Saturday night. The sea of faces comprised Yellow House people, creatives, friends, fashionplates and the kind of people spotted in the Sun-Herald's social pages. Adrian Rawlins came up from Melbourne to compere. Tiny's appearance sure made an impression in a bespoke suit made by Pitt Street tailor, Tony Bechini with fabric designed by Martin. Tiny's shoes were held together with gaffa tape and he carried a shopping bag. Under the musical direction of Nathan Waks, he sang old songs, new songs and songs from his Chameleon album, opening with Martin's favourite *Street Of Dreams*. Martin saw beyond the literal lyric and said, 'He gives it a different meaning'. [18]

Attendance was good but the concert didn't come close to breaking even. The Concert Hall seated 2500 and was probably half full. With no money in the Street of Dreams account the venue still had to be paid for and miraculously – yes, miraculously! - a royalty cheque for Martin's lyrics to *Tales of Brave Ulysses* arrived in the nick of time. Martin usually prompted the music publisher for payment but not this time. Martin wrote to Eric Clapton to thank him. 'This is the first time they've ever sent them spontaneously. It is what paid for the concert at the Opera House'. [19]

Two days later, Martin and Tiny got together at EMI Studio 201 and recorded four new songs: *The Bible My Mother Left For Me*, *Keeping My Troubles To Myself*, *The Last Mile Of The Way* and Tiny's own composition *Forever Miss Dixie*. The four songs read like a mini-summary of Tiny's career, especially the lyric, 'You only liked me best when I was playing the jester…' in *Keeping My Troubles To Myself*. Martin was overjoyed with the recordings, 'Religiously Tiny is the most powerful person I've met. It was unexpected because it was initially a musical interest. And then another side emerged.' [20]

The highlight of the following weekend was a concert at the Paddington Town Hall with the Conway Brothers band as Tiny's support act and backing. Mic was quite awed, 'I didn't know what to expect. There was no rehearsal. We had Peter Dean-Butcher playing t-chest bass, Jim Parnell on guitar (he was very very good), me and Jim. The guitarist had to follow whatever key Tiny was in and whatever he was doing. So they did - and we did. I'm not a good enough musician to follow someone just like that. I didn't know what was going to come next. I ended up playing washboard because I had no idea where he was going. We had no idea what was going to happen. We were in a state of shock.' [21]

Four days after the Paddo concert, Martin, Tiny and his entourage dined with radio personality John Singleton (Singo) at Eliza's Restaurant Woollahra. Singo teased Tiny about his religious beliefs and goaded Martin about his commitment. Martin taped the interaction and played it to visitors and friends.

Singo told Tiny, 'There's only two guys who are looked upon as having the same talent - going back 10 years – Brett Whiteley and Martin Sharp. Brett Whiteley is an independently wealth man. Martin Sharp is independently bloody unwealthy, unhealthy and his paintings are very hard to buy. And when he does them, he won't sell them. Do you suggest God's going to say, "Brett Whiteley at least you gave your talent a go and Mr Sharp you just kept it to yourself" or "Mr Sharp – well at least you're a nice bloke and because you have lack of respect for everyone you've met – you wouldn't give them your paintings because they weren't worthy of them! – well Mr Sharp, you're a good person and Mr Whiteley – you're a dickhead?"'

Tiny replied, 'What's most important in what you've just said is how the grace of God will judge Mr Singleton not how he will judge Mr Sharp.'

'Well that's my worry isn't it,' Singo replied, giving up. [22]

Still enthused by Richard Perry's recording of Tiny's Royal Albert Hall concert, Martin played it to all who called in – and there were many when Tiny was in town. Chris Cordeaux came back, Nico became a regular and Victor Rubin moved into Wirian and played the role of gatekeeper way too efficiently. Tiny liked visitors. He enjoyed the fuss. He made himself accessible and posed for the camera. William Yang snapped away, as did others. One of the classic shots was Roslyn Sharp's photo of Tiny in his stage clothes, strumming his uke while lying in Martin's ensuite bath. [23]

Having chalked up another successful Australian tour, Tiny planned to return the following year. The completion date of the film was a minor sticking point. Tiny told the press, 'The film should be out in maybe another year'. [24] The footage, which was once all about Tiny, was now also about Luna Park. But Tiny trusted Martin. They did a joint-interview with ABC Radio and the presenter described Martin's film as an 'open ended project which will go on indefinitely'. Martin blamed lack of financial resources, 'The film will be finished when its ready, but it's very unlikely that it will receive the support of tax schemes and film commissions and things like this because it's a bit too unusual, so it takes longer to make these things without that sort of advantage'. [25]

Tiny returned to New York and broke-up with his current love, Miss Dixie within 24 hours of arriving home. Home was now the Olcott Hotel, West 72$^{nd}$ Street on New York's Upper West Side, next to the famous Dakota Hotel where *Rosemary's Baby* was filmed and John Lennon was shot. [26] Tiny spent the next three months playing bars, clubs and vaudeville shows after which he signed a multi-city deal with Americana Hotels. Around this time Tiny met James 'Big Bucks' Burnett (known as 'Bucks') from Dallas Texas. Bucks would enjoy a productive relationship with Tiny and he got to know Martin as well. [27]

Tiny's American fans were surprised by the *Chameleon* album and frustrated that they couldn't buy it. Select tracks were popular with some independent FM radio stations, some were fascinated by Tiny's new image but the Post-Punk generation looked to acts like Boy George, Madonna, INXS, Prince and Michael Jackson. Even Martin was beginning to pay Michael Jackson lots of attention after the release of his *Thriller* film clip, loaded with occult imagery.

In an attempt to generate some funds, Martin held an exhibition at Hogarth Gallery Paddington. It was billed as 'Some Posters, A Few Prints and a Couple of Drawings'. Again, the room was packed with well wishers, many of whom hoped Martin would stop spending time and money on the film and get back to the type of cartoons and paintings that had consolidated his reputation during those halcyon 60s days.

The show was directed by Sally Burrows and Elizabeth Evatt, wife of well-known defamation lawyer, Clive Evatt. Saffron was one of his clients – 'absolutely dedicated to defending his good reputation'. [28] Clive's older brother was Herbert Vere Evatt – the judge, parliamentarian, writer and President of the United Nations General Assembly (1948-49). The Evatts owned Hogarth Gallery. They also owned 'Leurella', a big family home in the Blue Mountains. Clive inherited it from his father, Clive Evatt Snr. Located in Leura NSW it resembled Wirian with a tree-change.

The Evatts were curious about Martin's Dream Museum, which had not succeeded in finding a permanent space at Luna Park. In fact, between 1979-1982 there was no Luna Park. Clive commissioned Kingo to design a maquette for a Pop Art representation of Boofhead. Kingo's concept was passed to a tradeperson from Lithgow who cut out and installed a massive Boofhead in the Evatts' bush amphitheatre across the road from Leurella on the edge of an escarpment with breathtaking views of the Jamison Valley. Some locals thought the 12ft Boofhead statue ruined the landscape; others thought it was funny. Kingo explained, 'Clive Evatt commissioned me to do a sculpture on the front of Leurella. Somehow I never got to do it. Clive commissioned someone else – probably much cheaper. He would have shown them the small maquette which I cut out in 3D. It was a combined effort – Clive wanting to put something there and my idea of the fourth explorer - Blaxland, Wentworth, Lawson and Boofhead. I think they've done a jolly good job, by the way. Whoever did it - I'm really pleased the way it all came together.' [29]

This set a Pop Art theme, which blended well with the Toy Museum inside and the reclaimed railway signage in the gardens. Gradually, Leurella expanded into being the biggest toy museum in the southern hemisphere, displaying the best 20$^{th}$ Century toys – Tintin, Boofhead, Alice, The Mad Hatter, Barbie, Noddy, dolls, toy trains, etc. Undoubtedly inspired by Martin and Richard Liney's original Dream Museum, every time they went overseas, the Evatts brought something back to add to the collection. Clive and Elizabeth were serious art collectors too. Their collection included works by Brett Whiteley, Arthur Boyd, Tim Storrier, Jeffrey Smart and other A-listers. They had kept in close contact with the progress of the Yellow House artists over the years.

Back in Bellevue Hill, Martin ran out of money again. He wanted to pick up the master tapes for *Last Mile of the Way* from EMI but he owed them money. He was wondering how to solve this, when he met 'this rather strange woman' while walked to the Double Bay shops. She said, 'Hello, you're Martin Sharp'. Later she rang up, 'Can I do anything for you?' Martin said, 'As a matter of fact I'm a bit short of money…'. She lent him the money. Martin got his master tapes but he'd also acquired Mad Robyn. The mission now was to turn those tapes into vinyl before Tiny's next tour.

Then she called around. 'You're looking hungry,' she said and cooked boiled carrots, mashed carrots, food Martin didn't want to eat. Robyn Giffen was her name. Martin described her, 'a pathetic person who'd had a nervous breakdown and appeared like a shambling eccentric. When I was here on my own, she changed, she started stalking me around the table and asking me very weird questions. She was certainly getting strong and there was this act she was putting on, incredible to see, but it was impervious to penetration. I was half holding onto reality by tidying up and she was trying to break me from it. She started to stare at me and I felt myself going under hypnosis. It was like a snake charmer and I was going out. I admit I was weak at the time, I was terribly exhausted, the place was a wreck, everyone was overworked, the show had happened, the record had been done. Whatever it was – it was like she turned from this pathetic crone into this most powerful witch and evil force. I grabbed an old cross my grandfather had: "I know who you are, get behind me!" It broke the attack, she just cringed, she just frizzled up. She ended up in a mental hospital – broken up with her husband.' [30]

Then Russell decided it was time for him to move out. He said, 'I couldn't stay there forever, I couldn't make a living out of it. I had to start my own life.' [31] Roslyn Sharp expanded, 'Russell hitchhiked up to Cape Tribulation in Northern Queensland and gave all his possessions away before he left. I think he was extremely traumatised when my mother died, then our father dying, then our grandmother dying and Longueville being sold. He didn't know what to do with his life. He looked up to Martin a lot and Martin was kind to him, but some of the other people in the house were horrible.' [32] Russell eventually moved into a flat in Forbes Street where he lived for six years. He then moved to a place in Glebe from which he started a florist business, *Just For Love*. He made a good fist of the business and won some corporate clients.

\*

Martin kept watching – studying – the News. In October 1982 Lindy Chamberlain was found guilty of the murder of her daughter Azaria and jailed in Darwin's Berrimah Prison. It was an outrage! The whole country was split down the middle saying she was guilty or not guilty. The Free Lindy campaign found a voice on talkback radio and public hearings. Martin gave the case lots of attention. 'She's been made the Joan of Arc,' he said, 'I challenge you to do your worst. I'm not going to change my story one inch! This stuff needs a scholastic mind – especially Luna Park. I don't know the mathematics of it, I've only got the intuition. I'm learning a bit of the other. It is a crucible situation, there's so many possibilities'.

Martin gave the Azaria case it's own set of A4 files, He taped the radio programs, videotaped the television broadcasts and collected a stack of newspaper billboards. He believed the Azaria case had similar resonances to Picnic at Hanging Rock and the Ghost Train Fire. [33]

**The history of the case:** on 17 August 1980, 9-week old Azaria Chamberlain was taken from a tent at Ayers Rock (soon to be Uluru) by a dingo. The first Coronial Inquest held in Alice Springs, under Coroner Denis Barrett found a dingo took Azaria and that no member of the Chamberlain family was responsible for her disappearance. Those who understood the case saw it as a good result, though it did make the Northern Territory police look slack.

In November 1981 the Northern Territory Supreme Court quashed the first inquest and ordered a new one hiring the services of so-called forensic experts. Towards the end of 1982 Lindy, heavily pregnant, was found guilty of first-degree murder and sentenced to life imprisonment. Her husband, Seventh-day Adventist minister Michael, was declared an accessory and received an 18-month suspended sentence. Public opinion was strongly divided, even amongst Martin's friends. Sandy Gutman (aka Austen Tayshus) lampooned the case and included lots of Chamberlain jokes in his repertoire, like 'Azaria Chamberlain please make your way to the St John's Ambulance tent, your mother is waiting'. Ho ho ho.

Martin felt otherwise. He believed the treatment of the Chamberlain family showed deep flaws in the Australian consciousness. It showed immense prejudice towards women, contempt for the testimony of Aboriginal trackers and antipathy towards the Seventh-day Adventist (SDA) faith - an antipathy that Martin did not share possibly because in Victoria Cobden's hour of need, SDAs Noni Hedges and Peter & Anita Simmonds had been kind to her. Victoria Cobden was an outspoken defender of Lindy. [34]

Martin began collecting Azaria billboards. Martin had always been fascinated by billboards, like when Elvis died in 1977. Going back to 1966, there's a dozen billboards depicted on page 40 of his *Cartoons* book [35] and Martin had a stack of them, some of which he glued onto a huge backing board and turned into a collage. He did it for Elvis. And for Vincent he collaged postcards, pictures and clippings. Martin wasn't painting much but he was creating canvases and having them framed to exhibition standard.

One of the few pictures that he did start was a Luna Park clown face (Snow Job). He spent the next fifteen years nearly obliterating it with huge textured blobs of white paint (snow) reflecting his increasing frustrations with the bureaucracy.

# 4.
# UNPICKING THE CODE

*How many Martin Sharps would it take to change a light bulb?*
*None, he'd have it classified by the National Trust and he'd leave it there.*
Al Jones

By reading imagery as others read words, Martin was convinced he was onto something. 'It's like an iridologist saying, "I understand what's going on because I know what your eye is about".' [1] It was his 'contribution'.

Martin often felt weighed down with too many ideas, too many worries and not enough resources, 'I've got to turn all this into art – or bring it through – or at least "get" it'. [2] Martin was strident when Tiny was in Sydney. 'I'm making the film so people can see him as I've seen him,' Martin enthused. 'I have a fair idea of how good I am as an artist and my interest is to such a degree in Tiny Tim that I wouldn't be making a mistake about it.' [3] Five months later he languished, 'Sometimes the spirit is there, sometimes it's not. I suppose getting tired and rundown makes problems appear insurmountable'. Pointing to the stack of 250 cassettes of Tiny's phone conversations, Martin added, 'Maybe the best thing I've ever done is these tapes. Tiny said that to me once. So maybe it's going to just be the tapes and they'll be a curiosity - or something - later on.' [4]

Tiny was due back in August. Once announced, the tour became Martin's priority. Psyching up was a natural part of the process. Playing *Keeping My Troubles To Myself* at full belt was part of that. The four songs on this outsized 45rpm record are: *The Bible My Mother Left For Me, Forever Miss Dixie, Keeping My Troubles to Myself* and *The Last Mile of the Way*. The cover featured nothing other than a black and white profile shot of Tiny looking pensive, taken by William Yang.

Martin liked the image so much that he appropriated it for his Kinselas poster announcing Tiny's late-night concerts in September. (5)

Martin would constantly play that record. He would stand close to his punchy little Aiwa speakers, turn the volume to max, close his eyes and bow his head in an attitude of prayer, as the music spilled from his Inner Sanctum into the hall, anteroom and film editing room. Guests were often overwhelmed. Knock knock. Martin sometimes opened the front door, shyly sucking a cigarette with a whirlwind of music pounding in his Inner Sanctum. Or maybe Les Bean did the opening, her clothes painted Jackson Pollock-style. 'Ooo hellooo' she would say, 'he's in there'. Follow the music.

The entry hall was still full of fairground art and objects that appear to have been placed there for some forgotten reason. An 8ft tapestry of Tiny dressed as Pierrot, standing in the Luna Park dominated the back entrance wall. Clown heads. An upright piano. Philippe Mora's *Da Corner* painting, constantly moved around but never hung. For a time, a sex doll lay forlorn beside the front door. Someone brought it around and Martin left it where it was put. It was in desperate need of air. To the left Arthur Barton's *Loona Park* picture was being restored. To the right, the Inner Sanctum - where anything could be happening – gales of laughter, bursts of song or 'Eets beaootiful Marteen' - Willy de la Vega, effusing about Martin's 7ft x 5ft *Vincent Collage*.

Affectionately dubbed 'the Inner Sanctum' by friends and inmates, there was nothing 'inner' about it. Calling it 'Martin's Studio' might have been more accurate. It's where he spent most of his time. There was lots of bric-a-brac in this room: a Billy Tea poster, a plastic Michelin Man, his mother's painting, a Mickey Mouse telephone, Japanese prints, In-Out trays, a photo of his father in stagewear, records by Tiny, Jeannie Lewis or W C Fields, an outsized Goofy doll, a cardboard Prince Charles and Lady Di waving, a Peter Kingston chess set, a tangerine object, a coffee table book titled *Fairground Art* and several other beautiful books.

Scattered about the surface of the outsized former dining table (under which the Salami Sisters had lived) were bills, half-written letters, sketches, paint splattered coffee cups, news clippings, pictures, cut-outs, invitations, scissors, crayons – lots of stuff, including an African hand-held thumb piano known as a kalimba, the only musical instrument Martin ever played. The control panel was Martin's address/phone book, covered with doodles and as handy to him as the ashtray.

Martin was such a hospitable host that some guests felt puzzled at their reception. Scots College English Master, Peter Jensen could not grasp why this famous Australian artist would stop whatever he was doing in order to accommodate a mere drop-in like him. 'What did I do to deserve all this?' a glazed-eyed Peter asked after Martin played him a tape in which Tiny explained what he'd do if he were Pope.

Visitors might include Richard Neville accompanied by a very pregnant Julie Clarke, or Adrian Rawlins, or Margaret Fink - or a surprise guest like Joe P Rick out of the band Jimmy & the Boys. A couple of Cold Chisels called in too, wanting Martin to do the poster for their show 'An Evening with the Circus Animals'. Bill Lucas, an architect dressed in shorts and a short-cut silver jacket, dropped in and spun out. Cousins Roslyn Sharp and Katie Reid visited and danced. Russell showed up with state-of-the-art video equipment. Extras from *Mad Max 2* sat in the Inner Sanctum and didn't say much. Eventually a core group formed around Peter Royles and Toto Renshaw who called in drunk pretty regularly – two heavy drinkers with an audience of – say - six non-drinkers including Martin who was taping everything they said and did.

For a time it seemed Peter and Toto visited for the express purpose of creating spontaneous drama. Martin understood people's needs to perform, especially those who had been denied the conventional stage. He called it the 'Magic Theatre'. He'd seen it all before when a tramp named John Ivor Golding walked straight off the street into the Pheasantry - rapping - just hyper-babble - before leaving as quickly as he came after ensuring he did something shocking. Martin recalls, 'Bags and overcoats stuffed with newspapers. Harold Pinter got one of his characters from this guy.' [6]

One night Peter Royles smashed Martin's framed Picasso/Signac collage (the *Art Book* picture). Everyone was alarmed. What happens now? Toto threw Peter out. Martin brought him back. William was cheeky enough to photograph the pair, though at those sessions you wouldn't see Al or Marilyn for dust. Next night, Toto went head-to-head with Peter again. It was a 'from the uttermost to the guttermost' routine, each exaggerating their social differences. At one point, Toto tried to intimidate Peter, threatening to 'turn the head upon the neck'. In a blink, Peter clipped him. 'You got nothing!' Peter mocked.

'Do it again!' Toto exploded, 'Do it again! Do it again!' He kept repeating 'do it again'. Toto produced mace, 'You have stirred me up! You are an amateur!'

Martin intervened, 'I hope you would never use mace, knives or even a fist in this house, Toto'.

Peter switched the mood, 'Put some music on Martin, instead of this bullshit'. Martin played Elvis singing How Great Thou Art at ear-splitting volume. He was awed, 'I'd say Elvis is religious to the point where – well, you can hear by the way he sings his spiritual songs. That was his last concert.' [7]

Later, that same night, the subject of how Martin might fund the film came up and the possible sale of Wirian was mooted. Peter suggested a price of $1.5 million. Martin had other ideas, 'I don't think it's time at the moment'. Martin tabled his immediate financial requirementss, which were $400,000 to pay his debt plus $100,000 to keep the film going. He was on thin ice but the assets were still manageable. Martin never kept his financial problems secret, the possible sale of the house crept into the background of many conversations. [8]

Afterwards, Martin described Toto and Peter as 'archetypal figures'. Like Tiny and Les, Peter's drive to perform was beyond money and applause. If he didn't have gigs, he busked. If he had nowhere to busk he turned up at Wirian and played to Martin and guests whether they wanted him to or not. He performed drunk or sober, always with gritty passion. Songs like Don McLean's *Vincent*, Bob Dylan's *Just Like Tom Thumb Blues* and his own compositions. Session players and professional musicians were sometimes appalled when Peter was in full voice with Martin actually taping him. Admitting that Peter can be 'incredibly annoying' Martin added that he and Peter had 'a very close bond'. It was Peter, not those pro-musicians, who Martin wanted to record in a studio.

Martin was showing the film one night and Peter suddenly remembered what he'd heard that very night, 'I overheard guys talking at the Cross about how they burned down Luna Park and I never realized they weren't bullshitting until the next day when I read the papers.' This startled Martin, 'You've known that for years and you've never told me?' Peter explained that it wasn't until the film moved him to a certain degree that everything came flooding back. [9]

Martin taped Peter's account, had the tape transcribed and added it to other witness statements about the Ghost Train Fire. Never questioning that Peter might have been drunk or surreal, Martin took Peter's statement at face value and gave it to the Police. It read, 'I overheard a mob of bikies talking about the night and what they had done. I heard them say they went to the Ghost Train. One of them was talking about using lighter fluid to light the fire. They were all very drunk and seemed to know a lot about what happened. It wasn't until I read about the fire in the papers the next day that I realised what had happened myself.' [10]

Martin's new girlfriend, Yensoon Tsai came out of nowhere. Someone suggested she was married, that her married name was Robinson and she was part-owner of a fish and chips shop in New Zealand. William disliked their disbelief, which he found disrespectful. In his book *Sydney Diary* William describes Yensoon like this: 'She was from Taiwan. Her father was a classics scholar and a taoist priest who had raised and educated her in the ancient Chinese way.' [11]

Yensoon designed her own traditional Chinese costumes. She read palms, boiled up herbal remedies, quoted the *Tao Te Ching*, cast the i-Ching and evoked the spirit of an oracle. Martin liked her dish of fried duck. He said, 'There's always been a Chinese sympathy in this house. My grandmother used to have some Chinese help and some of the others too. There are a lot of fans here. Gifts and things. A sort of spirit was here from a few Chinese things. Then Willy (William Yang) came. [12]

'Yensoon has been very kind taking me to see Dr Ling an old Chinese physician who uses herbs to treat my kidney stones. He's a dear man, sitting in the back of a Chinatown grocery. They get on very well. Both are pleased they have met another Chinese who understands Taoism.' [13]

Cruising talkback radio stations late one night Martin taped a track, *Elvis Calling from Heaven*. The voice certainly sounded like Elvis or a damn good impersonator. For a time, Martin played it to visitors. One night, while playing the track, Martin was so overwhelmed by the spirit of Elvis that he prostrated himself before the speaker system. 'Did you feel that?' he said afterwards, finding his feet. 'I was thrown down!'

The following night, hopeful of recreating the same spiritual force, Martin played *Elvis Calling from Heaven* to Richard and Julie. The Elvis voice concluded: 'Ah hope you realise ah am with God now, he is my Manager, ah even have a Golden Guitar...'. When Richard's convulsions of laughter failed to dissolve Martin's reverential attitude, Richard snapped, 'Very touching, it makes me want to go to Hell!' Martin was sadly disappointed.

The following night Sociology lecturer, Robert Wolfgramm called in from Melbourne. Martin had enjoyed Robert's gospel music, particularly his *Refugee* LP. Robert did not crack up laughing when Martin played *Elvis Calling from Heaven*. 'What is it?' Robert questioned. Martin thought it might be Elvis communicating from Heaven. Robert was non-committal, which Martin took as agreement. As Robert was Fijian by birth, Martin showed him his great-grandfather William Kopson's late-19$^{th}$ century 'Fiji Diary'. Kopson was Martin's grandmother Vega's father. At the age of 20, Kopson left Sweden to seek his fortune and Fiji was part of his adventure. 'An *Illywacker* sort of character' is how Martin described him. He knew very little about his Kopson antecedent and summed him up with, 'he was probably seafaring – he made oars'. [14] Robert was fascinated by the authenticity of the 1870s document. In turn, he played Martin some demo tracks from his forthcoming gospel album, *Persecution Games*.

The Delltones too had an album in the pipeline - *Bop Til Ya Drop* - and Chief Delltone, Peewee Wilson, fancied a Martin Sharp cover, photographs by Jonny Lewis and liner notes by Tom Thompson. Martin had seen them perform at the Sydney Stadium in the late-50s, backing Johnny O'Keefe and playing their own set. The Dellies certainly knew their Elvis catalogue and Martin thought they were ideal to join with Tiny on *Are You Lonesome Tonight* at the late night show at Kinselas. Martin and Peewee had no difficulty reaching an agreement: the Delltones performing with Tiny and Martin doing their album cover. Martin's cover was lurid pink ultra hip 50s-style, which perfectly matched the songs.

Then the Cranbrook School asserted its construction rights, which meant guests could no longer park in the Wirian driveway. Everyone, except Martin, now parked outside the gates in Victoria Road, with Martin using the reduced car space to rest his $1800 Peugeot that had long died.

Martin created a new poster for model, Maureen Turquoise's fashion show at Sydney Textile Museum Mosman. It was one of the last posters he did using the services of McGregor Screenprints. For the next 15 years or so he used Stephen Lawson, a former Cranbrook student. (Tim Lewis was one year below him.) Unlike Martin and Kingo, Stephen had never got along with art teacher Justin O'Brien. 'For some reason Justin and I didn't click,' Stephen said, 'Justin put me off art entirely. He corrected and changed everything I did. But when Peter Brown came along, I got on famously with Peter.'

Stephen had a printmaking business in Kent Street Sydney. In the early 70s, Stephen and his girlfriend Lucinda Strauss, painted the rear stairs of the Yellow House. A decade later, Stephen and Martin reconnected. Stephen explained, 'Richard Liney had a place down the road called the Architecture Gallery. He brought Martin into my studio. Martin rang up one day and asked would I do it? The first one was *Tiny Tim Kinselas*. That was a street poster. That *Kinselas* poster is MG litho paper. I used to always prefer printing on the rough side because that made the look and feel of the print better. Martin quite liked it but when we did the Fine Art Limited Editions they were Art Paper, which is 100% cotton.' (15)

Producer, Hayden Keenan had done a lot of work with Martin on *Street of Dreams*. His film *Goin' Down* had its premier screening in Sydney. Martin didn't attend although he was interested in the film because it was about the hardcore goings on in the shared house where Roslyn lived in Potts Point. In the interim, Roslyn had lived in London and New Orleans. She worked as a radiographer and had a strong interest in photography. (16)

Then Tiny arrived.

Eight fans gather at the airport to welcome him, accompanied by his manager, Neil Hollander, who talked with a New Yorker's drawl. When Tiny got through the gate, Martin shyly presented him with the *Keeping My Troubles To Myself* record, after which they were locked tête a tête. Astonished travelers stared in disbelief as Tiny casually ambled through Sydney's international terminal at 9.30am.

Martin arranged a meet-and-greet function on the same day. Tiny and Mr Hollander were expected at Wirian at 2.00. Guests started trickling in at 1.00 - guests with showbiz and art connections dressed for the occasion, nibbling whatever Les Bean offered from a tray as she ballerina-ed her passage around the room. At five-to-two there was a knock. It was Peter Royles drunk. Seconds later Tiny arrived in the same doorway. Seizing the moment, Peter drew him away, 'I wanna show you something Tiny' and he whisked the Eternal Troubadour into the Dream Museum and shut the door leaving guests, and even Mr Hollander, wondering where Tiny went.

Five minutes passed. Another five. Then KER-RASH! The door to the Dream Museum burst open and out bounced Peter on one leg, holding his shin and saying fuck rather a lot. Tiny was in a flap because he couldn't handle the sight of blood. What happened? It was all about Peter showing Tiny his new Fender Twin amp, which he picked up then dropped on his shin. It was a deep graze. Martin and Les sorted it out - Tiny was escorted around the room meeting the Delltones, radio presenters, ABC people, journos and Yensoon, who made a quiet impression. (17) Les left a different kind of impression. Some thought her crazy - but what would they know? Les took on quite a lot of the 'responsible' stuff around the house, including cleaning. Also, she didn't drink, allowing no other explanation for her Dada performance routines than her will to do them.

Les had a private schooling where she excelled at horse riding and ballet. She would have been an excellent ballerina but she had the wrong sort of figure. In Wirian, she frequently pranced from room to room doing *petit saut* and *petit pas*. That was normal. To add to the performance, Les played several musical instruments by randomly plucking or banging them. Every week she would perform at talent shows in Paddington's gay clubs. Every week she'd come last. Tiny accepted her as part of the general ambiance. Mr Hollander hated her. [18]

One memorable night, Les swanned into the Wentworthville RSL Club, past security in her painted clothes. She hit the dance floor as Tiny was breaking into *Babyface*. Les swirled into her quazi-ballet routine and others joined her. With Tiny in full flight, people started dancing, cavorting, having fun. Horrified, Mr Hollander called security, had Les ejected, took out an AVO against her and threatened to cancel the Kinselas shows should Les be admitted. 'I don't want that woman within 50 metres of Tiny!' he exploded. Although he liked her, Tiny was too browbeaten by Hollander to intervene. [19]

The following night Tiny played the Castanet Club's Funny Festival in Newcastle, north of Sydney. Mr Hollander didn't attend, Les did. She danced, gyrated and did her crazed ballerina routine when the band - the Castanet Connection – broke into exciting but disorderly version of *Rock Around the Clock* with Tiny in full cry. A helluva moment! After the show, Les was literally mobbed by admirers. After Tiny - she was certainly the star that night.

Martin wasn't there but he arranged for the Castanet show to be taped. He studied the tape and fixed on Tiny's take on the Men At Work song *Down Under*. 'Did you hear that?' said Martin, focusing on the lyric, 'you better run you better take cover'. He interpreted this as a Jeremiad on the city of Sydney for its unwillingness to remediate the situation at Luna Park. Martin believed an admission of corporate guilt and a memorial to the victims would make a solid start. Luna Park was always in Martin's thoughts but with Tiny in town, Tiny was the immediate focus. Down Under, eh? [20]

After the in-store appearances, clubs and ordinary bookings, Martin always organized at least one 'Art' gig for every tour, inviting friends, cousins, artists and non-RSL type people to attend. Redolent of the *Chameleon* album and *Wonderful World of Romance,* Tiny's four late-night concerts at Kinselas (11.00pm-1.00am) were like charming 1940s nights. Naturally enough, there were crazy moments too.

Photographers went wild when the Delltones joined Tiny on *Are You Lonesome Tonight*. So did Peter Royles. He scrambled onto the stage yelling 'Tiny! Tiny!' This was way too much for one audience member, who grabbed Peter by the neck and down they went. *Do you gaze at your doorstep and picture me…crash…*two tables down, eight drink-splattered guests, broken glass underfoot. This was surely a bridge too far? Les was among those who berated Peter afterwards: 'Martin is paying for all this and you do THAT!' Several friends advised Martin to kick Peter out for keeps. But Martin appreciated that the arrival of an international star can cause a surge of energy to which some people are drawn. Instead of banning Peter, Martin booked him as Tiny's support act on the following night. Peter played out the interval, absolutely sober. [21]

Back home, Martin introduced Tiny to his mother who lived in an apartment in Elizabeth Bay. She was charmed. Returning to the film editing room, he showed Tiny the rushes of the film, which included lots of footage of the Ghost Train Fire. This seemed okay with Tiny. The completion date was the only niggle. Ever keen to get Tiny into a studio, Martin arranged for him to record the raunchy AC/DC song *Highway to Hell*. The name Denny Burgess came up as a muso who could coordinate the session. Denny (and brother Col) had a strong Rock CV - going back to the Throb, the Masters Apprentices and even AC/DC. Martin contacted Denny and asked him to put together Tiny's backing band, which he did, assuming the recording would run more-or-less like other Rock sessions. However, the first thing Denny saw when he walked into the Sun Studios (near Central) was Yensoon in full traditional Chinese attire, 'She didn't say a thing the whole time we were there'. It took him aback. 'Hmm…this is going to be different,' Denny reflected. [22]

Denny continued, 'We learned *Highway to Hell* but it was changed around. We realized we had to follow Tiny. We couldn't play a set thing because he'd change it each time. It was incredibly interesting - I came out of there going, "This guy is amazing" because he was so different - different attitude to recording, different way of doing things.' [23]

As well as recording and performing, Tiny was on a constant round of media interviews. One of the most successful was with actor Kate Fitzpatrick who concluded, 'He should be declared a National Treasure by the US Government'. After the interview she whisked him off to the Botanical Gardens where Tiny was photographed singing *Tiptoe Through the Tulips* amongst the poppies. [24]

Through all this activity, it's difficult to believe Tiny found time to take a break but when he did – usually late at night - he would sit around Wirian's kitchen table with Martin and maybe Al, William, Marilyn, Jonny, Yensoon, Fergus, Anne-Louise, Nico, Peter, Les Bean…whoever was in the house at the time. He'd strum his little uke, sing a bit and talk about his latest Miss.

Tiny's last appearance before heading home was Ringling Circus in the southern Sydney suburb of Revesby. The idea was to film Tiny in a cage with a lion. But Tiny was afraid of everything – mice, cockroaches – he was even afraid of Jane, Martin's somnolent corgi. Tiny showed up at the Circus with Martin and Yensoon, he greeted the film crew, saw the lion and froze. (This was one mangy and submissive lion!) Tiny agreed to enter the cage if the lion tamer came in too. It really was a non-event and the Australian press got a pretty lame story, but that's not how it came across in America. Unexpectedly, the American media picked up on the 'Tiny in the Lion's Den' story. When he got back to New York, Tiny's agent announced that he had 18 months of appearances at the Great American Circus. Tiny was required to perform a 10-minute medley after the trained bear and before the elephants. [25]

The 10th Anniversary celebrations of the Sydney Opera House were held after Tiny had gone. Martin's poster was sold (in two editions) from the Opera House gift shop and he was invited to attend the Cocktail party for 400 friends of the House at which Jill Wran, wife of the State Premier, was Guest of Honour. To celebrate the occasion on 20 October, ABC Radio broadcasted a day-long series of programs about the history and personalities of Sydney Opera House. The Sydney Symphony Orchestra played and there was a cocktail party in the evening where Lin Utzon, daughter of Jorn Utzon, the architect of the masterpiece, delivered an impressive address that Martin described as 'magnificent'. Lin was a ceramicist whose work was being exhibited in David Jones Gallery Sydney at the time. She became one of Martin's most valued friendships. Like Martin, Lin had been a student of East Sydney Tech (National Art School). Her ceramic works were exhibited all over the world - Copenhagen, New York, Oslo, Beijing. Whenever she came to Sydney, she always came to Wirian.

Towards the close of the year, Martin started preparing an exhibition, to be held in 12 months time at Ivan Dougherty Gallery Paddington. Martin collaged news clippings, cartoons and billboards about Luna Park, intending to mask his message for receptive eyes only. His canvases began to clutter up with words, like his Vincent Collage. Anyone who took the time to read everything would have the entire Ghost Train saga in detail from Martin's perspective – which would have taken hours. Through a labyrinth of eastern and western mysticism Martin was seeking answers. He revisited Jeannie Lewis' *Clowning Calaveros*. 'Once again a child had to be the victim'.

'The kids in the fire…' said Martin '…and Azaria Chamberlain.' [26]

Martin was also contemplating the song *Dingo* by Gary Shearston. Martin picked a prophetic voice in Gary's Dingo song of 10 years ago – 'Run dingo run'. In the early-to-mid 60s Gary had been instrumental in shaping an authentic Australian voice in folk music. He moved in London and wrote the novel *Balkenna* and had a Top 10 hit with the Cole Porter song, *I Get A Kick Out of You*. Peter Paul and Mary recorded his song *Sometime Lovin'*. Gary returned to Australia, studied for the Anglican priesthood and kept recording new material, which Martin enjoyed. [27]

Martin sketched a dingo in the jaws of the happy/sad face of Luna Park when he drew the cover for Robert Wolfgramm's new Gospel album, *Persecution Games*. [28]

# 5.
# DEVIL IN THE DETAIL

*Martin's paintings are like symphonies - like music.*
*And music is the greatest art that humankind has invented.*
Roger Foley

Martin started the year creating three '1984' posters, two for 'Sydney Festival '84' [1] and a cover/poster for the January POL magazine. [2] Having designed more than 15 posters over the past two years [3] Martin was moving away from that form of expression. Using Stephen Lawson's services, Martin transitioned from posters on street quality paper to prints on 100% cotton art paper. [4] He said, 'I'm trying to get away from posters. To get your head in that space you've got to gear up into a whole different ballgame.' [5]

Martin's father, Dr Henry Sharp, died 23 January, two days after Martin's 42$^{nd}$ birthday. His wife, Dorothy told Martin that his father had left him nothing. His mother was furious but Martin was okay with that but bothered by the speed of the burial, 'He was very swiftly put in the ground. I understood why we couldn't love each other – it was because I wasn't the child of Henry and Dorothy, I was the child of my mother. I think because a Dad is a Dad, love is still there but it couldn't happen on this worldly level to the degree that it should have. When he died all the love that was inherent in my father was freed and it could flow on. His spirit came to me. He came as soon as he could. It was great. It couldn't be better. You can't lose your family. You never really lose your father. It's impossible. At his funeral the next day - I was smiling!' [6]

After his father's passing, Martin made a resolute effort to take care of his stepmother Dorothy. Cousin Roslyn helped. She explained, 'Martin felt an obligation to keep an eye on Dorothy. He would regularly ring me up. (He loved talking on the phone.) If he had to take Dorothy out for lunch he would ask me to come along as a conversationalist.' This continued for the next 15 years. [7]

Henry was born in 1908 in the Old Candelo Hospital, 22k south-west of Bega NSW. Martin's grandmother Elizabeth (Bessie) was born in Bega in 1886.

In March, Martin crammed his grandfather Stuart Ritchie's trunk with Luna Park documents and took a trip to Bermagui, on the coast from Bega. It was mostly a study trip, family history was a convenient sideline. Martin's focus was to oppose the proposed demolition of Coney Island to make way for a new roller coaster ride. It was also to conceptualise his next exhibition – titled *Luna Images* - to be held at Ivan Dougherty Gallery Paddington in August, 'I went to Bermy to filter through the Luna Park material, these events that are caused by plotting, not caring for kids, carelessness, living a human life – the way of the world.' [8]

Martin spent a week on the south coast, a short drive from several dairy farm holdings once owned by the Sharp-Ritchie side of his family. At the turn of the century Martin's great-grandfather's brother, William Ritchie (1840-1896) held oyster leases and ran cattle a 10-minute drive south of Bermagui in an area known as the Murrah. Slightly further south Martin's great-grandfather, Henry Lucas St George Ritchie (1843-1905), had a farm/gold mine in Tanja. Martin checked out both areas. There was no visible trace of his ancestry - or of anything else really, other than farms, paddocks and wonderful waterways.

Martin went for occasional swims at the beach and he met the locals, like sharkmesher and a former abalone diver Allan Broadhurst. Allan described their meeting, 'Martin seemed really interested in what we were doing. In my case, I was a fisherman but he's an international artist. I would struggle to come up to his level. He didn't let that enter the equation. Instead he came down to mine where I was the champion and he wasn't. He talked about fishing as a teenager, Port Hacking that's for sure. He had early childhood memories of enjoying the solitude of recreational fishing.' [9] While this conversation took place, Allan's little daughter Kate got her crayons out, sketched the face of Luna Park and presented it to Martin. Along with other child art, he hung it with the other *Luna Images* in the August exhibition.

On his return, Martin watched the Frank Moorehouse TV drama, *Who Killed Baby Azaria?* And he looked for Ghost Train fire parallels in the Lionel Jeffries film *The Amazing Mr Blunden*. Martin then checked the Michael Barker documents, re-read his correspondence with the Barker family and pondered the meaning of the sacred blue kingfisher. Then he sorted Luna Park news articles, material from the Inquest, letters and child art. From these he made big collages that he asked Fergus to deliver to Acme Framing St Peters. Martin designed their business card.

Jo's health was deteriorating. She could no longer manage her self-contained Elizabeth Bay apartment, the sale of which provided her with a comfortable budget to renovate upstairs in Wirian where she could have her own rooms. Even though Street of Dreams was broke, Martin spent big on these renovations. Of course, the renovation money came from Jo whereas Street of Dreams was Martin's problem. Again he asked the Australian Film Commission (AFC) for support. AFC sent a representative who watched the film and declined. He also approached

AVCO Finance for a second mortgage. AVCO extracted a lot of financial information and also said no. [10]

Meanwhile, Wirian was going a bit mad. Someone called Philip moved in and started dealing speed. He only lasted three days before Martin ejected angrily. The cycle of Wirian inners-and-outers and callers seemed just as fast: Philippe Mora, Richard Liney, Margaret Fink, Robert Wolfgramm, Jonny Lewis, Tim Lewis, Peewee and Carla Wilson, Denny and Clare Burgess, Sky McCreadie, Steve Mackenzie, Isabelle Morse, Mad Robyn, Jeannie Lewis, George Gittoes, Toto Renshaw, Pilot Pete, Fix-It Bob, Clayton Simms, Marilyn Karet, Peter Royles, Richard Neville, Julie Clarke, Al Jones, Nico Flamer-Caldera, Yensoon Tsai, Les Bean, Harold the Kangaroo, Beth, Fergus, Sue, Marro, Robbie, Gary and Garry – were all there.

Some came with a purpose, like architect Alex Popov who drew the plans for Jo's renovation. Others were simply curious, like the well-known New York Pop and graffiti artist Keith Haring, who was in Australia to create temporary murals in Melbourne and for the Art Gallery of New South Wales. Haring sat quietly in the Inner Sanctum, reading, sketching and awaiting Martin. But Martin didn't show up. So Haring gave stickers and badges to everyone who sat with him and talked. He retreated a bit when Les strode through the house proclaiming, 'Get his autograph! He's famous! He's famous!'

Around this time, Tiny met New York glamour piece, Jan Alweiss – Miss Jan – who moved into the Olcott Hotel NY with him and his mother Tillie. Miss Jan couldn't abide living with Tillie and promptly moved out. Tiny and Miss Jan remained married for a decade but they didn't live together. Martin played a tape of Tiny explaining all this.

*

Meanwhile in Epping Sydney, with twenty-two thousand subscribers, Phil Ward's *Small Business Letter* had become Australia's most successful business newsletter and the cornerstone of his Australian Newsletter Publishers (ANP) enterprise. For a businessperson, Phil was a rare bird, not primarily motivated by money and business success. He poured his profits into the Free Lindy campaign.

Phil and Michael Chamberlain had studied theology together at the Seventh-day Adventist Church's training centre, Avondale College in Cooranbong NSW. When Lindy was pronounced guilty, Phil knew they were innocent and launched a private investigation into the case, which resulted in the publication of his book *Azaria, What the Jury Wasn't Told*.

Not only did Phil write that a dingo took the baby, he even said which one: Ding, the one that park ranger Ian Cawood and his wife Val treated as a wild pet. Notwithstanding the 'don't feed the dingoes' signs, Phil claimed the rangers broke their own rule and kept feeding them. In August 1980, there were drought conditions at the Rock and dingoes were frighteningly audacious. They were hungry enough to enter tents and attack at least two children prior to taking Azaria.

On the fatal August night – according to Phil - Ding broke into the Chamberlain tent, picked up baby Azaria, snapped her neck and carried her east to Anzac Flag Pole where he put her down because he heard commotion from the camping area. The noise Ding heard was the panicky start of the search. So Ding changed direction and headed for somewhere 'safe' – the Cawood residence. According to trackers Nipper Winmatti and Nui Miningerie, the dingo entered the Cawood property, but couldn't say what happened next because they were stopped at the Cawood fence. Shortly afterwards, Peter Elstrom, a young pilot from the city, spotted someone burying something in the Cawood backyard. Whatever it was, the wild life must have dug it up and consumed it before sunrise. This and more was in Phil Ward's book and Martin was convinced Phil was right. (In 1988 the book attracted a $500,00 defamation case, resulting in an out-of-court settlement to seven people.) [11]

Michael Chamberlain was less certain about Phil's theory. His views shifted back-and-forth over the years but in 1984 he said, 'I personally do not think that anyone was involved in the disposal of Azaria's body. However, that does not mean that I don't think there's been a cover-up of some kind'. [12]

Martin taped late night talkback radio programs about Azaria and collected the Chamberlain broadsheets, put aside for him by the Double Bay newsagent. Martin was fascinated how headlines were so easily manipulated, with shout-lines like '**LINDY GUILTY**' in big print and 'witness says' in small. 'Often people don't buy the paper – but they do read the broadsheets. Whilst the paper may cover itself editorially, broadsheets are unquestioned. In a few words a libel has been published – but I doubt ever prosecuted. This could be important evidence because it is before the judgment is handed down by the Courts.' [13]

Martin held the same exhalted opinion of Michael Chamberlain as he did Jenny Godson. These people were special, having walked the Valley of the Shadow of Death and come out the other side. Keen to connect, Martin found Michael Chamberlain's contact details and mailed him a copy of Tiny's *Keeping My Trouble to Myself* record. Michael agreed to visit Martin and was welcomed at Wirian by everyone except Sanderson - who skulked off. At the time, Sanderson was working for Haydn Keenan on the film *Pandemonium*, the tackiest Azaria film of all.

On arrival, Michael had that haunted-hunted look from having suffered too much media attention. He was jumpy, as if expecting a journalist to suddenly spring out from behind a clown. Michael had never been in a house like this before, one with its own film editing room and private toy museum. Clearly this was not another trap. So Michael settled down and asked Martin about the pieces from the funfair. The reply inevitably led to the events surrounding the Ghost Train fire and into Carl Jung's concept of synchronicity. Michael listened, in his thoughtful way, when Martin played the Gary Shearston song *Dingo*. He was shown all the Azaria articles, tapes of Free Lindy talkback radio, TV news videos, Martin's drawing of a dingo in the jaws of Luna Park as the cover art for Robert Wolfgramm's *Persecution Games* LP. Michael was nothing less than astounded. He didn't disagree with anything. He simply didn't comprehend Martin's motivations. Why the stack of 'Azaria' billboards? Why Tiny Tim posters adorning most walls, 500 Mickey Mouse figurines, blueprints of Jan Utzon's Sydney Opera House – why?

On his way out Michael walked past the LJ Hooker For Sale sign propped near the door - what was that about? Martin dropped the news that the place was on the market. 'Don't sell this house…' said Michael in an off-the-cuff manner.

'Did you hear that!' Martin stressed after Michael had gone. 'He told me not to sell the house!' Later that night, around midnight, after a short ceremony, Martin gathered together all live-in Wirianites and announced the house was off the market. The LJ Hooker For Sale sign was taken down, signed and dated by Martin - who arranged for Fergus to get it framed.

From Seventh-day Adventist minister Michael Chamberlain to former-Seventh-day Adventist minister the controversial Dr Desmond Ford, Martin drove to Macquarie University to hear Ford talk. Undeterred that the esteemed Biblical exegete had never heard of Tiny Tim and had no involvement in the Azaria case, Martin gave the Doctor of Theology a signed copy of *Keeping My Troubles to Myself*. [14] On his way out, Martin checked his big Tiny Tim painting that the university had commissioned almost a decade ago. It was hung in a stairwell. Martin wanted to touch it up.

Martin's *Luna Images* exhibition at Ivan Dougherty Gallery expressed his 'take' on the fate of the Park. It was all there. The changing face, starting with Rupert Brown 1935-1945, Arthur Barton late 60s-1973, Martin 1973-1981 and the 1982 fibreglass face. Anyone who took on the microscopic task of reading every word of newsprint would have gained a comprehensive summary of Martin's current metaphysical thought about the fire. Martin admitted his medium was too dense, 'It's a bit of a complicated exhibition to understand. It takes a lot of hard looking.' Abe Saffron's name, though small, was peppered throughout. The devil was in the detail. [15]

Phil Ward was back in the news, this time for being physically restrained by five policemen during a Chamberlain press conference. Admiring his pluck, Martin invited Phil to visit Wirian and when he did, Martin took him to see his *Luna Images* exhibition. Martin personally walked select guests around the exhibition room, talking about each piece, hoping they might grasp what he was trying to express. Sometimes he was a bit too optimistic. Impressing Patrick White was never easy - everybody knew that. Martin arranged a private showing for Patrick who brought Jim Sharman along. 'You're looking fantastic,' said Martin, opening the conversation. Patrick growled, 'Never say that to anyone, they might drop dead the next day. In fact, if you say that to them they usually do!' Martin handed him a copy of Phil's *Azaria, What the Jury Wasn't Told*. Patrick glanced at the cover, shoved it back and walked off, leaving Martin trailing him around the room. [16]

In the end, Martin was disappointed in the exhibition, 'People stayed away in droves. There weren't many Friends of Luna Park. I would have liked people to say, "Ted Hopkins' photographs of Luna Park are extraordinary". Or, "Arthur Barton's paintings are amazing" but it didn't get a critical response at that level. I'll have to accept the more esoteric feedback over the general public.' [17]

Meanwhile Luna Park management pressed on with their plan to demolish the Coney Island building. Friends of Luna Park had to act! Martin and Kingo strongly expressed their feelings to manager Hal Droga, who gave no satisfaction. Turning to the press was no better, the Sydney Morning Herald applauded the direction management was taking. In his book, *Luna Park, Just For Fun*, Friend of Luna Park, Sam Marshall described the drama, 'Plans for a massive Arrow Huss roller coaster running the full length of the Park are revealed. To fit it on the site, Coney Island would have to be demolished. Harbourside Amusements approaches the Museum of Applied Arts and Sciences to determine whether they will take the building. A report commissioned by the Department of Public Works on the importance of Coney Island recommends its retention'. [18] With the Department of Public Works onside, all was not lost.

In Sydney for his 1984 Australian tour, Eric Clapton decided to drop in on Wirian to look up his old friend. With no fanfare Martin introduced him to astonished friends, just 'This is Eric...' It wasn't an evening about past times, the difficult 70s. 'Patti Boyd' was off limits. Wine was forbidden. Instead, Eric sat through the film footage about Tiny after which Eric raised the matter of the dingo that had hit the news in England. Martin explained that the dingo did it. No body, no motive, no opportunity - Lindy is clearly innocent. Eric paid quiet attention and chain-smoked Rothmans cigarettes.

Knock knock. Peter Royles unexpectedly showed up carrying a new guitar. Not recognising Eric, Peter asked him, 'What do you do?'

'I'm in a band.'

'Then you'd know about guitars - what do you think of this one?' Peter thrust his new Takemine into Eric's hands, who played a few chords, handed it back, said it was fine and Peter went home.

Two nights later, Martin threw a grand party for Eric and his band. Everyone was there – OZ people, Yellow House people, Wirian people, media people, friends, Donald Duck Dunn (from Eric's band), Renee Geyer (Eric's support act) and so on. Les banged her drum, William took lots of photos, Brett Whiteley and Eric had a tête a tête that no one dared interrupt, Toto berated a young woman for no apparent reason, Wendy Whiteley confronted Yensoon – 'Who ARE you?' Peter Royles burst in - 'You didn't tell me that was Eric Clapton!' he accused Martin. Peter sang 'Wonderful Tonight' at Eric, which seemed to frighten him. And so the party progressed. Eric was long gone before it hit its rowdy climax. Later that week he and his band performed the Hordern Pavillion. Martin, Yensoon and a few friends were there.

Then 64-year old Harold 'the Kangaroo' Thornton moved in, with the words 'Greatest Genius' hand-painted on the back of his jacket. Harold made his mark in Amsterdam in the mid-70s where he painted the mural on the first Cannabis Café, even though he never smoked cannabis. His psychedelic pictures (Magic Realism) and his persona made him seem like an old acid-eater, even though he'd never dropped acid either. He was naturally, not chemically, eccentric.

Harold's greatest artwork was himself. Like Les, he painted his clothes, lilac suit-coat, even his little chapeau and its wooden doily. Sometimes he wore a chicken suit. He danced like an imp and he danced often. Notwithstanding their 30-year age difference, Les and Harold seemed fated to combine. Like Les, his songs followed no conventional musical structure. Now there were two of them coming last at Talent Quests!

To clear the end room for Luna Park research, the Dream Museum was temporarily moved out. Martin's working papers and files were moved in along with some eerie photos, menacing cartoons and two newly acquired comic books. Australian artist Trevor Weekes made pointed references to 'Mr Big' and the Ghost Train fire in an *Outcast* comic book published by Angus & Robertson in North Ryde. But the *Strange Days* comic was a puzzle. No one knew anything about its creator, British artist Brendan McCarthy, nor his Californian publisher, Eclipse Comics. One of McCarthy's segments featured a ship of fools, with the Luna Park face and towers as the ship's figurehead. Richard Walsh was involved in the publication of *Outcast*, which explains Luna Park coming to the fore. But – coming out of America - why would *Strange Days* care? [19]

Then Martin bought a photocopier and copied a lot of newspaper clippings and documents. While enlarging a picture 400% Martin noted the pixilated effect of blowing up newsprint. Enjoying himself, he worked over the best blow-ups with his Derwent coloured pencils. It gave him ideas for a portrait of his mother, a portrait based on the photo on display of Jo looking young and beautiful.

Martin spent time with Jo every day. Jeannie came to see her. As a little gift, she gave Jeannie a beautiful velvet cap with sequins and glass beads. Marilyn and Al Jones also kept her company. Yensoon became her part-time carer. Jo occasionally came downstairs. There would be an announcement before Martin assisted her passage down the stairs to the kitchen, where she would seat herself at the head of table and good-naturedly converse with Al, Marilyn, William – people like that. Les Bean would usually come up with something that put a smile on her face. Sometimes Russell brought her flowers. The kitchen often had lavish flower displays, provided by Russell's end-of-the-day flowers from his *Just for Love* (later, *Flower King*) business. [20]

The Wirian crowd was always shifting in or moving out. Marilyn moved out but continued working on the film. Fergus and William left too. Al moved into

William's under-the-house room. Dave Sanderson took a room in the upstairs servant's quarters and unexpectedly won a Daytime Emmy Award for Outstanding Individual Achievement in Children's Programming. It came from America in the mail. On receiving it, Dave raced upstairs to brag about it to Jo. Appalled Roslyn said, 'That crazy guy David Sanderson had come back from LA and won a film award. Jo was in bed. In exuberance he threw the award at her, it hit her in the ribs and broke her ribs!' [21]

Regular drop-ins included Peter Thompson who reckoned that he was a flight pilot, so everyone called him Pilot Pete. He played chess without rules. Any piece could move anywhere. One of Pilot Pete's musings was that Jesus drove a Citroen. Martin never had an easy time with Citroens. He bought a new Honda Civic that he kept for the rest of his life.

Straight from an asylum, Mad Robyn phoned Martin every night on the stroke of midnight. She seemed meek at first but could certainly turn forthright. Twice, she threatened to come around and torch the place if Martin didn't come to the phone straight away. Another time she introduced herself to a Wirian first-timer, announcing, 'I masturbated last night' where a simple 'hello' would have done. Julie, Richard, Kingo and others pled with Martin to monitor his houseguests. Julie feared Toto might do something dreadful. Richard thought the place was getting 'too mad'. Kingo couldn't stand the aggressive dogs, especially Mio the bull terrier who shredded a guinea pig on the lawn.

Some calm was restored when Garry Shead and his wife Judit Englert-Shead returned from Hungary. They had a commission to paint a 50-metre mural on eight panels of concrete on the Harris Street wall of the Dunbar Building of Sydney Technical College. [22] Garry and Judit were a friendly presence in the house, helping out, avoiding dramas, with Garry playing chess with Toto (and others) according to a conventional set of rules.

Said Garry, 'We came back from Hungary and moved from one place to another. I told Martin and he said, "Come and stay here". That's what we did.' Sometimes Martin and Garry sat up late and talked. 'The film was being made. He knew I was into esoteric/spiritual things - that was where we got this connection. Martin asked me for help (he probably asked many other people). I certainly had some definite ideas that Martin took on board. I'm quite aware that there were dark forces. I heard everything about Luna Park. I accept what Martin said. It's true! I just didn't want to go down that track too much' [23]

Martin barely ate. He smoked 60 cigarettes per day and drank endless cups of strong coffee. Judit kept him fed and Yensoon often switched the coffee to herbal teas. She also brewed up an ancient Chinese de-tox recipe that she regularly gave Martin. It smelled dreadful.

On the sixth anniversary of the Ghost Train fire, 9 June 1985, Martin attended a Requiem Mass for Jonathon Billings, Richard Carroll, Michael Johnson and Seamus Rahilly, the four Waverley College boys who died in the Ghost Train. It was held at St Mary Magdalene Catholic Church, Rose Bay. He came and went quietly and partook of the Eucharist.

Clayton Simms and Fix-It Bob from Bermagui, both came to Wirian for short stints as handymen. Mal was another Bermagui contact. He had done time in Long Bay Jail. There, he overheard a nasty group of inmates try to out-gross each other. The one that caught Mal's ear said that he'd 'torched the Park for Abe'. He sent word to Martin who set up a meeting. [24]

Martin was cooking up a lot of information in that end room, but no commercial press was interested in specifically linking Abe Saffron to the Ghost Train fire. They were probably worried about defamation and patently disinterested in synchronicity. *Rolling Stone* and the *National Times* said no, so Martin approached Fairfax journalists Max Suitch and Brian Toohey. They too declined. Everyone seemed indifferent to Martin's story then the Police took notice. This was most unexpected.

One night Mad Robyn had an angry confrontation with Pilot Pete. Claiming he had raped her, she picked up Martin's phone and called the Rose Bay Police. Two young cops came around. Martin ushered them into the Inner Sanctum to discuss the matter but Robyn suddenly lost all interest in the rape, took Pilot Pete to the kitchen and left Martin to explain. So Martin brought out his Luna Park files and showed them everything - testimonials, legal documents, witness statements, pictures of the Minotaur, Mr Sin cartoons, the *Strange Days* comic. The young cops couldn't believe they'd walked into all this! They felt Martin should make a formal presentation to Superintendent Ernie Shepard ('the Good Shepherd') of the NSW Police Internal Security Unit (ISU) near Central Station, which Martin was more than willing to do. He asked Bermagui-Mal to come along too.

'I was hanging out with the Freddy Owens crowd,' Mal began, 'and they were bragging about what they'd done. One said he'd chucked his girlfriend out of a first floor window...'.

Superintendent Ernie Shepard interrupted, "Hang on...I have a document about that case on my desk right now.' Just like that, Mal convinced them he wasn't making everything up. 'Go on.'

'Anyway this guy called Scar said, "I torched the Park for Abe".' [25]

Checking his files, the Good Shepherd said there were two 'Scars' currently in the New South Wales prison system and he produced mug shots. Malcolm picked one. Ernie Shepard promised to follow it up.

Although the *National Times* had told Martin they weren't interested in connecting Saffron to the Ghost Train fire, they ran a story that was almost as accusing. Journalist Patrick Howard linked six other fires to Saffron-linked properties in 1980-81, shortly after the Ghost Train fire. Like Luna Park, these buildings were part of the fringe entertainment industry, distantly connected to Saffron. The question of arson was raised in all cases. [26]

The next newspaper report was not so good. Headlined, 'Good Shepard Dumped', Shepard was removed from the case. The report read, 'The replacement of Superintendent Ernie Shepard as head of the NSW Police Internal Security Unit has surprised and angered many of his colleagues. The Sunday Telegraph has learned that Mr Shepard and his wife had received a number of death threats in recent weeks. During the 10-months he occupied the top ISU job – charged with rooting out corruption in the force – Shepard's unit has taken action against 19 police, the majority on charges of conspiracy to pervert the course of justice.' (27)

With the removal of the Good Shepard, the ISU investigation was over for Martin but the matter did not end there. Independent NSW MP John Hatton made a speech in State Parliament claiming that Saffron was the beneficial owner of the park. He reopened the Inquiry by raising questions 'of any relationship between one or more of the directors (of Harbourside) and Mr Abraham Saffron'. Those lingering suspicions simply would not go away. (28)

One evening John Barker came to Wirian in a fluster and told Martin about a death threat he'd received that afternoon. Martin got him to make an official statement, which read, 'At about a quarter past three today I was sitting at my desk at the Housing Commission. I get calls all day from people wanting to know how much they've got to pay off on their house. This one said, "Is that John Barker?" I said it was. Then a voice said, "Stop going to Martin Sharp's or you'll wind up like your brother". That's definitely what he said and he said it slowly, in an older voice. I remember him as being very articulate. Everything pronounced and punctuated. And then there was silence'. (29)

Who would do that? A serious hitman wouldn't mess around with phone calls. No, it was an insiders' threat, someone who knew Martin's relationship with Michael Barker. Who could it be? John said, 'I never felt truly threatened though our dear friend Martin was certainly very concerned in the light of the ghost train fire and Michael's death. (30)

Martin was very concerned indeed. Under the heading 'Luna Park – A Case of Arson' he issued the following statement which he photocopied and handed around. 'A threat was received yesterday afternoon (31 May 1985) as a telephone call to John Barker. It was received at approximately 3.00pm at his place of work. He was threatened that if he didn't stop coming to see me, that he'd "wind up like his brother". Michael Barker was working as a photographer with the Friends of Luna Park. He was killed in a hit-run accident on 21 November 1980. Very few people know anything about my relationship with John Barker and we believe that this threat came from someone who is in a position to imply that John's brother Michael had been murdered. Prior to this threatening phone call we had not thought of his death as anything but an accident. I have been studying the history of Luna Park with John Barker, who has carried on his brother's work in respect to Luna Park. Not as a photographer, but in other ways. John was among those who believed that the fire in the Ghost Train on 9 June 1979 was an act of arson. And that the perpetrators were commissioned by Abe Saffron, who is now in control of Luna Park through his solicitor David Baffsky and his cousins Hal and Colman Goldstein who – with no previous experience in funfairs – won the lease from the NSW Government.

'There was a perversion of justice in the intimidation of witnesses when the Police constructed a case which gave the illusion of the fire being caused by an electrical fault. There was a lot of haggling over the lease and Michael Edgley is only the front man. They have shown themselves – in my estimation – to be insincere in their running of the amusement park, which they obtained through criminal means. The evidence includes the testimonies of Mona Smith, Les Dowd, Peter Royles, Malcolm Mead, Jimmy Anderson (ed: a crime figure, not Jim Anderson from OZ) and others. Anderson suggests that the gang commissioned to start the fire were the Loners. Ringleaders, Redman and Animal were arrested soon afterwards and put away on charges of stabbing and rape. The remnants of the gang joined the Comacheros and were part of the split who formed the Banditos, which were involved in the Father's Day Massacre. The fact that John Barker has today been threatened implies that we are indeed onto something with this case'. [31]

Everything had built to a crescendo. Something had to give.

Martin retreated into himself. He drove around the streets of Double Bay checking out numberplates. Three days of this and Martin claimed to have 'solved' the case!

Abe Saffron had three cars.

Numberplates: ABE-111, ABE-222 and ABE 333.

Add it up = 666.

Martin also pointed out that 666 was the number of the free bus on a loop between Town Hall Station and the Art Gallery of New South Wales. Six-six-six indeed! Could anything be sillier? Some friends made fun of Martin.

'These things are deliberately chosen,' answered Martin. 'Pentacle necklaces, 666, $13, tattoos and when you see a personalised numberplate – someone chose that!' [32]

On 5 December, Abe Saffron was arrested at his home on one charge of 'conspiracy to defraud the Commonwealth' between 1969 and 1981 and 12 charges relating to false income tax declarations between 1975 and 1981. [33]

# 6.
# TIDYING UP

*Martin did the cover of Bop Til You Drop because of the show we did with Tiny Tim. Synchronicity and coincidence!*
**Peewee Wilson (Delltones)**

'What are you working on Martin?' guests would ask. The answer was always 'tidying up'. Tidying up was Martin's process for distilling information into themes. It might be a simple task like putting cassettes back into cases or delving into diaries, poems, personal letters, Vincent's letters, old encyclopaedias or his own family history. Eventually some document would point to a core theme - and that's the path Martin would follow next.

And so the Luna Park documents got filed, the newspaper clippings catalogued, the Tiny Tim tapes numbered while the film progressed ever so slowly. Editors came and went, none more faithful than Marilyn, who spent a lot of time in the film editing room, the room where Martin now stored his growing collection of Tiny Tim memorabilia, latest 45rpm releases from America - like Tiny's rendition of the Mr Ed song from the TV show - and even a book about flowers titled 'Tiny Tim'.

Poems. Martin loved poems. Nine years before the fire, poet Laurie Duggan wrote, *Inside the amusement park scared and shattered, we clutch at gratuitous image discarded style...* when Martin discovered that he exclaimed, 'he was inspired by a visit to Luna Park!' But what could he mean? [1] Another riddle was the Bernard O'Dowd poem 'Australia' taught by Cheery Bell, the Cranbrook teacher cheeked-out by teenage-Martin in a high school painting - '*Last sea thing dredged by sailor Time from Space, Are you adrift Sargasso...?* [2] Closer to home was, 'The Meeting of the Waters' by Thomas Moore, a poem found amongst his father's papers. The lines, '*Sweet vale of Avoca…*' suggested a connection with his father's side of the family, 'Avoca' being the name of a former Sharp family house in Bega. <sup>(3)</sup>

The visiting 'Wirian kids' were growing older. Instead of having them playing in the Dream Museum, Martin would put them to use by asking them to tidy it up - creative play. This often meant setting the figurines in new scenarios, like placing Alice in Wonderland in a Smurf kingdom, putting Obelisk and Asterisk in a Star Wars setting, etc. <sup>(4)</sup>

Figurines continued to capture Martin's interest. He was pleased to complete his Beatle set. He was one short until Peter spotted the fourth in a junk shop, which he gave Martin. Martin sifted through his grandparents' cabinets, checking out heritage figures that he remembered from childhood. He found Grandmother Vega's frog orchestra that had been broken and professionally repaired. Martin scratched away at the reparation, returning the frog orchestra to its authentic broken self. 'I'm taking off the repair, I think that's more powerful', he explained. 'It's a bit of a rash move I know – especially that somebody paid the restorer a lot to do that'. <sup>(5)</sup>

Most of Martin's 60s friends had been making a living from their art for the past 20 years. Some even won awards. Those 60s opinion-makers had become an extremely successful group of comrades in arms. They had spent that decade protesting, challenging and arguing with the powers-that-be. They were now running the show. Eric Clapton, Germaine Greer, Barry Humphries and Robert Hughes, were bona fide stars.

Richard Walsh was director and publisher of Australian Consolidated Press (ACP). He oversaw *The Bulletin, Australian Women's Weekly, Cleo, Australian House & Garden, Wheels* and another 55 Packer-owned magazines. Richard Neville invented his own job, a 'futurist'. Evolving from his daytime TV appearances, Richard presented a half hour Channel Ten show - *Extra Dimensions* - about sustainability and human potential. Whenever Richard appeared onscreen he got enthusiastic Wirian support - as did Martin's cousin Andrew Sharp, who played the suave Dr Andrew Baxter in the prime time show, Young Doctors.

The filmmakers were impacting too. Albie Thoms' book *Polemics for a New Cinema* sealed his position as Australia's champion of underground film. <sup>(6)</sup> Philippe Mora was directing films, working with stars like Alan Arkin, Christopher Lee and Christopher Walken. <sup>(7)</sup> Peter Weir directed Robin Williams in *Dead Poets Society* and Harrison Ford in *Witness*. Bruce Beresford directed *The Fringe Dwellers* and Phillip Noyce directed *The Hitchhiker* TV series.

Kathy Lette was well on her way to something big. *Rocky Horror* star of stage and screen, Little Nell (Campbell) opened a fashionable nightclub in Manhattan. Her younger sister Cressida was acclaimed for her woodblock prints of landscapes, interiors and still life. Jeannie Lewis represented Australia in the Cervantes International Arts Festival, Mexico. Lin Utzon was gaining a huge reputation in Europe as a ceramicist. George Gittoes and his wife Gabrielle travelled to the Northern

Territory to make a series of documentary films. Roger Foley – Mr Fogg – successfully introduced creative Lightshows to the corporate and private world Australia-wide. Bruce Goold created prints for Mambo Graphics and fine art galleries.

Gary Shearston enjoyed Top 10 success in England with Cole Porter's 'I Get A Kick Out of You' (1984). Returning to Australia, he shocked friends by studying for the Anglican priesthood. He became the Rev Gary Shearston and ran a parish in rural New South Wales (with his forthcoming *Aussie Blue* CD under wraps). Tim Lewis managed a heritage-listed pub in the Rocks - the Hero of Waterloo. Trying for an alternative lifestyle, Greg and Suzie Weight bought an acreage near Glenorie, a rural suburb on the edge of Sydney. Greg was doing portraits of Australian artists. He also lectured in photography, as did William Yang and Jonny Lewis.

After leaving Wirian, William lost many of his negs in a house fire. Recovering from the loss, he researched his Australian-Chinese heritage (dating back to the 1890s) and developed his own style of storytelling in a theatre environment. [8] Jonny came up with something different too. Inspired by Pete Townshend's *Face the Face* record, he started capturing the faces of absolutely everyone who came through the door of his Bondi studio: Martin, Brett, William, Albie, Thelma Clune, Justin O'Brien, Peter Royles, James Ricketson, Michael Glasheen…

After completing the Harris Street Mural, Garry and Judit Shead moved into an apartment in Double Bay where Garry toyed with the idea of illustrating a children's story before settling on a better idea – portraiture. He painted a portrait of Toto for the Mahlab Art Prize and won it. Garry also fired a salvo in the direction of the Archibald Prize with his 1986 portrait of Martin. The following year he and Judit moved to Bundeena where Judit encouraged him to focus on his painting. She later returned to her own art, creating exquisite sculptures.

Even minor players were making the front pages, not always for the right reasons. Sallie-Anne Huckstepp was found murdered in Centennial Park on the same day that Lindy Chamberlain was released from prison. That evening, Martin watched a one-hour TV Special about Azaria and reminisced about Sallie-Anne. Around 11.00pm Les and Harold danced through the front door. Hellooo, we've arrived!

Hushed tones: 'Guys, this is what's happened to Sallie-Anne…'.

That steadied them down.

At Wirian, the cast had varied a bit. A recovering junkie called Antony moved in to dry out. He was a quiet young man who did a bit of gardening. One night he went back to old haunts, jacked up and died of 'accidental overdose'. Martin was convinced it was a hotshot. He loathed heroin. He called it 'Satanic'. William and Al were gone. Yensoon and Marilyn stayed off-and-on. Dave Sanderson re-connected with Peter Draffin, which brought Draff back. Les Bean and Harold had become the oddest couple in town. With some success, Harold entered his portrait of environmentalist Dr Bob Brown - *Dr Bob Brown and Green Old Time*

*Waltz* - in the Archibald Prize. Another contender was Les' portrait of Martin, which was not hung.

Old friends like Kingo, George, Richard, Tim, Marro, Jonny and Margaret dropped in regularly for a coffee and a chat. People like Sam Marshall and Sandy Gutman too. Lin Utzon stayed at Wirian when she was town. All were treated to Tiny's latest offering, 12-minutes of *Highway to Hell* which was exhausting to listen to. Every week or so, Tiny would phone Martin – reverse charges - from anywhere in the world. They'd talk for an hour or more and Martin would tape it. Much of Tiny's talk was what Martin called 'preaching'. The rest were sex fantasies, which were getting creepier.

Tiny talked like this, 'I've never tried this, but my fantasy would be – there's something called a Love Pillow – they hang from the ceiling and the woman straps her legs in there just like a swing. I'd like to have a woman hang from the ceiling and push her, you know, with the tongue while she's hanging'. [9]

Sometimes Tiny talked creepy but he didn't mention to his Australian friends that he was working on a B-grade horror film called *Blood Harvest* in which he played a harmless but creepy clown called Mervo. Maybe he was being Mervo, looping those schlock-horror film ideas into the conversation. Or maybe not. He startled people with too much sex information. More startling was Tiny's response when asked about his impact on Martin's religious beliefs. He said, 'I don't know that side of him'. [10] How could he not know that side of Martin? Everyone else did.

In the mid-80s the three most arresting graphic companies in Sydney were the Ink Group, Mambo Graphics and Ken Done Enterprises. With a staff of two in a small inner-Sydney office, Linda Langton and Jonathon Lee set up a greeting card publishing business they named the Ink Group. Within two and a half years they were flying. In 1984 the Ink Group had 130 employees and the pick of Sydney's artists, Ken Done amongst them. Linda approached Martin who didn't exactly refuse. He just never got around to saying yes. [11]

Located at the Rocks, the Ken Done Shop was a big hit with tourists. Ken and his wife Judy designed every type of fabric you could put in a bathroom or on a bed. Ken portrayed Australian capital cities like sunny Yuppie paradises on a leisurely weekend. He took a shine to Harold the Kangaroo and gave him an exhibition at his Moore Park Gallery. The art world had no idea what to do with Harold - maybe that's what he and Ken had in common? Colourfully-dressed, Harold would show up at art openings, make a splash, turn heads - but who the heck was he? Thanks to Ken Done Gallery in Surry Hills, Harold had an outlet for a time. [12]

And Mambo. Mambo Graphics was launched in 1984 in Alexandria Sydney by Dare Jennings and Andrew Rich. By the mid-80s teen fashion was about skatewear and Mambo was right on track. (Martin disliked their rival 'Natas' - in a mirror it read as 'Satan'.) Mambo's Farting Dog t-shirt (artist: Richard Allan) was an instant hit. There was a loose connection between Mambo, Regular Records and the band Mental As Anything - and all were friendly with Martin. Of course there was talk of a Martin Sharp Mambo top, which (again) didn't lead anywhere commercially. [13]

No one was more surprised than Peewee and Carla when the Delltones won a Gold record for their retro *Bop Til Ya Drop* album. 'I would have been happy if it just charted!' Peewee exclaimed, 'That's all we expected. It'd been 15 years since we'd released a record. Carla rang up K-Tel and they said, "it's bolted, it's pouring out of the store". For about two weeks you could not buy it. The cover definitely captured the feeling of it and it came about because of the show we did with Tiny Tim. Synchronicity and coincidence! Martin did our cover - and the first book that gave us a real lift into another lifestyle was the *Politics of Ecstasy* – Martin did that cover too!' [14] 'Synchronicity and coincidence' always found a sympathetic ear in Martin. For creating the cover image that contributed to the success of *Bop Til Ya Drop*, Peewee and Carla presented Martin with one of the plaques.

Notwithstanding an unmanageable private life, Brett Whiteley canvases were soaring in value and he won the Wynne Prize again. Importantly to Brett, he had credibility amongst the Rock fraternity. Dire Straits' live double album cover featured his multi-panelled masterpiece *Alchemy*. Dire Straits named the album after that painting, and guitarist Mark Knofler produced and played on Dylan's first gospel album, *Slow Train Coming*. So maybe it was 'Alchemy' that drew Dylan's attention to Brett's art? On his 1986 tour of Australia, Dylan agreed to a press conference in Brett's Riley Street Surry Hills studio. 'No wives man!' Brett urged Jonny Lewis when he invited him over the phone.

Jonny described that press conference, 'I drove Martin there. Michael Driscoll and Brett sat together, Mart and I sat next to each other. We arrived long before Dylan got there. There were a lot of eager people. The questions were crudely monitored. Martin had only one question for Dylan.' [15]

'I asked him, "What do you think about Tiny Tim?", said Martin. 'He answered, "What can you say about Tiny Tim?"' [16]

Jonny continued, 'Martin adored Dylan. He thought Dylan was extraordinary (like we all do) but he wasn't going to drop Tiny Tim. Brett was shameless in his pursuit of Dylan. Martin couldn't give a shit, really. I remember Brett jumping to his feet giving this mad rave about where did inspiration came from? Do you drag it down from the heavens? Dylan just looked at him very nonchalantly and said yes or no – a one word reply.' [17]

Next, Dylan played the Sydney Entertainment Centre with Tom Petty and the Heartbreakers. Starting with *In the Garden*, Dylan ended with *Knocking On Heaven's Door*, signaling his gospel phase was not quite over yet. Australian director Gillian Armstrong filmed the concert for an HBO Special on general VHS release. [18]

The morning after the concert, Jonny rang Brett who said, 'I can't talk man, I can't talk – Dylan's coming around to see the studio, ah gotta go, gotta go'. Jonny continued, 'I rang him back later, "How did it go?" Brett said Dylan went through what he had in the studio and said what thought of it. I remember Brett saying, "Man, he's got teeth like a horse!" Brett could be very funny.' [19]

Martin was under the impression that Brett and Dylan remained in touch after that meeting. He said, 'Dylan was very interested in painting - he'd ask, "How do you do that?" Brett wrote him a long letter on how to paint. That was probably the last thing Brett wrote. Someone should track it down - see that Dylan got the letter.' [20]

In March, Martin attended a 'paint for peace' paint-in along the covered walk-way to Sydney Opera House and painted Boofhead. Kingo, Garry and Judit, and many others painted too. Arriving with a bit of a fanfare, Harold and Les danced and painted simultaneously, which amazed the gathered crowd.

Back at Wirian, Martin re-painted his *Kold Komfort Kaffe* Nimrod poster on a big canvas and he organized his major works for his coming Progressive Retrospective exhibition to be held at Roslyn Oxley9 gallery in Paddington. Dave Rowe attended that show.

Dave had a music industry background with Polygram, BMG and Sony in mastering and production. He had a formidable personal archive of musicians he admired, among them Gary Glitter, Tom Waits, Elvis and Tiny, the latter being the reason why his flatmate Helen Theodore, suggested he should go to Oxley's. 'I went to see the exhibition,' said Dave. 'The weirdest thing I could never fathom - because I didn't know much about Martin at the time - was that he had the huge "For Sale" house sign in his exhibition. There was a lot I didn't know about Martin - but I could tell that he loved Tiny from the posters and the music in the exhibition. That was it for me!' [21]

The Oxley exhibition was a raucous affair. Martin dedicated it to his mother and first teacher, Jo. And it was opened by his second teacher, Justin O'Brien. The works were obscured by the massive crowd of people straining to see fragments of Luna Park, Laughing Clowns, popular memorabilia and a wide variety of Martin's paintings, collages, posters and film clips. Hippies, socialites, students, artists and bohemians attended. As fast as one wave of visitors got out, another surged in, all stuck limpet-like to the walls as they inched their way around the gallery. Arthur McIntyre from The Age enjoyed the show, he wrote Martin as, 'Beneath the flip-pant, seemingly loony, veneer of a lovable eccentric exists a man-child who, unlike Warhol and his factory clones, really cares about the purpose of his art beyond the degenerate function of cynical commercial exploitation.' [22]

Oxley's was a 'progressive retrospective', like all Martin's exhibitions. Martin exhibited 97 items – 17 contemporary paintings, 10 pictures from schooldays, 16 collage works, 31 prints and posters, 14 original poster artworks, seven 'objects', the Nimrod series of seven and Tiny Tim records for sale. It summarised Martin's past, pointed to future directions and reminded Sydney that the Martin Sharp name could fill a huge exhibition space twice-over and still spill onto the street. [23]

After 'Oxley', Martin started a painting that became *Pentecost*. He took the composition from his own collage in *Art Book* and repainted the Matisse and Magritte images in his own meticulous style, replacing the dark chair of the Matisse original with Vincent's chair. He also positioned Magritte's dove in the foreground – hence the title. (24)

Stephen Lawson printed it. He said, 'Martin was inspired by the Matisse *Red Room*, all the elements exactly there - the chair, table, rug, the positioning of the window. Martin would be refining that image all the time. The window for example in *Pentecost* eventually becomes Calvary, the hill with the cross on it. He kept that religious side of himself very discreet for a long while.' (25)

Jo Sharp was diagnosed with liver cancer and diabetes. She rarely got out of bed. Marilyn, Yensoon and Martin took time out to go upstairs, sit with her and talk. No more chats around the kitchen table, her room became her whole world. In her decline, Jo started 'seeing things' and Martin, who took hallucinations seriously, feared his mother had been possessed by the spirit - or the essence - of her disease. He wrote, 'I believe that the spirit which possessed my dear mother in these times was using her as a window.'

Jo didn't believe in the supernatural, yet she claimed to have been lifted to the ceiling by people in her room. Martin wrote, 'Jo (my mother) was not a person to hallucinate and, though highly imaginative, she was not a vocally spiritual person. Indeed, she would say, "The only thing up 'up there' are possums in the roof." (Which there were.)'

Yensoon wrote in her diary: 'Looking up at the ceiling with her right arm raised in the air, Mrs Sharp suddenly saw seven little Chinese men descend from the ceiling. They were three feet tall, all of them wearing Chinese coolie hats with a round brim. Their bodies were round, each of them wearing a different color: red, green, blue and yellow. The yellow little man seemed to be the leader. He gave Mrs Sharp a stern and icy cold look. As if a hole was bored into her heart and she shuddered. His subordinates were much more genial to her. They smiled at her and the blue little man touched her hand, murmuring words of comfort. She found that he had a slimy and soft body. The leader motioned his subordinates to lift Mrs Sharp up to the ceiling and then put her down onto the floor. She protested and ordered them to put her back to bed, but to no avail.

'In a trice, she found herself in a verdant park. The sun was setting. Although the surroundings were a joy to her eyes, no living things were visible, only the wind was sighing amidst the trees. It struck a note of desolation to her. She felt a sense of despair. The little blue man presented her with a blue silk flowing robe, which she happily put on because it was her favorite color. The moment she put it on the sun suddenly sank beyond the horizon and they lifted her up in the darkness, at which time she lost consciousness. Upon regaining consciousness she found herself to be in her own bed.' After this episode, Jo's condition declined rapidly.

As death approached, she lapsed into hypoglycemic comas. To bring her out of it, the doctors fed her barley sugar. There were several disturbing episodes during this period. In this state Jo would adopt two personalities - cheerful and cooperative or duplicitous. Martin wrote, 'She appeared possessed by an alien - hateful, intelligent, cruel, arrogant, despising help, physically strong. (My mother was very frail.) Palpably evil, the whole atmosphere of her room would change. It was most upsetting. Jo would have no memory of these experiences. Her doctor would sidestep the issue when I tried to talk about it. I thought it was very important to discuss but no doctor would. If I'd known more about exorcism I think I would have attempted to do it.' (26)

Jo Sharp was ambulanced to St Lukes Hospital where she spent her final weeks. The last thing Jo heard was Rev Allan Moyes radio broadcast, which closed with the Irish Blessing (May the road rise up to meet you). Jonny and Martin were present when she died. Her last words were, 'I've been talking to God for the last four hours…' Afterwards Martin said, 'I wanted her skeleton to put in a glass case with her walking stick – just a skeleton and a stoop. The years had stooped her. "The Artist's Mother." I really did want it. I couldn't get a clearance for it'. (27) After this Martin referred to himself as a 'childless orphan'. Robbie Tarling, a friend who knitted a pink Mickey Mouse jumper for Martin, responded, 'He's surrounded by his children but they're not his flesh and blood!' (28)

For all Martin's achievements, there remained only one more thing Jo wanted of him – a child. William Yang had confronted Martin with Jo's hopes - 'The child – isn't it?' Ruefully Martin admitted, 'I guess so, yes'. Jo had gone. Still no child. (29)

After Jo's death, Martin read his parents' love letters. Although his mother had told him that 'the marriage was all over on the honeymoon night…' Martin believed the letters showed otherwise. He played a lot of 30s and 40s music and allowed himself to drift into sadness. He also replayed the tape of Jo's funeral service in which Martin's childhood friend and neighbour, John Gregory-Roberts, delivered the eulogy before a rendition of Jo's special song, *Hello Young Lovers*. Martin wept. He read her diaries questioning, 'who is she writing for?' as he carefully noted comments about his childhood, OZ trials and bygone years. Ruminating over the past sparked in Martin an unlikely renewed interest in his Yellow House *Catalog*. He wanted Phil Ward to publish it. Phil, the business newsletter publisher from the Free Lindy campaign. Many publishers would have seized the opportunity, not Phil. He had no idea what Martin was talking about. Publisher Tom Thompson did.

As a 16-year old schoolkid, Tom would visit the Yellow House when he came to Sydney. A fulltime journalist in the mid-80s, with the assistance of his wife Elizabeth Butel, one of Tom's projects was packaging books for Penguin Publishing. Tom explained, 'Elizabeth was trying to do a book on Luna Park with Martin and

Kingo, but neither of them would ever get to the table with a contract because they all had their other things to do.'

A radio program called *Growing Up in the 60s* was Tom's next idea. He decided to publish the material as a slim 90-page book. Martin agreed to do the cover and pictures. Then Martin changed his mind, 'Tom, I can't do the cover, I'm caught up in (whatever painting he was doing)…'. Tom said, '…from his existing artwork Martin wanted me to choose anything relevant. I chose some pictures, paid him $200 - but I still had no cover. A friend of mine said "I'll do it in the style of Martin" – as a way of homaging him.'

Tom selected five pictures that had previously been published in OZ magazine and Craig McGregor's *People, Politics and Pop*. His idea of reproducing Martin's popular mid-60s Pop Art illustrations appealed to another author, who made the same request. Again, Martin said yes, providing he didn't need to draw anything new. [30]

Les moved out with Harold when she inherited enough money to buy a tiny flat in the back of Kings Cross. Then Yensoon moved on, leaving behind an all-male cast. Alcohol was taking its toll at Wirian and Martin - who never drank - was running out of patience with two or three drunks. Sometimes Wirian seemed like a Lonely Blokes Club. Sanderson became so morose that Martin kicked him out. Some guy called Paul was a regular visitor. Within the year he was charged with rape and sentenced to nine years jail in Risden Prison Tasmania. 'I can't throw him out,' Martin bleated, 'he looks like Vincent'.

Peter Royles didn't drink as much as before but he still had occasional breakouts. Peter had a creative force that seemed to push him to self-destruct out of sheer frustration. Recognising this, Martin wanted to get him into a studio and record an album but Martin could neither afford the time nor the expense. 'Martin loved me and hated me - didn't he?' questioned Peter, who continued drinking at the Bondi Pub less regularly. Peter wanted to dry out, get a driver's licence, buy a vehicle and move away. In exchange for painting the house, Martin bought Peter a Dormobile, which he parked outside Wirian in anticipation of passing his driving test. [31]

Then Peter Draffin moved in. He was AA (Alcoholics Anonymous), which meant he didn't drink at all - but on the rare occasion that he did, watch out. Things started well between Draff and Martin. At his best, Martin thought Draff was a gem. Richard Neville often popped in with daughters Lucy or Angelica. Richard was on the Speakers' Circuit and he'd call in after addressing some corporation about ethical business practices and environmental issues. He continually teased Martin with cheeky remarks about 'the regression of the Renaissance Man' and the 'Cosmic Crime-buster'.

Jo's Will: Martin poured through the trusts and accused the trustees of not acting in his best interests. Jo's estate was $1.7 million. According to Martin, $105,000 of that money was locked into a system that he couldn't unlock. Yes, he got his hands on some money from the brokers' trusts and sliced $750,000 off his mortgage, but what about the rest? Did the money go to beneficiaries like the Flying Doctor, Kings School Parramatta or even the Cat & Dogs Protection Association? He needed to know. [32]

Although Martin was telling friends he didn't plan to paint much more after *Pentecost*, the photocopier brought him back. Art - Martin reckoned - was the only way he could express his point of view. [33] He had continued to experiment with the photocopier ever since he'd bought it. He enlarged newsprint pictures, enlarged the enlargements, and kept going until he got what he wanted. He dubbed his process 'Art Journalism'. After a while he started colouring them, using crayon and linseed oil. Copying Martin's technique, Peter Royles did the same, with surprisingly good results.

Martin started a picture of the Ghost Train fire victims, hung in cruciform – four down, three across. He linked the number seven to the Willie Nelson/Ray Charles song *Seven Spanish Angels took Another Angel Home*. Like the Ghost Train fire, the Milperra bikie massacre was another example of seven plus one deaths.

Always keen to know what Martin was up to, the Sydney Morning Herald ran a story about Martin's toy collection, a sample of which generated interest in the Oxley9 exhibition. The SMH photographer snapped Martin in a striped Russian sailor's top, seated at the bottom of Wirian's central stairs. Beside him is a Kewpie doll and behind him, a painting of the Luna Park face by a 9-year old boy. The journalist was interested in all the Luna Park memorabilia that was saved from oblivion, Martin answered, 'They're not really mine, I'm just keeping them. They are part of the history of Australian comic art'. [34]

Further changes were afoot. Peter Royles passed his driving test, Draff consulted the i-Ching and assisted Martin with Luna Park research ('about bloody time!' said Martin). Paul became more irritating than usual Martin. And as if to fulfill Richard Neville's 'Cosmic Crimebuster' heckle, Martin wrote, 'I've worked out the government corruption angle. The dark forces got many of the politicians' children on heroin and then had them right in their pockets, having the ability to kill them by altering the doses. (Button's son dead, Unsworth's son dead… so it goes). To think that drugs wasn't even an election issue, the most important issue of all. Inflation = black money, that's the economic effect of heroin on a country.' [35]

The most surprising news of all was that Les was getting married. Aged 52, her prospective beau - Gareth - was a Cranbrook sports hero when Martin was at school. A veteran of three marriages, Gareth worked in advertising in Malaysia for 12 years. Martin picked out one of Jo's rings for Les and the wedding was held in a private ceremony in October. Martin was Best Man and Les' sister Penelope was the second witness. Harold was hopping mad. After this, Les Bean stopped being Les Bean. She didn't paint her clothes any more. She and Gareth moved to Coffs

Harbour where he had 28 acres of land. No longer a crazy eccentric, in time Les evolved into a successful businesswoman.

Martin gained two important assignments before the year was out. The artistic director of the 1982 Adelaide Festival, Gavin Henderson, returned to England where he took up the position of artistic director for the 1988 Brighton International Festival. Henderson had commissioned Martin's 1982 Adelaide Festival poster and wanted one for the Brighton Festival,. Since Jo's death, Martin had toyed with the idea of returning to England. When the Brighton Festival agreed to put Tiny on the bill that clinched it for Martin. He was going in May.

Martin's second major piece was a tapestry 3m x 6m in size, commissioned and donated to the State Library of New South Wales by Mr and Mrs Jim Bain. Martin created and editioned the print, after which four young weavers at the Victorian Tapestry Workshop spent six months weaving the design into an art object. The picture centred on the Sydney Harbour Bridge and the Opera House. The Southern Cross soars across the top and Luna Park is on fire. The tapestry was a summary document, comprising symbols from Martin's journey as a citizen of the country. He presented the blue groper, blue kingfisher, Captain Cook's Endeavour, 'the Moon is a harsh mistress', Uluru and the dingo. The tapestry is edged with the words from the Bernard O'Dowd poem, 'Australia'. Martin named it 'OZ?' [36]

Russell Sharp commissioned and sold Martin's posters when he wasn't being the Flower King. He said, 'I was living at Wirian at the time this was being created. I sat up all night while Martin cut it out. It was printed by Steven Lawson. There were only 87 in the edition. We each took a third and it sold out in three months @ $300 each'. [37]

# 7.
# THE BRIGHTON CUT

*When you meet people with Martin you don't know whether you are meeting someone off the street or somebody famous. He didn't differentiate.*
Roslyn Sharp

Australia was very parochial, even in the late-80s. 'Making it' in Sydney might mean nothing in Perth, Brisbane or Melbourne and vice versa. Sydney lionised Brett Whiteley; Melbourne was all Howard Arkley. Sydney adored Margaret Olley; Melbourne had Mirka Mora. Until the advent of the worldwide web, very few – like cartoonist Michael Leunig – bridged the Sydney-Melbourne gap with ease.

Philippe Mora's younger brother ran the William Mora Gallery in Melbourne central. In 1988, William took an educated risk by exhibiting two artists from Bundeena, a waterfront village on the outskirts of southern Sydney where George Gittoes and Garry Shead had settled. They both had outback themes. George showed his Northern Territory collection. And Garry exhibited his *Outback Ballad* paintings dedicated to his father. Both were a great success.

RAW was a collective of Melbourne art students who shared an inner-city house and wore black. Having heard stories about the Yellow House, they bailed George up at his opening and questioned how they might turn their live-in collective into an art environment. Dave, Pasqual, Walter and others listened most attentively to his replies. [1] Moments like this must have impressed George that the Yellow House concept still had legs.

Artistic director for the Brighton International Festival, Gavin Henderson contacted Martin again, broadening his request from one poster to a 'Martin Sharp poster exhibition – the London Years'. This became a possibility, at least for a couple of months. Then Tiny declared an ultimatum: he would not perform in

Brighton unless the film was screened as well. Martin and Tiny had a standoff over this one. It was Martin who backed down. The film was more than enough work, a poster exhibition would be too much, especially as Henderson wanted Martin to pen a short piece as well. So it was all go! Go! Go! On the film.

To add to Martin's concerns, in April, Luna Park was closed 'for renovations and repairs'. The investment company changed its name from Prome Investments Pty Ltd to Luna Park Investments Pty Ltd, which sounded sinister and required whatever scant attention Martin could spare. There was Wirian to manage too. Clayton from Bermagui moved in and helped with maintenance, Al Jones came back and Peter Draffin was there too. Draff eschewed technology and believed the progress of humankind ended with the Industrial Revolution.

Draff lasted eight months. He said, 'I stayed there in 1988. Martin had someone working on the Tiny Tim film called Deanne (Judson) and I had this raving infatuation with Deanne. She didn't have one for me. I remember Martin working on the Brighton poster. That's one of his best posters I think.' [2] Draff confessed that his 'manic, drunken behaviour' was unacceptable though he was angered by the way Martin handled it. He wrote, 'No one gives Draffin the old carpet-out-from-under and stays mates!' [3] For a time, Martin and Draff went separate ways.

Martin, Marilyn, Paul Healy, John Barker, Sally Fitzpatrick and others worked tirelessly to complete the film in time. From a feature length, freeform documentary loved by friends, it needed to be structured enough to engage a generic audience at a public screening at a major arts festival. This edit was known as *The Brighton Cut*. [4] Some have thought it to be the finished product. It is not. Martin wrote, 'The Brighton Cut' will not be the final cut…more a trial…' [5]

Exhausted and cutting it fine, they only just met their deadline. Carrying the film, with no margin of time, Martin caught the Sydney-to-London flight but there was a delay. Martin explained, 'I was flying over with the film. It was meant to be shown that night in Brighton, We were going over Afghanistan or somewhere like that. I had a window seat. I always love the window seat to watch what's going on. All of a sudden I saw what looked like a big fire - it just went zzzzonk! - past the window and I knew I'd seen something happen. Then they said we had to go to Amsterdam where I was stuck when I was supposed to be showing the film.' [6]

On arrival, Martin was driven straight to the screening. There he met up with Aussie friends - Marilyn, Al, Nathan Waks, his wife Candice, Harold the Kangaroo and cousin Roslyn. Roslyn was living in London at the time. Martin invited her to photograph the event. She said, 'I was going to Brighton anyway because an old boyfriend was in the comedy section. It was fabulous but I kinda felt sorry for Martin that there weren't more people there. He introduced me to Richard Attenborough who was very warm towards Martin. They obviously were very fond of each other. Richard Attenborough hung around for the whole concert. I'm sure I would have met others too but when you meet people with Martin you don't know whether you are meeting someone off the street or somebody famous. He didn't differentiate in how he treated them.' Roslyn had a lengthy conversation with Tiny about moisturisers. [7]

Patron, Sir Richard Attenborough sat with Martin and watched Tiny's full marathon. Martin recalls him drawling out just one word to sum up Tiny's act - 'er-maaazing…'. [8] To the press Sir Richard enthused, 'They employ me to encourage people to give money to the festival, but I do like to see events when I can'. [9]

Tiny had arrived well before Martin, bringing his new wife Miss Jan. Just eight days before, Tiny had been in Dallas Texas headlining the third Mr Ed Musical Festival – 'Edstock' - organised by James (Bucks) Burnett. In 1984, 'Bucks' recorded Tiny singing the 'Mr Ed' song and he released it as a 45 rpm single. Bucks again took Tiny to a studio where they laid down the first takes for what would become Tiny's *Girl* album (1996). This happened the week before Brighton, [10]

For someone in terrible physical condition, Tiny certainly had boundless energy. Two boxes of Callard and Bowser butterscotch sweets were all he required to prepare him for his record-breaking romp through the history of popular song. After a quick prayer and a dash of makeup, Tiny hit the stage. Anchored by musical director Nathan Waks, Marvin Lewis (piano) and Al Jones (keyboards and piano accordion), the band just kept going and going…! One hundred and thirty-eight songs later, Tiny broke his own record and reestablished his World Non-Stop Singing Record for a Professional Singer. 'World Beater!' read the newspaper headlines.

Commenting on Tiny's endurance, his third wife Miss Sue said, 'Tiny had three times a normal person's energy. Even when he was old he had tremendous stamina. He could stay up for several nights in a row without affecting his performance too much. He was able to sleep sitting up in almost any kind of conveyance – whether it was a car or a plane or anything. He didn't have a lot of muscle strength but he was a big person and in some ways he could just go on and on like the Energiser Bunny. I suppose there was probably a lot of determination there to just keep going. I don't think he had much of a plan. He was just winging it, making it up as he went along. He was good at that kind of thing – thinking on his feet and figuring out how to get the audience interested and involved, and keeping them involved.' [11]

Brighton's *Evening Argus* wrote, 'Brighton Festival achieved a world record late last night when Tiny Tim sang for three hours, 11 minutes and 30 seconds without a pause. He smashed his own previous title which he gained nine years ago in Sydney with two hours and 15 minutes warbling the classics of the previous century. With a large and enthusiastic Zap Tent crowd cheering him on, he broke the three-hour barrier with All My Lovin', part of a Beatles selection and finished up with falsetto Tiptoe Through the Tulips and finally We'll Meet Again'. [12] After dueting with her husband on the closing song, Miss Jan herded Tiny back to their hotel and kept him to herself. 'She was difficult,' said Martin who was suffering with kidney stones during the festival.

In the end, Martin regretted that after such a big effort the film was not shown to advantage and that the marathon didn't really peak. Summing up he said, '*The Brighton Cut* was projected in a theatre. The light wasn't very strong in the projector. It was a bit of an uncomfortable night. The marathon lacked a bit of sparkle. We didn't have Adrian (Rawlins) there for the introduction to the marathon, so everyone noticed the difference between someone who could do an introduction for Tiny and someone who couldn't.' [13]

Other times Martin felt more positive, declaring it 'a great concert'. He had mixed feelings about the *Brighton Cut* of the film, but he was nonetheless pleased it had gone that far. 'The film needs a lot more work, though I would stand by what exists as the *Brighton Cut*. I had a great trip. I can't say it was a triumph, though TT's Marathon certainly was. IS.' [14] Reviewer Steven Puchalski wrote about the film, 'Although newcomers might be perplexed, it's all so unique and inspired that I couldn't stop smiling, as it captures his (Tiny's) humanity, hilarity, and belovedly twisted lifestyle. It's not difficult to imagine that Tiny Tim was an off-stage weirdo, but it's gratifying to see it chronicled for posterity, while realising he actually exceeded expectations.' [15]

And so, Tiny and Martin parted ways, Tiny returned to the States with Miss Jan and Martin spent a couple of months in London staying with Zandra Rhodes. [16] Having finished his stint with the Great American Circus, Tiny signed with Donnie Brooks for the '30 Years of Rock N Roll' tour. Donnie Brooks was an early 60s pop star with hits like *Doll's House, Mission Bell* and *Memphis*. He continued to accept all recording offers, which was the habit of a lifetime. The *Girl* album with Bucks was in abeyance and the film *Blood Harvest* was released to pathetic reviews. Critics praised Tiny's as Mervo the Clown as the only good thing in the film. Martin approached its producer Bill Rebane about brokering a distribution deal for the *Street of Dreams* film but Rebane couldn't generate interest. [17]

Meanwhile, in Sydney, Dave Rowe couldn't get enough of Tiny. He had attended the Oxley 'Progressive Retrospective' the previous year and loved Martin's Tiny Tim posters. When radio station 2-Double J played the Brighton marathon in its entirely, Dave taped it and wore the tapes out playing them. He wanted new copies. 'Ring Martin Sharp, he'll have it,' said Helen Theodore, the flat-mate who had told him to attend the Oxley9 exhibition.

'You can't just ring Martin Sharp!' Dave responded.

Apparently, you could and Dave did.

Martin invited him over.

Dave: 'I walked in – didn't get the tape, got a job!'

Dave Rowe's great-great-grandfather was Alfred Rowe, better known in the 1880s and 1890s as circus man, the Great Onzalo. Said Dave, 'Martin had written an article in *Quadrant* magazine (1977) and he mentions the Great Onzalo walking across what would become the Sydney Harbour Bridge. Martin states that, "they built the Harbour Bridge in his footsteps". Well lo and behold it turns out that it was my great-grandfather! (He went under the name of the Great Onzalo. His real surname was Rowe.) I would learn that Martin liked to synchronise all those connections.

'The second connection was that the same man, (the Great Onzalo) was the first to ever bring a gramophone to Australia. He imported one and charged a penny (or something) for people to have a listen in this tent. No one had ever seen one. It was like Sideshow Alley at the circus. Martin kept adding these up. I came to realise that connections mattered. I took him over some scrapbooks and things. I was so excited that he was as big a fan of Tiny as I was. I recall that day. He was so patient.' [18]

Having worked for Polygram, BMG and Sony, Dave could handle every production aspect of music - tape transfers, post-production, mastering, re-mastering, promotion and importantly, dealing with record companies, which is how he got to know Martin Fabinyi co-founder of Regular Records. The Regular Records label was initially created to manage the band Mental As Anything. It grew to include many acts like Kate Ceberano, Icehouse, The Reels, Austen Tayshus, and it was about to include Tiny Tim. As Martin's new assistant, the Brighton Marathon tapes were Dave's first task. Three hours-plus of Tiny's marathon was non-commercially viable from a record company's perspective, so Martin agreed they should produce an edited version, staying true to Tiny's marathon effort. Dave tightened it into one exciting hour. For a while it seemed this would be the product. Martin changed his mind at the last post. Said Dave, 'We edited all the best bits and made it one long marathon. We did a great edit. We had a nice smooth-flowing mini-marathon. We had the master ready to go into production and he left me a note, "Dave, let's release the whole tape". It suddenly went from one to three cassettes.'

Martin didn't want it cut back at all (except Tiny's final duet with Miss Jan for copyright reasons). He designed a black and white cover and Dave made it a commercially available 3-cassette pack. [19] 'I just felt the whole thing was too long to be commercially successful and Tiny agreed that the marathon would be too much in its entirety'. [20] Another idea was to release the Chameleon LP to CD, a project that would drag on for ages.

Clarifying his standing at Wirian Dave said, 'I was honoured that Martin asked me to work on this project, I went there to work on Tiny's music not for any other reason. A lot of people were doing what I was doing there. A stream of people worked on the Tiny tapes. He had set up a room, which we'd converted into an office. It was the room beside Martin's Inner Sanctum, which he loved because he could hear my edits all day long. What he didn't like was that whoever called in would hear what I was doing, hang out and chat. There's a lot of work that doesn't get done when you're continually interrupted.' [21]

In August George organised a Yellow House Reunion dinner at the Art Gallery of New South Wales. There was a proposal afoot for a reconstruction of the original rooms inside the gallery. 'A George Gittoes idea,' wrote Martin in a letter, 'Can't say I'm that keen – doing it once was hard enough.' Suddenly switching subjects in the next paragraph he added, 'The Tapestry looks great at the Library.' [22]

Hung for all Sydney-siders to enjoy, the *OZ?* tapestry overpowered the reception area at the State Library of New South Wales with its size, beauty and complexity. Through the windows, it could even be glimpsed by passing traffic. The prints too were a commercial success, which is more than can be said for the 3-cassette edition of the Brighton Marathon. Unable to get a record company's interest, Dave released it for Martin as a Street of Dreams production, which basically meant that Martin gave them away to friends.

'I'm trying to tidy up the house,' Martin continued the letter. 'Got a student called Jessica coming any moment. Something on The Bad Boys of Australian Art! The house is quiet at the moment - so much to tidy up and sort out it's almost overwhelming. (a) The film (b) Luna Park (c) Dream Museum (d) Mum's things (e) my Art (f) Tiny's Tapes (g) my life...'

The Brighton Cut behind him, Martin got back to tinkering with the film. He continued, 'The cutting room is being prepared for the next cut of the film, got Tiny's wedding footage in London at last. They hadn't forgotten me over there and it was great to see old pals again and new ones too. Zandra Rhodes was an absolute trooper & put me up, so I repainted her mural. Nicholas Roeg really adored Street of Dreams. Very encouraging. Didn't see Eric. Mick Jagger asked me to his party here.' In his brief attempt to launch a solo career without the Rolling Stones, Mick Jagger came to Sydney for a concert and gave Martin a fistful of free tickets, which Martin distributed among friends.

He continued, 'Tiny was great. I wish he could have come to London he would have loved it. His wife Jan came...we didn't really take to each other although I tried. They've separated now. Tiny says, "I've never known such peace!" Marriage still seems a million miles away for me – though my heart doesn't stop longing. I got flu and jetlag when I returned – I have just surfaced to "Tidy Up Before Art" mode. Palace of Art, Bricks of Boredom. Yensoon seems quite a lot happier and stronger. She been going to a Free Catholic Church & associated Lodge and loves Masonry, which she says comes from China. Draffin & daughter Christabel have just arrived.' [23]

Martin announced that Tiny was coming to Australia in May, so once again was all hands on deck. Martin had a stack of Tiny's live music from which to create a new release and he selected the 1983 recordings of *Highway to Hell*. Maybe Dave needed an assistant? Dave didn't think so. Martin got him one anyway.

Wendy Evans worked at Westpac Bank. Dave went there one day to cash a cheque. When Wendy saw the signature she exclaimed, 'I know Martin Sharp!' Back at Wirian, Dave checked with Martin, 'Do you know this Wendy Evans?'

He said, 'It doesn't ring a bell'. What she meant was that she knew his artwork. But because Dave had mentioned Wendy, the next time Martin went to the bank she opened with, 'I was talking to Dave about you…' and for some reason Martin drew some inference that there was a connection between Dave and her. 'Next minute she was employed!' said Dave. [24]

Like Dave, Wendy worked on the Tiny Tim tape transfers on-and-off for years. When things got rough between Dave and Martin, Wendy might take over. And when Wendy had other work, Dave would step back in. Dave and Wendy were quite different in their approach. Although not professionally trained, she did many hundreds of hours of safety masters, which to Martin were invaluable because he'd use them as listening copies.

Tiny was always optimistic about his new releases. Released in America, *I Saw Mr Presley Tiptoeing Through The Tulips* was a curious single that suggests Elvis might still be alive somewhere, at least that's what a few US journalists thought Tiny meant. Martin played it for a time, chuckled about it then shelved it among his ever-growing collection of Tiny Tim ephemera. His Australian release of Tiny's *Highway to Hell* seemed more appropriate, giving Martin a reason to reconnect with its musical director, Denny Burgess. Commenting on their 1983 sessions Denny wondered if that wrapped up his relationship with Martin, '…but then Martin rang us up and said, "That went really well, we'd love you to be Tiny's band when he comes back'. That's when we started to see Martin at various times.' [25] So Denny and his partner Clare became regulars at all Martin's events.

The murder of Lady Winifreda Ashton, widow of artist and former director of the Art Gallery of New South Wales (1937-1945) Will Ashton, captured Martin's interest for a time. A serial murderer had killed six elderly women in the Mosman area. When the police tracked down 'Granny Killer' John Wayne Glover, it was revealed that he lived next door to Barbara Thiering, wife of the Chaplain of Cranbrook School when Martin was there. Thiering's book *Jesus the Man* didn't impress Martin at all. He couldn't see anything other than fiction in what she called the 'pecher' method of Biblical interpretation, a code that defied all logic. 'I think it's rubbish,' said Martin. He didn't want the book in the house. [26]

John Godson's widow, Jenny – who reverted to her family name Poidevin – had remained close to Martin after the tragic loss of her husband and sons, Damien (6) and Craig (4). She spent hours with Martin going over the evidence and concurred that the Ghost Train fire had been deliberately lit. In February, she told *New Idea* magazine, 'I believe that - because the people who did it are evil, motivated by greed - there is an evil essence in there. Nine years ago I wouldn't have conceived I could think anything like this, it would have all been foreign to me. But after my own experiences and my reading, I believe there is evil in the universe which has the power to control people and situations.' The magazine featured a picture of Martin holding up the photograph of the minotaur beside her two boys. The magazine's headline was, 'The Luna Park Tragedy…a link with the occult?' [27]

George, Greg, and as many of the original Yellow House people as they could attract, started conducting regular meetings with an aim to persuade the Art Gallery of New South Wales into holding a Yellow House Retrospective exhibition some time in the future. With Tiny only a couple of months away from arriving, Martin wasn't particularly engaged in the Yellow House revival group. He attended no more Yellow House strategy meetings than necessary but Albie ensured that Martin received all circulars and was kept right up-to-date.

In April, Tiny returned to Australia. Martin always marked Tiny's arrival with the release of a new record. The original idea was a 45rpm single, with *Highway To Hell* as side A and either *Mickey Mouse, Forever Miss Dixie* or *Last Mile of the Way* on side B. In the end, with the support of Regular Records, they released a cassette single (cassingle) with *I Love Rock N Roll* on side B. Martin did the cover art, which was also printed as a promotional t-shirt. [28]

Tiny's *Highway To Hell* was perhaps the last-ever cassingle released on the Regular label. Never achieving the universal acceptance of vinyl records, in the 80s cassingles became popular thanks largely to the Walkman and car audio players. The CD format of the future would mark a big change in the music industry. Significantly it resurrected the back catalogue of every major artist, as the buying public updated their music collections to this new format.

The MTV film clip was another 80s phenomenon. MTV (Music Television) was an American cable TV show guided by 'video jockeys'. Every music release required an accompanying film clip. Martin sought the assistance of filmmaker Michael Glasheen to address this new challenge. Michael captured the pace of the music by filming the Sydney to Newcastle motorway as the 'highway' (…to Hell). It was screened on MTV and gradually tricked up into the version currently on youtube, with Tiny singing and AC/DC visuals on the power chords. [29]

Arriving in Australia to the usual Wirian reception, Tiny performed RSL Clubs and Martin organised a gig at the former Kinsela's club, renamed Kakadu, where Tiny sang a mini-marathon which included *Tiptoe, Whole World In His Hands, Mame, Wabash Cannonball, Amazing Grace, Heartbreak Hotel, Somewhere My Love, Loverly Bunch of Coconuts, Roll Out The Barrel,* and a couple of Aussie tunes - *Waltzing Matilda* and *Tie Me Kangaroo Down Sport*. The Doug Anthony All Stars played the late-night show; Tiny played the late-late night show.

To launch the *Highway To Hell* cassingle, Martin organized a private function at Wirian. The place was packed with friends, artists and celebrities, including Garry, Judit and Gria Shead, Denny & Clare, Draff, Harold the Kangaroo, Ros Oxley, Roslyn Sharp, Al Jones, Clayton Simms, Toto Renshaw, Craig McGregor and radio personalities Danno and James Valentine. Channel 10's *Good Morning Australia* was there filming. Martin and Tiny were innundated with at least 70 well-wishers before Tiny returned to the States and took up where he'd left off with the Donnie Brooks' 30 Years of Rock and Roll tour. Before leaving he told

Martin to clean the house up and to either marry Yensoon or terminate. It was Tiny's most understated Australian tour. Everyone was still drained from Brighton.

Before the year was out, there were two more new releases for Martin's friends to enjoy, Gary Shearston's 'Aussie Blue' CD and the Tiny *Marathon* triple-cassette pack. The *Highway To Hell,* Glasheen/Sharp video was aired on MTV and Martin started working on an album cover for Regular Records' celebration of 10 years in the business. Martin's 3-piece Boofhead band image was used for two LP records (*Greatest Hits* and *Hits That Missed*), the video and the boxed set. Tiny's *Highway to Hell* was track 4 on *Hits That Missed*. Production was credited to Martin Sharp and Al Jones. [30]

Over the years, Martin had mostly kept the details of his love life under wraps. He opened up to friends but didn't want these matters widely discussed. Not that he minded for himself, he said, 'but out of respect for the women involved'. Martin always expressed affection for past loves. His exes mostly stayed in touch for years after the romance was over. and maintained good relationships after relations ended. Martin wrote long letters to Eija Vehka-aho who lived in Europe, he supported Cressida Campbell's exhibitions and Victoria Cobden was invited to the Tiny Tim shows, Eric Clapton's party, opening nights and everything else Martin came up with. His tryst with Yensoon was a private matter. William knew the details, not many others did. As a muse, Martin painted Yensoon at least twice. A huge black on white portrait was hung beside the front door. He also painted her nude, which he kept out of sight upstairs. He later destroyed that picture.

Now, and for the next seven years, 48-year old Martin would fall in and out of love like a teenager. The average age of his sweethearts was early-20s and they were mostly platonic muses. After Tiny left the country, Martin told everyone that he was keen on Emma Walker. It started when one of Martin's friends, writer Edda Walker was dying of cancer at the Sacred Heart hospice. Edda asked friends to bring something beautiful to her room and Martin brought his picture *Pentecost*. That's how he met her daughter Emma, an aspiring young artist who came to live at Wirian. He wanted to marry her but wanted to follow Tiny's counsel and remain chaste. About sex, Martin said, 'If you don't scratch it, it doesn't itch'. [31]

Martin developed a fascination for paintings of young women. His first subject in this series came after he photocopied a photograph of his mother as a young girl, he blew it up and over-painted it. Since her death, Jo's room remained untouched. Everything was as it was when she was alive – her books, pictures, 1941 diary, comb – everything. Martin's portrait was a beautiful tribute, after which he cast around for more subjects. He was interested in the beauty expressed in that first blush of youth. 'I'd like to do for young girls, what Justin did for young boys', said Martin, who Justin had painted as a 15-year old high school student. Justin's portrait of Martin always had pride of place on the Inner Sanctum end wall.

Martin added, 'I still want to paint great nudes. I'm trying to work out if it's a temptation or a genuine artistic urge. Possibly both.' [32]

# 8.
# THIS IS NOT THE YELLOW HOUSE

*The Yellow House Gallery was never recognized by the art establishment because it was too difficult to categorise, too difficult to market and too subversive to ever be accepted.*
**George Gittoes**

'Although it was not recorded in any conventional history, the Yellow House remained strong in the oral history of artists,' wrote art critic Joanna Mendelssohn. 'Even before its demise it had taken on a legendary quality, and its stature grew in the telling. Many of the younger artists who came there found it an important impetus to their creative life. Most who worked there found that, although intense, the experience of working in a communal way, and keeping their individuality as well as losing it, was worth the pain'. [1]

In the early 70s, 57-59 Macleay Street Potts Point wasn't the only performance art space in town. They were popping up everywhere. Now-forgotten places like the Workshop in William Street, the House of New World in West Ryde and the like. The difference was that the Yellow House was run by artists, those other venues were run by hippies, who were creative rather than artistic.

Eighteen years later, the Yellow House artists were still friends. There had been many small get-togethers, but 1990 marked their 20th anniversary. There was a pervasive feeling that they could link arms, come up with an idea and 'put the band back together'. After all, the key players were still around, still talking to each other and in good artistic shape. Could they expand the Yellow House idea from something ephemeral, regional and generational into filling a significant gap in the history of Australian art? In the early-70s, hippie art was everywhere. Yet it left not a trace in the late-80s art textbooks.

George did a head count – most people liked the idea, but not everyone. Musician Nic Lyon, thought once was enough. He reckoned, 'We'd had a bellyful of it all!' Although Nic didn't involve himself, George ensured his name was listed in the Catalogue along with the others. (2) A few others had moved on too, especially Brett. The main thing was that there was a core of interested participants and no opposition to the idea of putting a proposition to the Art Gallery of New South Wales, which they did.

Antony (Tony) Bond, Director Curatorial at the Art Gallery of New South Wales (AGNSW) in 1990, recalled the occasion, 'A small Yellow House delegation came to see me. George Gittoes, Greg Weight and Peter Wright came to see if I would be interested in doing this exhibition at the Gallery. They came first without Martin.

'I thought it was well worth doing, partly because of the anniversary but also because it was related to Sydney with a sort of international connection as well. I assumed they were trying to establish whether I was up for it and what the terms might be. They said, "We'd like to do an exhibition of the Yellow House" and I said, "What could that possibly be?" I don't think they were quite sure what it might be either but we workshopped it. We did a lot of workshopping before we came up with the concept of what it finally was.

'I could not have shaped it as an exhibition myself and I don't think they wanted me to. If we were not sure how we were going to work, there was the possibility of making an exhibition of all the works that had been shown at the Yellow House. That wouldn't have given a sense of what the Yellow House really was - but constructing the rooms would give us a sense of what the environment was. I thought we had to reinvent the whole thing and make it as engaging as possible.' (3)

It wasn't exactly a cold call. Greg was documenting art works at the gallery and George knew him from living in Bundeena when Tony was Curator for the Wollongong City Gallery. And Tony knew Peter Wright as a Hill End artist.

They did well to call on Tony. Not every curator was suited to handling their spontaneous, non-bureaucratic, freewheeling, charismatic, post-hippie, *laissez faire* approach to gallery art. You can't just throw together a major show at AGNSW at short notice. These things take time - sometimes years - in planning, negotiating and booking the space. But you can't do it, if you don't try.

Tony was charmed, fascinated and hooked. He just needed to get them to understand one small point: a show like this would not command a big budget because the gallery had no provisions for impromptu shows. The team agreed to call for sponsors and Tony would scrape together whatever funding he could. 'It was at relatively short notice,' he said. 'I just called in a few favours. Edmund Capon (Director 1978-2011) thought it was one of my crazed adventures I think!'

The meeting went well.

They said they'd bring Martin next time.

'He didn't do a lot of talking,' said Tony, 'he sat there with that look on his face'. Martin said very little because he had other priorities. There was a crisis at Luna Park. The park was shut and there was a serious plan to demolish it and hand the place to developers.

The key players name-checked those involved in the previous cartel, Harbourside Amusements. What Martin and others regarded as the 'Abe Saffron team' had certainly not given up. The next 12 months saw plans floated for restaurants, nightclubs, cinemas, cafes, a 200-room hotel, a 1200 space car park and an office block over Coney Island. Martin and Kingo joined architect Sam Marshall and other protesters to figure out a counter plan. Gearing up for more action, Friends of Luna Park, with fresh supporters, organised a public rally to mark the 10$^{th}$ anniversary of the Ghost Train fire. Performers included Gary Shearston, Ignatius Jones, the Castanet Club, Terry Serio and the Hummingbirds.

Martin feared the Yellow House retrospective would distract him from what he saw as more urgent matters. He said, 'I had to put aside the film for a while. I had to put aside Luna Park. I was worried the Yellow House was like a red herring to get me off those things.' Before the year was out, Martin and Premier Nick Greiner were guests on the *Vizard* TV show. Martin and the Premier had a backstage chat where Martin felt a satisfactory arrangement was reached about the Park. The following morning Martin received an official letter from Greiner saying the leaseholders had nine months to fulfill their current obligations and to re-open by 1 June 1990. [4]

Either way, the 20$^{th}$ anniversary of the Yellow House was neither here nor there to Martin but the date did coincide with something that was of major importance to him, the 100$^{th}$ anniversary of Vincent's death - 29 July 1890. Martin turned his attention back to Vincent's letters.

Looking deeper he concluded, 'Studying for the Yellow House show, the centenary of Vincent's death became very strong - I couldn't do anything else! The one thing that gave me the go-ahead with the Yellow House show was a letter I found in which Vincent said, "Jesus Christ is the greatest artist" and I thought that was an amazing statement coming from the greatest painter. That was the main part of the show. I did a few paintings myself but they were by-the-by. I couldn't repeat myself. I wasn't interested in reconstructing anything myself. George was – and he had an absolutely valid reason – inspiration. I was not inspired to recreate.' [5]

George and Greg formed the nucleus of the Yellow House Artists committee. Tony and the artists felt they should reconstruct elements of the Yellow House at its best. Martin disagreed. He felt they should commemorate Vincent's death. Tony said the space could accommodate both. The Yellow House committee could manage the entrance, the walk-in and the central area. And Martin could have the big back room where he could do whatever he liked.

Tony described their discussion, 'Martin did raise the Van Gogh anniversary. He did suggest, "Why don't we organize a Vincent van Gogh exhibition to coincide with it?" I explained that was a little bit far-fetched. That would have taken 4-5 years. You can't just do it instantly. "…but if you want to commemorate it yourself, that's fine…". Martin basically got a free rein in that respect.' [6]

The artists formed sub-groups and stayed in touch through circulars and meetings, which became a semi-regular event. They sometimes met at the gallery, sometimes at Wirian and sometimes at the Hero of Waterloo, a pub in the Rocks managed by Tim Lewis who had played a tiny role in the original Yellow House. 'I certainly wasn't involved like the others. I certainly was not a prime player,' he clarified. Back in Yellow House days Tim was in his 3rd year as an art student at East Sydney Tech. Jonny Lewis had invited him to meet Martin. Martin handed Tim a brush and got him to paint two Magritte figures in the *Magritte Room* after which he never stopped asking Tim to paint.

In 1973, Tim painted *Art Exhibition* alongside Martin in Jo's house in Cranbrook Lane. Tim worked with the team at Luna Park, lived at Wirian in the mid-70s and managed the place when Martin went to London and Paris. Martin and Tim knew each other well and, in 1988, here was Tim serving drinks to the Yellow House committee at the Hero of Waterloo pub, tenanted by his family. [7]

Other meetings were frequently held in Tony's office at AGNSW. 'It was usually three people at any one time,' said Tony: often Greg, not Albie, sometimes Roger, never Brett, not Kingo ('I don't think he was a meetings person.') and always George. 'George was taking the running quite a lot. What Martin didn't want to do - George would do that,' Tony explained. 'Having separate meetings with other people - doing the rooms for example - George would pull that together. It needed to be as collaborative as possible - but the way things go, somebody's got to have that sort of chutzpah.' [8] Martin felt the same way, 'George was the boss of the Yellow House exhibition at the Art Gallery of New South Wales because he was the only one prepared to take it on!' [9]

Key committee members were Peter Kingston, Dick Weight, Arthur Karvan, Albie Thoms, Roger Foley, Bruce Goold, Mick Glasheen and Frank Elgar. Everyone missed the presence of Jonny who was in Paris working with French master printer Pierre Gassman. Bruce held up Jonny's portrait to include him in the group magazine photo. [10]

Decisions, decisions. Should they snap-freeze the best of the Yellow House or keep it open-ended? Martin wanted it open-ended, which was not going to work in the gallery. Security issues would be a nightmare. Tony didn't need to say a word. George disagreed with Martin and everyone on the committee agreed with George. An open house 70s-style 'happening' was a thing of the past. The consensus voted: 'This is OUR show!' [11]

Said Tony, 'We got a kind of game plan, which was essentially to construct it around the rooms but Martin was quite keen to open it up and to have as many people as possible who had shown there or been involved. I said, "I'll leave that to you Martin". We left that end space relatively free so he could literally curate whatever.'

'The idea was to recreate the rooms of the Yellow House. The rooms were quite tightly managed and I was working with the people who initially worked on the rooms. I didn't see the originals so I didn't know how they looked then but Greg had some good photographs of the rooms. I suppose the question was – *do we make it an exact replica of what it was or do we try and fix it up a bit?* That proposition had never really been asked in the past because normally when you're creating something you're selecting, you're not re-making. But with a show like this - actually reconstructing the environment - my instinct is not to do it at all really, but if we're going to do it then maybe we make it as good as we can in the space.

'The original was very atmospheric. We could not have all that atmosphere. For example, we could not have impromptu musical performances within the space. So we would try to make the best of it. We worked through the floor plans and to my amazement (because there was clearly quite a lot of competitiveness) we actually came to an agreed distribution of space where we would build the walls and where the rooms would be constructed within the Project Gallery on the ground floor of the gallery.' [12]

The Statement of Intent was drafted by Albie, listing dates (July-October 1990), aims, room installations, supervising artists, performances, AGNSW role, curator's role, artists' roles and a budget of $225,000. [13] Albie suggested lifting the artists' personal fees from $20,000 to $30,000, given that they were individually responsible for so many things – locating artworks, painting walls, loan documentation, helping to install props, supervising installations, assisting in preparation of the catalogue, assisting in fund raising and assisting in publicity.

Greg had taken all the best photographs of the Yellow House in its prime. These shots were used as primary references for reconstructions. His picture of the Stone Room was the Catalogue cover, with spreads throughout capturing the ambience. [14] Joanna Mendelsson was invited to write the introduction to the Catalogue and Tony wrote the preface (but he omitted to give himself a by-line). [15]

'This is not like curating a normal exhibition,' Tony explained. 'Normally an exhibition would be my conception. I would design the show. I would invite artists to participate and I would polish it as well as I possibly could to give the public the best experience of that work. But in this case I was listening, trying to manage this team. Martin on the other hand wasn't really fussed about the team and I wasn't there to try and manage Martin.' [16]

'For me to put the Yellow House into the Art Gallery of NSW is like putting the Loch Ness Monster in a zoo!' Martin erupted. He wasn't prepared to drop all cooperation but he certainly complained a lot. Martin admitted that at one stage he got 'abusive' with the Gallery. 'How can you put the Yellow House in an art gallery?' Martin mocked, 'The Yellow House was a joke on art galleries!' [17]

Martin's refused to have anything to do with Administration. His terms and conditions included working nights - sometimes he didn't arrive before midnight. Tony accommodated Martin with special security arrangements allowing him to work (and smoke) in the Gallery until the early hours of the morning. Mostly he came on his own but once the word got around that Martin was there, other people started turning up. Some came to keep him company, others brought one of their own pieces to hang. Martin never questioned whether or not it hung in the original Yellow House. Martin never questioned anything.

'He wouldn't say no to anybody,' said Tony. 'Anybody who rocked up with a picture under their arm – Martin took it in. This made the registration process and security (documenting everything that entered the building) very difficult. It's a miracle we didn't have major problems with works being mislaid or works not being documented. It could have been a nightmare because I didn't have a registration-person on all the time. What was Martin doing at 3.00am? I have no idea. Nobody complained to me.

'Martin was interested in opening it up to all the players, which I think was appropriate in the circumstances. From a curatorial or a museum point of view, it was pretty unusual. We did have a consultation with a couple of the others whether or not I should be in there editing. I wouldn't have known where to start! My intuition was, "Either I curate it or Martin does. And I don't think it's going to work if I try to edit what Martin's doing." I can't remember Martin doing much by way of editing, he just sort of fitted it all in. In the end, the rooms worked well and the kind of chaos of Martin's curated room captured some of the spirit of the time. There were a lot of works there at one point, an awful lot of works.' [18]

The centerpiece of Martin's open door policy was the constant presence of Harold the Kangaroo – who never had anything to do with the original Yellow House, he was in Amsterdam at the time. Martin arranged for Harold to set up his easel and paint his psychedelic fairground art tableaux within the show. Harold, in multi-coloured clothes, crazy chapeau and silly little beard, hammed up his role. Whereas the actual Yellow House artists were more retiring by nature, Harold chatted to everyone. Without missing a paint stroke, he told passing young women they were beautiful and danced like an imp as required. Said Martin, 'Harold was a great contributor. He was there every day throughout the whole show with his hat out for money. He was the exhibit I'm sure they hated most, but the people loved him.' [19]

Another performance piece was an upright piano that came from Roger Foley. In the 1930s, one of Roger's aunts had traveled the world as a concert pianist. 'She actually met Adolf Hitler…' said Roger, '…but that's another story. I put the piano that I inherited from her in the middle of the exhibition and Martin wrote a little sign that said, 'Please Play Me'. Every kid that went past had a bit of fun. That added a sense of liveliness and fun.' [20]

The commemorate Vincent, Martin had to conceptualise something new. He needed an assistant: Tim Lewis! Tim - now working in a horrible Surry Hills pub because the lease held by his family at the *Hero of Waterloo* had expired, jumped at the chance. 'I find painting lonely in a way,' said Martin, 'that's why I enjoy working with Tim – we share a bit. Vincent said artists should work together – not necessarily on the same picture – but they can work together on similar things.' [21]

'I wanted to get back to painting,' Tim said, 'then out of the blue Martin rang. He asked me to help him with the Yellow House recreation at the Art Gallery of NSW. Do you want to come and help us?' YEAH!! [22]

Tim moved back to living and working at Wirian. He worked alongside Martin on a collage inspired by Vincent's letters after which they painted a series that included Martin's copies of Vincent's Dr Gachet, The Artist on the Road to Tarascon, Self Portrait and others – all in lurid colours.

There was plenty of media coverage in the lead-up to the exhibition. George often spoke for the group, chatting to Philip Adams on ABC radio like old mates. Others were also interviewed, including a reluctant Martin who talked up the show. Privately he may have complained, but publicly he didn't break ranks. In June, he told the Good Weekend magazine, 'The Yellow House was the best thing I've been involved with'. [23]

The Winter edition of *Art and Australia* magazine featured the splendidly illustrated, 'Yellow House, a Brief History' again by Joanna Mendelssohn. It published four of Greg's photos, Martin's 1969 picture of Vincent's Chair, George's 1970 *Self Portrait* and Brett's rarely seen 1970 *Portrait of Martin Sharp in the lyrebird tradition*. [24] FMG magazine ran a feature in which Albie explained the original ideas that inspired the place, 'Van Gogh had the idea – a community of artists in the south in the sun. Martin Sharp had the place – an old art gallery in Sydney's Kings Cross within two Victorian houses that could be used as studios, residences and exhibition spaces. It was called the Yellow House.' [25]

The *Australian magazine* too ran an article. 'Viva Vincent' by Berwyn Lewis featured seven of Martin's pictures, Vincent's self portrait by Tim, Brett's portrait of Martin and a current photo of George in a yellow jacket reconstructing his Puppet Theatre inside the AGNSW. Some hefty claims were being made. Nikki Barraclough credited Albie's launch of the Ginger Meggs Memorial School of Arts as the start of the 'later revival of Australian film'. [26] Jonny told the Australian magazine that the ideas for Nimbin and the Aquarius Festival came out of the Yellow House. [27] Art investment writers joined in too. *Australian Business* magazine featured the Yellow House artists in their investment section called 'Collectibles'. Maybe they were all right. [28]

The opening – at last! - at the end of July. Emblazoned across the entrance was a Roger Foley light show with the words, "This is NOT the Yellow House" in the style of Magritte. 'It set the right tone. Roger stressed, 'One of my installations was a projector installation on the front of the building. With very powerful projectors I wrote across the top of the entrance to the Art Gallery of NSW… It wasn't the Yellow House! The gallery had white walls and the Yellow House didn't know white walls!' (29) That established, visitors were ready for a highly innovative exhibition.

The opening night was another occasion where 'everyone' was there – artists, art students, poets, musicians, critics, journalists, socialites, art bureaucrats and people who were simply curious – basically what Nic Lyon described as 'a gathering of the clan'. Significantly a lot of visitors brought along their teenagers. After all this time their kids got a handle of what their parents had been telling them about over the years! Tony Bond described the spectacle, 'The opening night – there was a lot of spontaneity about that. An amazing crowd! There was an incredible atmosphere and there were a lot of people who hadn't seen the gallery, dressed up to the nines – performing really!' (30)

After speeches, there was music. Martin wanted his Fijian friend Robert Wolfgramm to sing his song *Emmaus*. Robert lived in Melbourne and no longer performed. Anyway, George, Greg, Roger, Albie – none of them - had heard of him. (31) Gary Shearston sang songs from his latest CD, 'Aussie Blue'. *Crafty Old Captain* was one high point. And Jeannie Lewis sang *Gary's Song* from her 1973 hit album, 'Free Fall Through Featherless Flight'. After this and some speeches, visitors walked through the Entrance Hall where Martin's *Catalog* was displayed in a glass cabinet. Then they swarmed into the rooms.

They saw: the Cloud Room painted after Magritte, with stage for performances, a display from Martin's *Artoons* and some of his *Incredible Shrinking Exhibition*. The Bonsai Room 'presented by Brett Whiteley'. The Stone Room by Peter Kingston with a tribute to George Greenough. The Magritte Room displaying works by Magritte, Martin, Bruce Goold and others. Mary in the Bathroom, a mannequin installation by Tim Burns. Spookyland, an ultra-violet environment with artworks by Peter Wright. The Fogg Capsule, a lightshow environment by Roger Foley (aka Ellis D Fogg). The Black Room featuring white sculptures by Judy Sale and Tim Burns. The Infinity Room, a photographic display by Greg Weight. The Puppet Theatre by George Gittoes. The Whaam Wall and Fur Tunnel by Albie Thoms. Corridor displays were by Antoinette Starkiewicz, Franklin Johnson, 'Hop, Liney, Hobby and Paolozzi'. Martin curated his own space up the back, featuring the Vincent-themed pictures he had worked on with Tim as well as other works. (32)

Films screened were: *The Yellow House Filmmakers' Cinema* by Albie Thoms, David Perry & Aggie Read, Garry Shead, Peter Kingston, Mick Glasheen, Chris McCullough & David Lourie, Bruce Petty & Peter Weir, A&C Cantrill and George Greenough. *Yellow House Cinematheque* mixed classical and avant-garde works with primitive cinema. *Yellow House Associated Films* by Paul Cox, Antoinette Starkiewicz & George Gittoes, Jim Sharman, Albie Thoms, Tim Burns, Albert Falzon & George Greenough. And a preview screening of Martin's film, *Street of Dreams –Brighton Cut*. (33)

Artists officially included in the Catalogue of Works for this incarnation of the Yellow House were: Tim Burns, Magdalene (Marie) Briebauer, Roger Foley (Ellis D Fogg), Juno Gemes, George Gittoes, Joyce Gittoes, Mick Glasheen, Bruce Goold, Franklin Johnson, Peter Kingston, Jon Lewis, Tim Lewis, Vivienne Pengilly, Peter Powditch, Julia Sale, Martin Sharp, Antoinette Starkiewicz, Albie Thoms, Greg Weight, Richard Weight, Brett Whiteley and Peter Wright. [34]

Adrian Rawlins came up from Melbourne for the spectacle. He expounded the significance of the Yellow House in his public address and afterwards to anyone who would listen. Roger filmed Adrian inside the reconstructed Stone Room talking with authority and flair. Here's just a sample, 'Absurd as it seemed at the time, this claim that Martin was genuinely responding to Vincent van Gogh's vision was in fact true. And in the Yellow House we found people prepared to create the most beautiful art for no reward. They did these great rooms and these true surrealist and romantic works in three dimensions, in four dimensions even. And they never had one thought of reward. The psychedelia of the late-60s was a reflection of a social movement which really had begun in 1848-1850 when European nations threw off traditional monarchies and embraced a truly democratic view of human potential. We saw in the poetry of Walt Whitman, various movements like the Chartists and the Suffragettes, where people really thought what we now call "People Power". Martin Sharp's involvement was to a romantic and transcendental love, which he saw manifesting in the work of Vincent van Gogh and in artists like Tiny Tim, the most cosmic artist we'd ever seen. All of that fructified in the Yellow House. Martin's art, Martin's posters - genuine psychedelia which he'd done in England in 1966-67 - still stand as the greatest expression of Psychedelic Art that was ever created.' [35]

The Yellow House exhibition generated quite a bit of momentum. It appealed to a younger audience too. Jason Whalley's high school band performed a cover of *Tales of Brave Ulysses* in 1990 when no one else was playing it. Recalling those days, the singer of Frenzel Rhomb said, 'I had only heard the Yellow House being talked of in reverent, hushed tones and had a vague idea that it was basically some squat in Kings Cross populated by a bunch of old hippies where anyone could walk off the street and paint a wall. It wasn't until seeing the Yellow House retrospective in 1990 that I realised I was right - but also completely wrong. As a 17-year old kid the concepts they were exploring and the psychedelic art blew my mind. The idea of this loose collection of artists doing whatever the hell they wanted in a shared communal space was both inspiring and exciting.' [36]

Aside from magazine articles, television coverage and radio interviews, it spawned two more Yellow House exhibitions - the Josef Lebovic Gallery (1990) and the other at Michael Nagy Gallery Potts Point (1999).

Josef Lebovic had built his gallery business up from scratch. He started with one of the first stands in the Paddington Market Bazaar and quickly graduated to buying Picasso prints in London and reselling at a tidy profit. Twenty years later, he'd bought-and-sold his way up to owning a smart gallery in Paddington that specialised in quality prints. Josef knew all about the 60s-70s art scene in Sydney and London. Some of the artists counted him as a friend. Unlike the AGNSW, Josef's Yellow House exhibition had pieces for sale. He was disappointed that Martin was not more commercially-minded.

'The reason Brett sells and Martin doesn't,' Josef explained, 'is that Brett publishes books of all his posters and prints. Each poster is dated and the editions are numbered, so collectors know exactly what they've got. But nobody knows how many posters Martin has done and nobody knows when he did them.' (Another three decades would pass before Michael Organ of the University of Wollongong would attempt a definitive listing of Martin Sharp posters/prints.) [37]

And so in August-September, concurrent with the AGNSW exhibition, Josef's exhibition included works by George Gittoes, Bruce Goold, Franklin Johnson, Peter Kingston, Garry Shead, Martin Sharp, Antoinette Starkiewicz , Greg Weight, Richard Weight, Brett Whiteley and Peter Wright. The featurepiece for Lebovic's ad was Martin's *Vincent* print of the collage that he gave Jeannie (all those years ago). [38]

Praise did not come from all quarters. Some felt that Martin had moved from appropriation to straight copying. He didn't care. Martin replied that he never created a new image when one was already doing that job. Still, he didn't count his contribution a total success, 'I don't think the paintings succeeded. None of the pictures are really finished. The criticism is exactly what Vincent did, whenever he wanted to make a spiritual point he went outside his own work. He painted copies of Millet's paintings, Delacroix' paintings. I'm not really a painter, I'm an occasional painter. Vincent was a painter, that was it - nothing else – (and a writer). Sometimes I paint but realise that to paint properly it's something like being a musician, you've got to do it all the time. I can bring out an image and sometimes I can paint them well but it's an enormous effort. I try to copy, but Tim can DO it!' [39]

The Yellow House retrospective enhanced the legend of every artist involved. They were all proud of the achievement. Said Greg, 'I think the *Retrospective* was timely - 20 years after the Yellow House itself and 100 years after Vincent's death. Those two anniversaries and the re-creation attracted huge attendances and, in a way, it proved the popularity of the place. It proved the synergy that the artists had, which was quite unique because we had a very constructive relationship. There was camaraderie among the group that encouraged the furthering of ideas. The thing is, the same group doesn't live forever – the Beatles were only five years I think. The individuals can't sustain, can't tolerate each other - or something. But the period of time that the Yellow House existed, those that were there really did cooperate with each other. That I think was the strength of it.' [40]

Tony was pleased too. Another of what Edmund Capon called his 'crazed adventures' had proven right. He said, 'I don't think anybody had any anticipation of it being a success. I was always told "it's a kind of niche really - it was a moment" - but I thought it might actually be quite popular because so many people had talked about the Yellow House during the time I'd been in Australia.' [41] In its long history of exhibitions, the Yellow House retrospective was the best-attended contemporary show held at the Art Gallery of New South Wales to 1990.

# 9.
# COURAGE MY FRIEND

*I never imagined that you could paint a picture longer than an hour or two.
Martin taught me that art takes as long as it takes.*
Joel Tarling

    *Abalone Diver (The Lost Hokusai)* was Martin and Tim's next picture. The possibility of Art Exhibition 2 was on the cards. Martin explained his tight artistic relationship with Tim, 'I'm the producer – if you like – Tim's the performer. I found the image, I've got the canvas, I've got the prints, I've got the studio, I've got the place to allow the picture to grow in – and a wonderful painter who's patient and humble enough to work on another person's image - which is a great thing I have with Tim after Art Exhibition. We'll both sign it.' [1]

    *Eternity* was their next canvas, commissioned by Remo Giuffré. His 'general store' - named after himself - was located on the corner of Oxford and Crown Streets Paddington. It had a big street presence. It stocked a range of 'unique and thoughtful' items from Westclox fob watches and sleep masks to the type of t-shirts students - not skateboarders - might wear. Describing himself as a 'creative strategist' Remo was inspired by Arthur Stace's 'Eternity' motif. And who better to depict that than Martin Sharp? Remo commissioned a traffic-stopping 5-metre Eternity picture for his shop window, inside was a range of Eternity t-shirts, postcards and prints. [2]

    Tim and Martin both worked on the *Eternity* canvas, Tim painted the blue background, Martin painted the yellow calligraphy. To make the blue background seamless, Tim overpainted the 'Eternity' motif, later to bring 'Eternity' back to the foreground. He said, 'I did layers of blue washes in that painting. As a result you get this luminosity coming through. It has a depth. In order to do these washes,

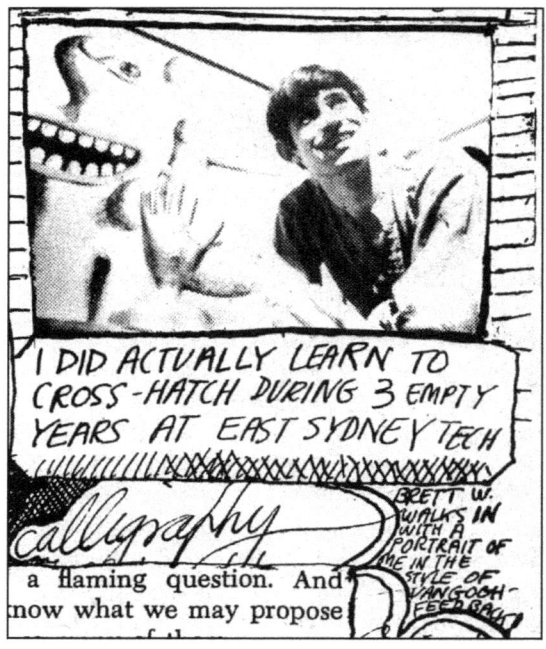

*(Top) From Cartoons (Scripts 1967); (Lower) Detail from Catalog (Arcana 1971, p7) Courtesy UOW*

*Walsh, Sharp and Neville from Catalog, p6, courtesy UOW*

*(Top) The OZ Editors (from OZ 1); (Lower) the cover of OZ 11 (1964), courtesy of UOW*

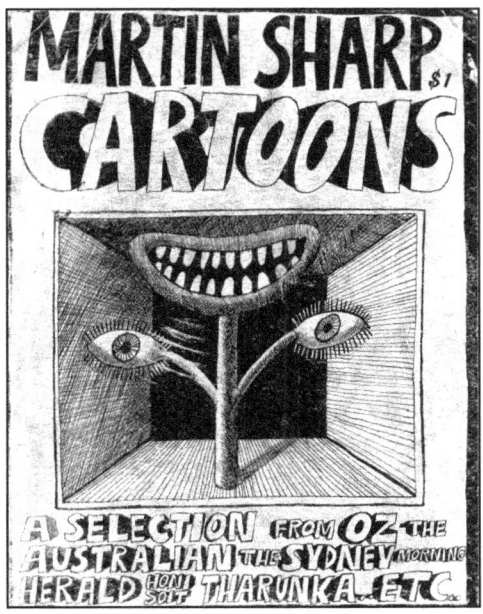

*(Top) Sharp cover for Pop by Peter Draffin (Scripts 1967); (lower) From Cartoons, courtesy UOW*

*Sharp covers for the Cream's Disraeli Gears (1967) and Wheels of Fire (1968), courtesy UOW*

*Sharp cover for the last issue of Sydney OZ (1969)
courtesy of UOW*

*Jim Anderson, Felix Dennis and Richard Neville
"admire" the Schoolkid's issue of London OZ 28*

*(Top) Albie Thoms, Martin Sharp and Richard Neville (photograph by Jonny Lewis); (Lower) OZ Schoolgirls "team"*

*Martin Sharp in the early stages of painting Tiny Tim's Non-Stop Singing Record (courtesy David Pepperell)*

*(Top) Tiny Tim's Chameleon, using a photograph by William Yang; (Lower) Martin Sharp with Tiny Tim in Sharp's Kold Komfort Kaffe setting (photograph by David Pepperell)*

*(Top) Ted Hopkins, innovator at Luna Park, with Martin Sharp (photograph by Jonny Lewis); (lower) Luna Park fire in full blaze*

*Martin Sharp at work on the Luna Park face*

*Martin Sharp outside Luna Park on 31 May 1981 (photograph by Peter Adams)*

*Martin Sharp at the Luna Park exhibition 1984
(photograph by Jonny Lewis)*

*Jenny Godson with Martin Sharp's paintings of her family (photograph by Peter Royles)*

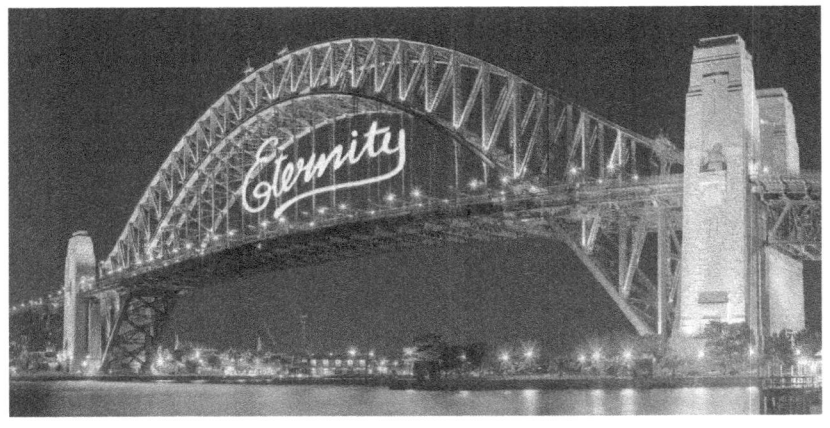

*Arthur Stace (above) and Sharp's homage (below)*

you can't leave traces of the yellow. Sometimes I painted over the whole lot. One day, Martin came down from upstairs and the "Eternity" had gone. He totally freaked out. He related it to Patrick White's death, (30 September 1990). He was very superstitious about things like that. The next day it was all fine.' [3]

Early in the year Tim's sister, Sally Swinn, introduced Martin to 29-year old Paiwan Phongsitthisak with the possibly of employing her as a housekeeper at Wirian. Usually known as Pai, she was also nicknamed Pepsi. Her best friend was 'Tiny'. Martin said, 'Tiny is doing a Pepsi Cola commercial and her name is Tiny. Of course I notice! Names and coincidences are starting to emerge. I can see a similar pattern with the Luna Park Fire.' [4]

Pai was born in a small village on the border of the Mekong River, Laos. This once-great river was fished-out and Pai was raised poor. She wanted to earn money to raise her 5-year old son whom she had adopted to her brother. She met an American who took her to Bangkok. Pai worked as a dancer and a German guy brought her to Australia. 'I suspect there was a drug connection,' said Martin, 'possibly because he was shot'. In Sydney, Pai worked at the Birds of Paradise Club, Kellett Street, Kings Cross. One night, 42-year old real estate agent, David Smedley took a real shine to her. Smedley was dangerously possessive. He stalked her. Said Martin, 'He was violent towards her and made her do things sexually which she found extremely unpleasant. He actually said, "If she doesn't toe the line she's got to go back to Thailand because I've got the power over her visa".' [5]

To distance herself, Pai rented an apartment near Centennial Park but Smedley moved in, she couldn't get away from him. Late one night, Pai rang Martin in a distressed state. Smedley had been hitting her again. Martin hastened to the rescue. He located her near a phone box, drove her to Wirian and gave her a spare bedroom to sleep in overnight while Smedley jealously awaited her return. [6] Gria Shead became one of Pai's Wirian friends, she elaborated, 'It was a horrific time. She'd been beaten by that cretin, she was terrified. She said, "He's really dangerous, I've got to get away from him." So we told Martin. "Could Pai stay with me?" (I was living at Wirian.) He said she could. That was good, that was hopeful, that she could get away from this man. So she did move in.' [7]

Al Jones had formed a band, Al & the Gators, and he vacated the room under the house. It was convenient that Pai should take over his room. Meanwhile, Wirian was its usual hive of activity. Martin gave Ken Done some Tiny Tim music and phoned Michael Chamberlain for advice about whether or not to sell Wirian. He then began a small picture – about the size of a record cover - that he called a 'study' for his big canvas, *Artist on the Road to Tarascon*. [8] Willy De La Vega kept Martin company late into the night. Dave Rowe worked on the music. A singer called Patricia came and went. Greg and Suzie Weight broke up so Greg moved in and started cataloguing Martin's works. Gria carved linocuts in the Dream Museum. Pai told Gria about the dark side of Smedley. Gria said, 'I helped her get a

Restraining Order. I was only 17! I'd never done anything like that before but she was in danger. And sure enough she really was'. [9]

Tim urged Martin to keep Pai's situation at arm's length. Recalling his days managing the pub in the Rocks, Tim said, 'That guy used to come down to the Hero of Waterloo and say frightening things to me. I had a bargirl working for me and he'd get really threatening because he fancied her. I was scared of him!' [10]

Martin's relationship with Cranbrook School fluctuated with changing headmasters. He was annoyed that they weren't paying their contribution to the jointly-owned fence, yet with some reticence Martin took a talk for the Art Department. He said, 'I've gone back and talked about Tiny Tim once - but I'm not too hot at giving talks otherwise I wouldn't probably wouldn't paint. Some artists are good at talking, I'm not particularly'. [11] Martin always had time for students, as evidenced when Year 12 student, Joel Tarling, spent a week doing Work Experience at Wirian. Joel said, 'There was something really lovely about Paiwan being there. She cooked amazing Asian food, the kind that Martin liked. She kept Martin well fed, the house clean and everything was ticking over.'

What was work experience at Wirian like? Many students did it. Day one - Joel 'just moped around the house and weeded the driveway'. Day two - Martin checked Joel's sketchbook. They selected a picture and Martin set him up to paint it. Later that afternoon Joel thought he'd finished. Martin took a look and told him he'd only just begun. Joel worked that image for the rest of his stay - a little improvement here, a little improvement there. He explained, 'After a couple of hours painting, I thought I'd be done but Martin kept saying I could do more. He got me painting it for the remaining four days. I never imagined that you could paint a picture longer than an hour or two. He taught me that art takes as long as it takes. Dave Rowe was in the same room as me, the Dream Museum room, doing the Tiny Tim *Rock* album. I was working under Arthur Barton's *Loona Park* restoration. I now look back and think, "I am so lucky to be working in the shadow of that!" Martin gave me a book every night. I tried to like the *Coles Funny Picture Book* but it didn't connect with me. The next evening he gave me the *Robert Crumb 1967 Sketchbook*. I started drawing that night in bed and it changed the way that I drew. When my work experience teacher called to check on me, she was over the moon. I'd never seen her giddy like a schoolgirl. She couldn't believe that she was going into that house. I got an Honourable Mention certificate for Work Experience.' [12]

While watching Tim breathe life into the Lost Hokusai canvas, once again Martin contemplated the meaning of the picture, 'The arrangement of those shells represents a third eye - this rock-like creature on the bottom of the sea. I was gradually working it out and then I thought, "That's Hokusai! The figure is the muse. He's living underwater." which signifies one world. The diver has come down from another world, taken this part of himself and is representing it above the water. The abalone is a symbol of female generative organs, also a symbol of unrequited love, because it's a uni-valve shell not a bi-valve shell (bi-valve is requited love and uni-valve is unrequited love). And then I realised this is an oriental equivalent of Botticelli's Birth Of Venus!' [13]

And Tiny? He had been recording an album in Burns, a small township outside Nashville USA. It's where you'd operate if you couldn't afford Music City and where Gordon Stinson ran his NGT record label and recorded Tiny's impressive Leave Me Satisfied album. Tiny had an ill-timed business argument with Stinson. It was over a $1000 cheque that was paid into Tiny's mother's account and bounced, so Tiny refused to promote anything until Stinson made this right. For the first time in a long time, a Tiny Tim single hit the Top 100 charts, entering at No 88 with a bullet. It was Leave Me Satisfied/I Wanna Get Crazy with You. Stinson was a small man with a big belt buckle, just your basic Good Ole Boy. He lived in a trailer on his property and the house was the studio and had gone to a lot of trouble to get this album 'right'. On national TV, he arranged for Country music legend Buck Owens to join Tiny on a performance of Tiger By the Tail, the song Owens made famous. [14]

Without Tiny's cooperation and promotional value, the single was dead in the water. Instead of rewriting the cheque, Stinson pulled the record and no one could buy it. It was just another Might-Have-Been moment for Tiny. 'How often does a Tiny Tim record hit the charts!' said a disappointed Stinson. This left Stinson with a lot of unsold records, a promotional video and a heap of merchandising material. Stinson knew of Martin. He was hoping to sell Martin a 50% share of this failed venture for $100,000. Martin didn't have that much disposal cash but he checked out the offer and half-wished he could proceed.

Martin was a popular subject for magazine writers. There was a constant trickle of offers. He had repeated offers to 'do a book' to which he was completely amenable if it was about Tiny (which no publisher wanted). Martin was also offered a contract for a book about Luna Park. He declined. [15] An autobiography? He declined that too. Tom Thompson and Elizabeth Butel had previously tried to interest Martin in having his OZ drawings published in a book format. Nice meetings, no product.

In 1989 Tom became publisher of literature at Angus & Robertson, which strengthened his negotiating position. Said Tom, 'Elizabeth and I went to Wirian every month for about three years mostly to get a book out of Martin. I then got to be publisher at Angus & Robertson and thought, "I'm equipped financially, I'll start all over again with him". And so we went to Wirian at another level. I made two packages for Martin to try and get him to the party. We offered him a contract with A&R to do the *OZ Book*. He wouldn't do it.' [16]

Martin had converted the Dream Museum room into a second workspace (for Dave, Gria and others). The heart of the collection was moved elsewhere and representatives of the Powerhouse Museum came to Wirian and checked it out. Said Martin, 'The Powerhouse Museum had a lot of ideas. All these little things represent something for everyone who goes into it. The Yellow House was like that, there was a doorway into it for everyone - no matter where they came from, no matter what their age - it had a point of access. The Dream Museum is like that. I think the Dream Museum should go to Luna Park. That's what it was collected for initially.' [17]

Around this time Martin encountered Abe Saffron in person for the first and only time. Martin had softened his position on Saffron's involvement in the Fire. He felt others were implicated too, perhaps even more so. [18] Martin came face-to-face with Saffron in a restaurant called DB's at Double Bay. Martin had an arranged lunch date with Karen Robson ('a brilliant show business lawyer') and Martin Fabinyi. He said, 'Walking towards this place looking for Fabinyi, I notice this person looking at me, smiling. I turned around to save us a spot and he – Abe Saffron – is sitting right in the middle of this restaurant where I was supposed to meet Fabinyi. I was taken aback. I walked in with Karen ("We've got to meet Fabinyi here anyway…"), shook his hand and said, "Hi, how are you?" It was a strange meeting, quite good-natured in its way. What was I to do? Keep walking? Go somewhere else? It could have been set up of course – couldn't it? Or was it just chance? The thing was – it was as if Saffron was expecting me'. [19]

The Luna Park Trust people visited Martin too, checking out the pieces he had purchased or salvaged from the Auction. They planned an exhibition before the year was out, while also reconsidering the status of the Park, which was torn between restoration and development. A third player entered the ring. Representatives of the Eora Aboriginal tribe asked the Government to build a $300 million cultural centre on the Luna Park site. Martin was never going to disagree with them.

Then came the heartbreaking news that Eric Clapton's son, Conor, died after falling 49 storeys from an open window in a New York hotel. The accident happened during a visit from the housekeeper who had opened the window in order to clean it when Conor wasn't in the room. She was unable to stop the boy from playfully darting past her. Martin expressed immense grief about the pain his friend and former flatmate was going through.

Martin had met Marianne Faithfull in the late-60s. She was with Mick Jagger when he and Richard Neville called on Mick's house to raise money for OZ maga-zine. Marianne became friends with Martin's girlfriend Victoria Cobden when she accompanied Mick to Australia to film Ned Kelly in 1970. They remained in loose contact ever since. To celebrate Marianne's Blazing Away tour, Martin held a huge Wirian soirée in her honour. All Martin's friends were invited, the OZ crowd, the Yellow House people, Tiny Tim people - new friends and old. It was a big night at Wirian. Wine, music and cake. After this, Marianne and Martin frequently chatted on the phone. She sent him demos of her newest recordings. He gave her a print of Eternity, which she hung in the bedroom of her Paris apartment.

Martin had always painted portraits. Fictional ones in high school, real ones now. He had painted Chica Lowe, Polly Seidler, his mother, the victims of the Ghost Train fire. He now began a series of pictures of young girls. Amber Mackenzie was an art student. She shared a studio space alongside Luke Sciberras at the National Art School and agreed to sit for Martin. All the preparatory drawings were done upstairs in his verandah studio off his bedroom. The picture didn't come downstairs until Martin captured the essence of what he was after.

Amber described Martin's process, 'He ran off a lot of Polaroids. He just wanted my face. He was quite specific about my hair. There was a point where it could have been a nude. He asked politely, would that be comfortable for me? There was nothing weird about it. He was an utter gentleman, I said no. In that first session, I could feel he was seeking what he was trying to do. He found it in the second session and clicked in. That was quite relaxing for me because I could feel his artistic tension and I sorta felt a bit responsible for it. He started painting Minyo Weight around the same time. Minyo's portrait was more Botticelli and mine was Modigliani.' [20]

Occasional visitor, Ian Reid (owner of the Yellow House premises in the 1970s) summed up his thoughts, 'I think Martin's muse was nubile young women, best stated in that beautiful painting he did of the young woman in the Hokusai pool. *Abalone Diver* - I thought - moved towards his essence.' [21]

While painting Amber and Minyo, Martin continued working quite steadily on *On the Road to Tarascon* (later named *Courage My Friend*). Paiwan cooked beautiful Asian food. Willy de la Vega visited often. Distinguished artist, Judy Cassab painted Martin for the Archibald Prize. And Emelia Gypsy Fire wanted Draff to ghost her kiss-and-tell account about her alleged tryst with Bob Dylan. Richard Neville was simply fascinated.

Good news for Coney Island. In August came a serious proposal for a 3-stage development of Luna Park – stage one, refurbishment as an amusement park, scheduled for completion September 1993 at a cost of $18.4 million. Heritage items like the Face and Coney Island to be fully restored. The Palais de Danse to become a reception venue. The Crystal Palace to house a café, restaurant and a nightclub. A nightclub? Would alcohol be served on the premises? Martin wasn't pleased and immediately got on the phone to Kingo about that!

8 November, a gloomy Friday night.

Paul Healy finishes his work and leaves Wirian.

Gria goes out.

Tim goes out.

He says goodbye to Paiwan, in so doing he is the last Wirian person to see her alive.

The film *Performance* is on TV.

Martin returns home after attending a roast for John Singleton, says, 'Then I come home to a real roast!'

He plays a tape about Weary Dunlop and works on a commission called, *Fragments of a Funfair.*

Willy de la Vega drops in. They talk about Luna Park and Weary Dunlop. 'Willy understands why I love Weary,' said Martin, 'it's a bit naff but it's sincere'.

Around 3.00am the dogs bark.

Maybe Gria or Pai coming home?

Martin and Willy smell something.

They run to the room under the house.

Martin yells. 'Grab the fire extinguisher!'

They run past the ringing phone, 'Hi – this is a call for Tim Lewis from America…'.

'Not now!'

Flames at Pai's window.

Martin bursts in, extinguishes the flames.

Can't breathe. Can't see.

Then he does see.

Two people lying on the floor.

Pai, uttering her last gasp.

The other – a male - stands up.

It's Smedley, almost unrecognisable, clothes and hair burned off, skin translucent.

'Don't worry,' he says, 'Everything'll be all right'.

'You monster!' Martin cries.

He rings for an ambulance.

Four times, he rings for an ambulance…

'…and the next thing we see is him, walking the drive, covered in ash – pale blue, maybe a little jockstrap on – like an Indian monk – bald, completely unrecognisable, except the voice is the same. And calm. He's in a trance. He'd gone down, knocked her out and poured petrol over them both.'

Three fire engines arrive but Martin and Willy have already extinguished the fire.

Two ambulances and Police.

A policeman enters Pai's room and says, 'We've got a Code 4 here'.

Some guy with a video camera from Channel 9 arrives.

Smedley walks to the Wirian gate.

'Where are you going?'

'I'm leaving'.

Willy insists, 'You've got to stay'.

Smedley crosses Victoria Road, leans on a telegraph pole, 'but he had no skin, no clothes, all burned off'.

Smedley died 2.00pm the following afternoon. [22]

Journalist Mark Riley reported, 'A 29-year old Thai woman who was burned to death in an apparent murder-suicide on Saturday dreamed of saving enough money to bring her young son from her small village to live with her, according to her employer. The woman was a housekeeper for the artist Martin Sharp and lived in a downstairs flat at his Bellevue Hill mansion. She and her former defacto husband Mr David Smedley, whom she left two weeks ago, died in a fire at Mr Sharp's house soon after 3.00am on Saturday.' [23]

The following weekend, Father James (Jim) of Christ Church St Lawrence Broadway, conducted a Catholic-Anglican-Buddhist mass at Wirian. Around 50 people attended.

The *Luna Park – Fragments of a Funfair* exhibition was held between December-February in Sydney's Hyde Park Barracks. Most of the North Sydney councillors were present at the opening. Its 148 exhibits centred on photographs by Ted Hopkins and works by Arthur Barton. Greg Weight and Peter Kingston were well represented and Martin exhibited his *Fragments of a Funfair* print. [24]

Some of guests knew Pai and their reflections overshadowed the 'Just For Fun' celebration for which the organisers had hoped. Adding to the gloom, Martin toppled the second 'F' in his *Fragments of a Funfair* print, It now read: *Fragments of an Unfair*.

*

At the close January 1992 Martin took a trip to Bermagui with Richard Neville and Julie Clarke. The Nevilles did a house swap with a couple on a picturesque property called Umbi Gumbi on Lake Cuttagee. While there, Martin unsuccessfully tried to quit smoking.

Tim 'held the fort' at Wirian during Martin's brief absence. Jonny moved in and so did jack-of-all-trades Terry Stanton. Tim was surprised that Martin took a break. 'When I lived with him at Wirian – he might go out once a week, maybe once every two weeks,' said Tim. 'He might go to an opening or something like that. Other than that he'd rarely leave that living area where he had the big table. People would come to him.' [25]

Martin returned in time to attend the opening of Kingo's 'Cartoon Boxes, Paintings, Etchings, Chess Sets and Snakes and Ladders' exhibition at Australian Galleries. Martin and Brett were photographed together for the social pages, perhaps for the last time. Brett told Martin he had a dream in which Satan said to him, 'If you're kind to anyone, I'll kill you'. [26]

Martin and Tiny discussed another tour of Australia. This was to be the only time Martin brought Tiny out without a promoter, footing the bill himself. Martin had money on previous tours and Tiny was $short. This time it was the other way around, Tiny had contracts for two well-paying ads – Pepsi Cola and Budweiser Beer. Martin's finances had always been a bit borderline but previous tour expenses could usually be balanced by the arrival of a *Tales of Brave Ulysses* royalty cheque. This time, a bit more than that was at stake.

Tiny's tour coincided with Martin's exhibition at Australian Galleries. So did Bob Dylan's tour. In March, Dylan was playing Sydney the day after Tiny was due to arrive. Martin bought tickets for himself, Emma and Tiny. The plan was to orchestrate a backstage meeting between Tiny and Dylan after the concert, held at Sydney's State Theatre. Tim's Bob Dylan *Self Portrait* picture was hung in the foyer. It was so precise that the audience might have mistaken it for a blow-up of the actual album cover. Did Dylan see it? Maybe. As for the Tiny Tim-Bob Dylan meeting? That didn't happen. Tiny postponed his arrival date by three days because of commitments for the Budweiser ad.

In Sydney, it was all go. Martin asked Denny to put together a hard rocking band to back Tiny's Rock medley. Martin wanted a Vaudeville-type band as well, but switched to a Country band when Chris Löfvén, bass player and manager of the Prickles, applied to be Tiny's support. Chris and singer Steve Fasan called on Wirian and explained their intent. Dave said, 'A country band - we need one of those!' So they were in.

Dave got the media onside, *The Sydney Morning Herald, Drum Media, On The Street, Steve Vizard Show, The World Tonight* and Ray Martin's *Midday Show* where Tiny appeared with Chad Morgan. 'Everybody wanted him. Tiny Tim has left an amazingly good trail over the past nine years he's been here. There wasn't a bad word about the guy.'

Back at Wirian the core team comprised Dave, Terry, Tim and work experience student Blazey Best. Pitt Street tailor, Tony Bechini made Tiny's suits and Miss Scheherazade kept his heart aflutter.

Said Dave, 'I truly think Martin tried to stay out of it as much as he could, rather than cause confusion. Martin has to get a credit because he brought Tiny out, but as far as everything running smoothly is concerned it has been Terry Stanton, Blazey Best and myself. Tim's always been there to help. He's very talented computer-wise. My observation is that Tiny has to make decisions, which he doesn't want to make, so you have a recipe for disaster when Martin leaves the decision-making to Tiny. Martin himself can find it difficult to make business decisions. He's shy in that sort of way. They both need damn good organisers. The pair of them should be millionaires - they certainly deserve to be. The pair of them are a couple of angels, they really are.' (27)

Tiny was in Sydney when *Sharp On Paper* opened at Australian Galleries. The show was packed to the walls with smokers spilling on the street, where Martin joined them. The 90 pictures on exhibit included the Elvis collage, portraits of Amber and Minyo, *Film Script*, the Luna Park Crucifix, *Fragments of an Unfair* and a range of works dating back to 1965. Also on sale was Tiny's Brighton Marathon triple cassette and the *Highway to Hell/I Love Rock N Roll* cassingle. Tiny struggled through the crowd to reach the microphone where he sang four songs including a poignant song for artists about 'being careful' when painting… *That Mother of Mine*.

After that Martin and Tiny went to Rich Studios where they recorded *Eve of Destruction* and *Rebel Yell*. The band was Denny (bass), John Botica (guitar), Claude Woodward (keyboards) and Col Burgess (drums). Said Denny, 'We didn't do any rehearsals, we just listened to the recordings of Bon Jovi and followed Tiny – Tiny would just say, "Do you know such-and-such gentlemen?" And off he'd go.' [28]

Martin was using his prints/posters as a form of currency. That's how he paid musicians and others. Martin offered to create a poster for Denny's stage band (Burgess Brothers) but somehow – with regret - Denny didn't get around to taking up the offer. Martin even paid his dentist with a print! But Tiny was someone Martin couldn't pay with art. He only wanted cash. Martin didn't have the money and hoped this tour would be 'like two artists working together' which was not in Tiny's thinking. Notwithstanding that over the years Martin had spent a couple of million dollars on Tiny, especially on the film, Tiny's management expected payment in full. For the first time, Martin's entourage saw an uneasy relationship between the two, with Martin asking friends and banks for loans that were hardly forthcoming. Good relations between Tiny and Martin never broke down. But it came close.

Tiny turned 60 on 12 April and to celebrate, Martin organized a big gig and a midnight after-party at the Paddington RSL Club which held 1000. They were just short of filling it. Martin pulled out all stops to make it memorable – Denny's Rock ensemble, the Prickles, an Ellis D Fogg lightshow, film crew and the birthday cake from the well-loved Paddington cake shop, *Sweet Art*. Roger wanted to project onto the stage, so everything had to be white, white sets and white stage clothes. Roger filmed the show independently of Martin. [29]

The Prickles first, then Denny's band. Then Tiny. It was another sensational night. *Highway to Hell* ran for a solid 8 minutes. The dance floor was going nuts! Someone called 'Miss Josephine' climbed onstage, grabbed Tiny and kissed him. Denny recalls that two Hoodoo Gurus – Brad Shepherd and Dave Fawlkner - were impressed. They brought Tiny out a year later. [30]

After the show, Martin and Tiny returned to Martin's Honda Civic to find that someone had broken a window and stolen Tiny's ukulele and Martin's tape recording gear. Hoping to prick the thief's conscience, because the thief may not have known they had taken Tiny Tim's uke, Terry Stanton wrote a press release and the newspapers ran the story. Martin organised the purchase of a new 'Martin' (brand) uke. The stolen uke was later found amongst the rubbish at the back of the club. Tiny and Martin went to the Festival Studios with Denny, Col, John, Claude and Miss Blazey (backup vocals) and recorded *You Give Love a Bad Name* and *Rock N Roll Medley* into the early hours of the morning. Later, more recordings - Tiny and the Prickles recorded seven Country tracks which included *I'll Never Get Married*

*Again, The Banjo Pickers' Wife* and *Courage My Friend*. Said Chris Löfvén, '*Courage My Friend* was probably best of the lot. Monica from the Prickles and Blazey were doing the harmonies. Steve Coburn helped Martin mix it.' [31]

Martin was in the studio by night and Australian Galleries by day. He was at the gallery when former abalone diver Allan Broadhurst walked in. On seeing the *Lost Hokusai* picture Allan blurted, 'Shit! That's an abalone diver!' Martin overheard, invited him back to Wirian and gave him a print - signed, 'to Allan, the fisherman'. Allan told Martin, 'Women were known to be the best divers in many countries, not just Japan. So that's absolutely true to form. It was early days of harvest because this is not very deep. She's bringing the catch up for the person in the boat. She hasn't got a bag so she's just one-at-a-time. It's a wonderful way of presenting it'. [32] Before leaving, Allan sat through Tiny's extended version of *Eve of Destruction*.

Once again, Dave was supposed to create a commercially viable product but he feared that no one was going to give it airplay. 'Twenty-five minutes of it is too long especially in an industry where we live by the 3-minute song!' [33] Guitarist John Botica was surprised too, 'If *Eve of Destruction* had been edited down it may well have been a hit. There was a really powerful four minutes to be extracted from that track. I'm certain it would have been an absolute worldwide radio sensation! But obviously, that was not the producer's thinking.' [34]

Advisers were usually frank with Martin but when it came to editing Tiny, he seldom backed down. Said Dave, 'I think I'm pretty hard-hitting when I speak to Martin, I hope I am. I won't lie to him. He says, "Tiny's such a handful". Tiny - like any artist - would be guided. It's simply that Martin lets him be a handful. Martin is brilliant, but not in the PR department.' [35]

\*

Even as his reputation soared, Brett Whiteley could not control his drug habit. On the night of 15 June, Brett checked into a motel in Thirroul, south of Sydney. Coincidently publisher Tom Thompson and Garry Shead were meeting in Austinmer, a kilometre away, discussing flipping Brett's Lawrence diptych, so that Garry's image would this time grace the cover of DH Lawrence's Kangaroo. Brett had already agreed. Garry was still not entirely happy about 'flipping the diptych'... Brett was found dead in the morning. Cause of death was 'due to self-administered substances'. Cressida gave Martin the bad news.

Art students made pilgrimages to Lavender Bay, sitting and drinking near the waterfront outside the Whiteley house, on the stretch of land later known as 'Wendy's Garden'. Brett was richly mourned, not always sympathetically, with many students suggesting an artist of such calibre had no right to squander himself on smack. Poet Robert Adamson eulogised him in his book Black Water and told the Sydney Review, 'our greatest artist is dead'. Michael Leunig wrote a poem about 'Burke and Wills and Whiteley too…' called Deepest Blue, Martin read it to guests while sketching a picture of the Little Prince against a blinding sky which he titled Thirroul. [36]

Brett was cremated in a private ceremony. Martin placed the bonsai-ed Morton Bay fig (from the Yellow House) on top of the coffin. He said, 'He was too much of a star, with all the pressures of stardom on him, which gets in the way of your work. He was trapped into the art gallery scene. He was the darling of the Art Gallery of NSW and all that sort of stuff. It was no good for him. I miss him in art. He brought many subjects to attention, which had never been brought into art in a contemporary way. Lyrebirds, Bex signs, all sorts of things no one was dealing with at all. I couldn't deal with the heroin side of it. I just didn't like that. He was very generous when he was free of it. He was wonderful.' [37]

Shortly after, Luna Park's $25 million the restoration was given the green light by the North Sydney Council with a view to opening as early as September 1993. The Luna Park Committee agreed in principle that a memorial to the victims of the Ghost Train fire should be built in the new Luna Park. Martin had strong views about the Memorial, above all it should not be seen as tokenistic.

Back home, Tim Lewis and Bernadette Trella got married and Martin was Best Man. The formal ceremony was held in Blackburn Gardens, across New Head Head Road and handy to Wirian where the after-party was held. Lots of friends gathered to celebrate – Greg, Sue, Dick, Willy, Marro, Marilyn, Mike (Bernadette's brother), Terry, Tim's daughter Tilly, Sky and Dave. He was out of sorts because Tiny's new management had turned down the release of the *Eve of Destruction* and Martin turned down the release a *Best Of* compilation.

One evening, Martin, Marilyn, Greg, Willy and Sky sat around the kitchen table while Martin read from a section titled 'Moronic Geniuses' in the *Encyclopaedia of Aberrations,* a book that Draff had brought to his attention. The section on Blind Tom – an idiot savant – fascinated Martin. [38] He suggested someone should write a book about him, an option not taken up – not even by Draff. A year later, author Dierdre O'Connoll called on Wirian and Martin asked her to look up Blind Tom in the British Library, which she did and got hooked on the idea. Quite a few years in the making, it was she who wrote the book, *The Ballad of Blind Tom*. [39]

Haydn Keenan's film *Pandemonium* was televised before the year was out as was Geoffrey Robertson's *Trial of OZ*. Neither impacted on Martin, although the outrageously handsome Hugh Grant playing Richard Neville triggered Martin's sense of the absurd! He just kept painting, which is exactly what he said he would not be doing.

The *On the Road to Tarascon* picture was still the current epicentre of Martin's oevre. He reworked it over the next 15 years and painted it three more times, adding Mount Fuji before settling on the final image, He titled it *Courage My Friend,* named for Tiny, Vincent, Paiwan, Eric, Brett, Jenny Poidevin, troubled friends – but mostly for sometime Wirian resident Patricia, who gave Martin a copy of the Koran and *Imitation of Christ* by Thomas à Kempis before killing herself. [40]

# 10.
# TINY TIPTOES OFF THE STAGE

*Tiny didn't like to go to the hospital, see a doctor or anything like that. That was unfortunate.*
Hal Stein (Tiny Tim's cousin)

At the start of 1993 Martin was hospitalised and put on a respirator. In that first week he said he didn't care whether he lived or died. He didn't want it known that he was doing a hospital stint but people found out anyway. He had lots of visitors – Jenny Kee, Danton Hughes, Cousin Katie, friends, helpers and pests. The colours of his deliriums fascinated Martin. He wrote about them in his ever-present notebook.

Luna Park Amusements Pty Ltd was formally given the go-ahead to develop and operate the Park. The Trust contributed some of its assets to the site and Whittingslow Amusement Group contributed rides and cash. While Martin was in hospital, the reconstructed face of Luna Park was lifted into position. The administrators were moving ahead promptly, which agitated Martin as - although the Memorial to the victims had been agreed to in principle – conceptually, it was unresolved. 'If you put that face up without a memorial there, you're just inviting trouble,' he said - even though he hardly breathe, let alone protest. [1]

Martin believed the Memorial – not the face - was the place to start restorations, 'I'm not going for the face at the moment. Without the Memorial it's like putting the Old God there again. They've got to have something beautiful because all those carnivals have got a dark side to them.' [2] He liked the proposal that Michael Leunig or Bruce Petty should design the Memorial.

Having lost 10 kilos, Martin was visibly frail. Although technically clear of emphysema, he still had a lung problem. 'Water on the lungs' was what doctors called it. Working at Wirian and 'holding the fort' with Marilyn, Dave Rowe summed up Martin's health, 'He hasn't declined, the major concern is there's been no major improvement. The lung is really crapped out because of 30 years of 100 smokes a day. He's in the process of having tests. They're going down into the stomach with tubes. That'll exhaust him unbelievably. There's been a stack of people going through and that's quite exhausting for him as well. Marilyn was a bit upset yesterday because she could see how tired he was. People were pouring in and he doesn't say no. We're going to tell them that there are no visitors until the tests are over. But he seemed really good, talking positively, talking about carrying on with things. It was good hearing him trying to run the ship from the bed.' [3]

Still, the doctors were reluctant to discharge Martin because they felt he was in no position to take care of himself. They kept him an extra week and told him to quit smoking as a matter of urgency. [4] 'Is Martin still smoking?' is what guests would ask. Sure, he was still smoking. Martin never minded smokers. His Inner Sanctum was always heavy with nicotine but smokers copped dark looks from Martin's protectors when they chuffed in his presence, 'Smoking helps you concentrate. I don't think my health is fantastically good but I don't think I can handle things without smoking cigarettes and drinking coffee.' [5]

To convalesce, Martin stayed with George in Bundeena, near Port Hacking. George had won the 1992 Blake Prize for his painting 'Religious Prayer' and after Martin's stay he would travel to Somalia to document the contribution of the Australian peacekeeping force. Garry and Judit Shead lived in Bundeena too, so Martin felt comfortable there and he surprised everyone by not hurrying home. After Bundeena, Martin went to *Happy Daze* in Blackheath where he stayed with Richard and Julie. He didn't smoke over this six-week period.

When he got back, Martin had Willy de la Vega and Terry Stanton for company. Willy had become increasingly religious, almost a monk. He quit smoking and only read 'scripture'. Martin read Scripture too, he also continued reading all 55 years of his mother's diaries. Like, Martin's birth entry, 21 January 1942: 'Having a baby is simple'. 22 January: 'I feel marvellous'. 8 February: 'Martin is a little devil'. Martin reminisced about the past - his father's return from the War when he was four, the breakdown of his parents' marriage, his Art Father Justin O'Brien, high school paintings which hung in his Inner Sanctum. He read through family papers, letters and documents. He even revisited his great-grandfather William Kopson's Fiji Diary from the 1870s. About Sitiveni Rabuka's 1987 coup he conceded, 'I can see his point of view'. [6]

Dave worked on the tape transfers, Marilyn worked on the film, Terry worked around the house, Willy worked on conspiracy theories and Kingo tried to reach a compromise with Martin in the negotiations concerning the Memorial. Meanwhile, Garry Shead won the 1993 Archibald Prize with his portrait of publisher Tom Thompson. George won the Wynne Prize for his work 'Open Cut'. And Roger Foley-Fogg produced a show on behalf of the artists of Australia, to show support for Paul Keating and the Labor Government in the forthcoming election. Throughout all this, Martin kept a low public profile but he did muster the energy to accompany Lin Utzon to the Sydney Opera House in April when she unveiled a bronze plaque in honour of her father Jorn. Recognition of Utzon's genius was an issue that ranked high on Martin's list of concerns, dating back to Art School days when the Sydney arts community was horrified that the NSW Minister for Public Works, Sir David Hughes, brought about Utzon's resignation. Martin lampooned Hughes in OZ.

Flames started appearing in Martin's pictures. He reworked *Pentecost* with flames. He was preparing it for entry in the 1994 Sulman Prize. Martin's printer, Stephen Lawson said, 'I did two versions of *Pentecost*. The original one didn't have the flames, and then the next version has got flames starting to come through.' [7]

As his health improved, Martin's interest in honouring the victims of the Ghost Train fire intensified. He became argumentative about the stance the Luna Park Reserve Trust was taking on the Memorial. Martin said it had to be on the very spot where the tragedy occurred and he brooked no disagreement. On 18 June he wrote to the Luna Park Reserve Trust withdrawing his support. The management quickly responded, disappointed to lose him. They wrote, 'From the Park's point of view it is a pity that we are not able to make use of your undoubted commitment and obvious talents. Let us hope that we are not for too long the poorer for it'. [8]

In this, Jenny Poidevin, wife and mother of three victims, added her voice to Martin's. To the Trust, she wrote: 'I sincerely acknowledge your need to commemorate on my behalf the memory of my late husband John and our sons Damien and Craig Godson. My feelings until now have been mixed, regarding an actual memoriam. Upon meeting with you some months previous I was forced to accept whether or not this memoriam was really what I wanted for them. I am sure now that this is what I would like for my family. It has been an extremely painful and difficult decision to make. I have no problem with the proposed redevelopment of Luna Park, I only hope and pray it is beyond the corrupting powers that previously pervaded its atmosphere. And what's more, extremely safe, allowing future families to enjoy the new Luna Park to its utmost. If my memoriam is to be considered I would feel it be placed on the original Ghost Train site. For me this would be more meaningful. I would be open-minded in this regard. I know life goes on in this regard and change is inevitable, please accept my best wishes in regard to the reopening of Luna Park, as I have previously presented my ideas for a memoriam please accept this as my wishes. I am more than happy to discuss any future possibilities. Yours sincerely Mrs Jennifer Godson née Poidevin.' Martin added, 'If they try to hedge on this, I'll be out of the place quick-smart!' [9]

Then Martin got sick again and returned to St Vincent's Hospital. Marilyn was placed in charge of Wirian. Helpers came-and-went and Martin was again overrun with visitors to his bedside. Shortly after his release Martin got back to battling his nicotine addiction, strengthening up and creating a poster for Tiny's *Rock* CD. He had to get well and get ready - Tiny was booked for another Australian tour.

A lot had been happening in the world of Tiny Tim. The song that made him famous, *Tiptoe Through the Tulips*, was re-released on a compilation LP called *Dumb Ditties*. For the first time in a long time, fans without an original copy could actually play Tiny's hit song. Next, *God Bless Tiny Tim* was re-released in Japan in CD format. Out of circulation since 1968, the album was released with its original cover and Japanese liner notes inside. Some interesting obscurities also popped up. Dave tracked down four songs by Tiny Tim & the Band recorded amongst Bob Dylan's Basement Tapes. He also tracked Tiny's contribution to the 1969 Beatles for-fans-only *Christmas Record*, another rarity. [10]

Nineteen ninety-three was the year that Cream was inducted into the Rock and Roll Hall of Fame, in Cleveland Ohio. The band performed at their induction ceremony. In his speech Eric said that the rehearsal held the day before was the first time they had played together in 25 years. The performance sparked rumours of a reunion, which did not take place in the 90s due to solo projects and family-first commitments. Importantly, the induction established that they could still sound good as Cream, and that they could co-exist in the same room.

Days before coming to Australia and right out of the blue, Tiny picked up the phone and reconciled with his old friend, Bucks Burnett. Bucks – you may recall – produced Tiny's *Mr Ed* single in 1984. He and Tiny started the *Girl* CD in 1988. Then Bucks and Tiny argued about Miss Stephanie Bohm and parted company because – as Bucks puts it, 'his unrequited love for Miss Stephanie was too great to allow him to work with me'. [11] In August, Tiny and Bucks sorted out their differences. Work on the album resumed.

With the *Girl* CD back on track, as the re-energised president of the Tiny Tim fan club, Bucks started a newsletter called the *Tiny Tim Times*. It offered updates on the latest releases, concerts, appearances and fan club news - a club that was surprisingly successful. It even included a few famous names, like former Sex Pistols' singer John Lydon, and David Cassidy (from the Partridge Family). [12] Martin signed up too. He liked the idea of the newsletter and the club, describing it as, 'small but genuine'. He and Bucks remained in touch.

Yes, Tiny was coming, but negotiations with Australian promoter John Kannis (manager of the Hoodoo Gurus) took a backwards step. Kannis would only pay a business class flight and Tiny insisted on first class. 'So we had to cop the difference,' said Martin. 'Luckily a cheque came through for *Tales of Brave Ulysses* – a cliffhanger. It just zipped in, in time.' [13]

Angry about Martin cutting it fine again with the dollars, Dave was getting emphatic, 'We have run out of money Martin, stop spending!' [14] Health issues. Money problems. Martin hit a new low. 'Maybe I blew it,' he said in despair. Wirian may have to be sold - it was back to this again - talk about Cranbrook School buying it or putting Wirian on the open market. Even the economic rationalists among Martin's friends didn't like those options, believing that selling the house 'would kill him'. [15]

The finances of Tiny's tour were underpinned by Hoodoo Guru concerts in Adelaide, Melbourne, Canberra, Newcastle and Sydney - hard rocking venues - the idea of which Tiny found unsettling. The Hoodoo Gurus were a Pop-Rock band with punk sass. Tiny was used to genteel audiences of a couple of hundred - not a couple of thousand plus mosh pit. *Tiptoe Through the Tulips* was a hit way before this crowd was born, they mightn't know Tiny Tim at all. As their Special Guest, Hoodoo Gurus' singer Dave Fawlkner planned to introduce Tiny, who would then play his 15-30 minute set before the Gurus took the stage. There was talk of the band backing Tiny for a couple of Rock songs. Martin surmised, 'They're fans of Tiny, of a sort. Dave Fawlkner said *Highway to Hell* was their favourite song.' [16]

Then, shortly before slipping into Australia, Tiny broke the habit of a lifetime, quit living in New York City and did an overnight flit to Des Moines. The New York mobsters had always kept an eye on Tiny's career. Starting with Frank Sinatra, then Caesar's Palace, through to present times, the mob was always in the background somewhere. (Maybe that's how it was in the American entertainment industry!) Tiny's career had been taken over by a former police officer Mr Connolly and Tiny was genuinely scared of him. Enter Stephen Plym, an entertainment agent in Des Moines Iowa. Plym had booked Tiny on-and-off since 1971. On his own admission, when he first saw Tiny perform, he described him as a 'national joke' [17] but this time around the wheel, Tiny was doing it tough, Plym saw an opportunity and offered to manage him. All Tiny had to do was slip quietly out of the Olcott Hotel and check into the Savery Hotel Des Moines, which he did. Having ditched his New York agents Tiny now found himself travelling without his customary management support. Dave Rowe stepped up as Australian tour manager.

Tiny arrived on Halloween, Martin noted that this was a quiet Halloween year, 'it didn't have much Satanic stuff on television. This year though it was on a blue moon'. [18] Said Dave, 'When Tiny arrived he was impressed we'd got the *Rock* album out. But when he found tracks that went for 30 minutes he said, "No radio station is going to play this!" Tiny suggested that it'd be best if Martin edited it down - but that was never going to happen.' [19] They were creating Art, not music. By now, everyone was getting the message that Martin never edited Tiny, who he thought perfect in 'his purest form'.

The Regular Records Christmas party was held at Iona, a 19th Century heritage-listed mansion on the Paddington side of Sydney's Kings Cross. Mental As Anything launched their *Chemical Travel* album, Dog Trumpet launched their *Strange Brew* single (with its Martin Sharp cover), Relic of Mary Lou launched their *Monster* EP and Tiny launched his *Rock* album in the new digital CD format. [20] The Iona event went off with a bang. Tiny sang and the bands strutted their stuff, climaxing with Reg Mombassa's backdrop unfastening itself from the back wall, floating down like a parachute and draping over the drummer. Everything else went to plan.

A lot of record industry people attended. Social pages photographer Robert Rosen was there too. And a new face, Satoshi Kinoshita who lived between Sydney and Tokyo. Dave described him as 'a mad Tiny Tim fan, a photographer in Japan. He comes to Sydney often. In his own right, he's a music producer'. [21] Satoshi saw potential for Tiny's music in Japan, as evidenced by the success of the Japanese re-release of the *God Bless* CD. Martin, Dave and Satoshi held several think-tank meetings about releasing the *Chameleon* album in Japan, which in time – (a long time) – paid off.

The *Rock* CD was an extraordinary burst of sound. Some tracks seemed never-ending, which accounts for the album's mixed reception. Some people hated it. Others thought it brilliant. Shortly before his death (4 December 1993), Frank Zappa announced that he wanted to release it on his own label. [22]

All the gigs went well. At the sold-out Newcastle venue Dave Rowe introduced Tiny because Dave Fawlkner didn't arrive on time. Dave Rowe was surprised by the excitement, 'I could barely get the intro out, they were just chanting-chanting-chanting, Tiny Tim! Tiny Tim! Tiny Tim! The Hoodoos gave him his 15-minutes and they loved it. Of course the mixer from the Hoodoo Gurus made that ukulele sound like a bass guitar! Every show Tiny was scared as hell to go out and every show he came off unscathed. He got a massive reception in Melbourne. He was so over-the-moon, he said to me, "I can't believe it! I can't believe it!" That's the way it went all the way through.' [23]

Talk about guts! Tiny was a diabetic 61-year old with a little uke, playing to a thousand or two drunken Aussie head-bangers. He was terrified at Selinas Coogee. Beer cans zinged around the room. 'They threw Tiny in the middle…!' Martin complained, '…with just his ukulele. Tiny described it "like being armed with a slingshot in the desert" - going out to face this antagonistic vibe'. [24] Dave saw it differently. To get the audience onside, Tiny decided to give away his *Highway to Hell* cassingles by throwing them into the crowd. 'This is HIS idea!' Dave stressed, 'Well, I'm sorry - in a pub environment if you want to start a missile throwing session throw a missile! It wasn't just at him. They were throwing things everywhere.'

If Martin was short of money before the start of this tour, his scant resources dried up until the money simply ran out. 'Martin wasn't paying me,' Dave explained, 'I ended up leaving because I had rent to pay. I had to get work - which Martin didn't understand. I said, "I can't believe you took this on when you knew you didn't have the money!" His solution was "just live here" (Wirian) - but I didn't want to.' [25]

Running out of dough didn't keep Martin from recording Tiny. He recorded *That's What I Want for Christmas* and *What a Friend We Have in Jesus* on mini-disk, which set up a Christmas theme and so *Tiny Tim's Christmas Album* started taking shape. Three days after the mini-disk session, Martin took Tiny to Rich Studios and recorded *People Are Strange, Satisfaction, I Am I Said* and *Rainbow on the River*. Peter Jensen – the English master from Scots College who used to drop in back in the early 80s - videoed it all for Martin because Pete was the only person Martin knew who could work the equipment. Later they recorded *Rudolph the Red-Nosed Reindeer*. [26]

Frances Greening (aka Angelica Tremblay) was a gospel singer and missionary who had returned to Sydney after working in Africa. One evening she decided to go to a pub because she'd never been in one before. That's where she met Peter Royles who told her about his wonderful artist friend. (She later changed her name from Frances Angelica Greening to Angelica Frances Tremblay, Tremblay being her married name.)

She said, 'I thought, "I've never been in a pub in my life" and there was one at Coogee. I saw men bashing each other up, so I went across the road to the chemist to buy some Band-Aids and I started fixing everybody up. Then I met Peter Royles. He was next to this really big guy who was a boxer. Peter was smoking a cigarette and putting it out on this guy's arm. He'd just hassle people. He said to me, "I want you to meet someone real famous – Martin Sharp". After a couple of months Peter said, "Martin needs a Gospel singer". I went to the studio. Tom Kazaz was the producer. He said he needed some vocals on the *Christmas Album* so I did it and met Martin. Then I went back to his house. I'd never seen art like it before.' Martin asked her to sing backup vocals on four tracks - *White Christmas, Silent Night, O Come All Ye Faithful* and *Mission Bell*. [27]

Two days before heading home, Tiny played the Rose, Shamrock & Thistle pub (known as the Three Weeds) in Rozelle. Denny's Rock ensemble backed Tiny, Dog Trumpet was his support act and Triple-J radio host Maynard was emcee. After the show, Tiny went back to Martin's kitchen and, just like old times, he pulled out his uke and sang to a few friends until 3.00am. Next day, he flew back to the States, back to Mr Plym.

With Tiny back in America, Martin focused on (1) Tiny's *Christmas Album*, (2) a possible Pop album and (3) lobbying for a Memorial at Luna Park. Guests came-and-went, including some of the old crew like Mad Robyn and Pilot Pete. The more respected guests included, Sandy Gutman (Austen Tayshus) and Lin Utzon. Martin threw a party in Lin's honour. Guests included Opera House advocates and politicians. The building was approaching its 25th anniversary with no clear plan to reconcile with Jorn Utzon beyond symbolic gestures. Martin was pushing for Utzon to receive a belated honour for his masterpiece. He accompanied Lin when she presented her father's scale model of the main hall to the Sydney Opera House Trust, its governing body. [28]

Meanwhile, the Tiny Tim news from America was bleak. After an initial burst of celebrity appearances like baseball matches, the Iowa Variety Club Telethon and TV interviews, Tiny had done the rounds in-and-around Des Moines and Plym could no longer afford his keep him at the Savery Hotel. Too frightened to return to New York, Tiny moved to Hotel Fort, a historic 11-storey building in need of renovation. Tiny's room was not much bigger than his double bed. The view from his window was a brick wall. Through Bucks and his newsletter, quite a few supporters got to hear about Tiny's plight and Martin was one of them. For the lead article of the January 1994 issue of the *Tiny Tim Times*, Martin wrote, 'Somehow we have all got to pull together to give Tiny our best support. I don't know how we can do this; perhaps we should hold a convention or develop some effective network'. (29)

Enter: two new players - English experimental musician and outsider artist, David Tibet, and deejay Ernie Clark who would soon run the official Tiny Tim website. Bucks and Tibet worked together on a new Tiny Tim release, *Songs of An Impotent Troubadour*. Through Bucks, Martin got to know Tibet with whom he discussed releasing recordings internationally or at least in England. While this was going on, Martin – via Dave Rowe – was in the early stages of discussing a Japanese release of *Chameleon* with Satoshi. So even though Tiny had struck a career-low, ideas for five new CDs, plus website, were being mooted by supporters.

In the end it wasn't Bucks, Martin, Ernie, Tibet and certainly not Plym, who rescued Tiny. Tiny found his own way to issue a cry for help. Ever a reader of the *National Enquirer*, Tiny called up the magazine. They sent over a journalist who ran a small feature about Tiny's dire circumstances along with a sad photograph. Plym was furious, 'Who's gonna want to book you now?' he barked. Heiress, Sue Gardner read that article. She had a teenage crush on Tiny in 1968 and reminisced, '*God Bless Tiny Tim* was the first album I ever bought. I remember trying to figure out whether I wanted to marry Paul McCartney, Paul Simon or Tiny. I guess I finally settled on Tiny!' (30)

Miss Sue contacted Tiny in his hotel and along with Dennis her fiancé they looked him up. They caught Tiny in full flight, talking, talking, talking late into the night. On the drive home, Miss Sue speculated that Tiny might sing at their wedding. Dennis reckoned it should be the other way around - Dennis should sing at Tiny and Miss Sue's wedding! That's how quickly Tiny and Miss Sue bonded. (31)

The main obstruction to Tiny re-partnering was the question of divorce, always a complicated subject in terms of Tiny's religious beliefs. There were health issues too. Miss Sue had delicate health and not in a strong position to take on an invalid. She did it anyway, despite a specialist explaining that Tiny was in the early stages of heart failure as a result of untreated diabetes.

In the summer of 1994, Tiny recorded *Prisoner of Love: A Tribute to Russ Conway*. Recorded in Tampa Florida, the band called Clang was under the baton of Paul Reller, Associate Professor of Music at the University of South Florida. Tiny has always aspired to record tribute albums of all the great songsters, he and Mar-tin even had a title, 'Twentieth Century Suite'. Tiny regarded this Russ Columbo tribute as his best album, 'Believe me, this is the greatest recording I have ever done, including *Tiptoe Through the Tulips*'. (32)

Within the month Tiny officially filed for divorce from Miss Jan, leaving him free to marry Miss Sue. It wasn't the only wedding announcement: Denny Burgess and Clare Barrett wed at St Patrick's Church at the Rocks Sydney. Martin and Frances (Angelica) were amongst the guests. Martin gave Denny and Clare an *Eternity* print as a wedding present and Clare was surprised how religious he seemed. She remarked, 'When he came to our wedding it seemed that he had a really strong Catholic faith. I found it so surprising that such an unconventional person had such a strong conventional religious belief.' [33]

Then the Bucks Burnett-Dave Tibet project *Songs of an Impotent Troubadour* sold a surprising 1500 copies on release. Wow. This was an unexpected boost. [34]

Tiny and Miss Sue tied the knot at Immaculate Heart of Saint Mary Church 18 August 1995. After the wedding, Tiny moved partly into Miss Sue's Minneapolis suburban home. Conscious of not taking advantage of his partner's financial situation, Tiny insisted on generating his own income. Within three days he was back on the road, within two months of the marriage, he was diagnosed with congestive heart failure. He refused to be admitted to hospital and never missed a performance. In the first 12 months of marriage Tiny was on the road 300 days. No matter how exhausted he was, off he'd go – to the next gig, anywhere in America and sometimes overseas.

A new album came about after Pink Bob heard one of Tiny's songs on a radio show. He didn't know much about Tiny but loved what he heard. Pink Bob researched 20 years of Tiny's music before approaching him to record on his Ponk label. The *I Love Me* CD was a combination of new recordings and rare singles. Songs include, *Another Brick in the Wall, She Left Me With the Herpes* and a rerelease of *I Saw Mr Presley Tip-toeing Through the Tulips*. [35] This CD was followed by *Tiny Tim Live in Chicago* for Bughouse Records, with a cover featuring the pink and lime green lettering of Elvis's 1956 album and with *Are You Lonesome Tonight* as the opening track. [36]

Then Tiny returned to Miss Sue, who lived in Minneapolis. Tiny was unlike everyone in his suburb except neighbour Johnny Pineapple who had a Hawaiian band and also played uke. One night, Johnny videoed Tiny talking about the history of recorded music for hours. He drank lots of beer and walked Johnny and his young son through past forgotten names of chart-toppers. Martin was sent a copy of this video titled *Musical History Tour*. It inspired Martin to consider cutting the film back to its original 1979 marathon. [37]

Tiny's last appearance in England was 16 December 1995. Organised by David Tibet, he released the concert under the title *Live in London*. [38] Said David, '*Live in London* is a recording of the show he did at Union Chapel which I've released, and that was the only time I saw him live and that was just a phenomenal show. Absolutely amazing.' [39]

In a short space of 18 months – from Mr Plym to Miss Sue – Tiny had a big upward shift in popularity. It wasn't chart-topping stuff, more a lift in credibility.

The ukulele was making a comeback and over the years Tiny had more than paid his dues. For a time he was seen as the godfather of the uke craze. There were uke festivals all over America, England and Australia and Tiny was hailed as one of the original ukulele troubadours, the performer who knew 10,000 songs and was still strumming. Tiny knew exactly who Arthur Godfrey was. Everyone else had to look him up.

In September, Tiny was the headline act at the Ukulele Expo held in Montague Massachusetts. He was accompanied by his friend, Mark Mitchell. Tiny seemed tired but he got through a one-hour video interview without incident. Then he walked to the mike, opened his mouth to sing, collapsed, fell off the stage and banged his head on the floor. Screams, pandemonium. Mark pushed through the crowd and comforted Tiny who was terrified of needles and even more frightened of being cut by the doctors. [40] This was all filmed and screened on the evening News. 'Felled like a tree,' is how Martin described him.

The doctors said Tiny's heart was functioning at around 40%. Because of his poor physical condition, heart surgery out of the question. They gave him a year to live if he took things easy. Tiny remained in hospital for eight weeks, during which time daughter Tulip visited and informed him he had four grandchildren and that she was a convert to the Jehovah's Witness faith. [41] Tiny begged her forgiveness for having been an absent father.

Discharged to Miss Sue's care, after a month of rest at home Tiny got restless, singing around the house, always wearing a tie even when dressed in his pyjamas. 'A man must always wear a tie!' he proclaimed. Miss Sue described those sessions, 'He always felt that he had to give God the first-fruits of his voice. So he never would sing his romantic songs unless he'd sung one hymn. Sometimes he'd say, "I want to sing a song for you but I can't yet because I haven't sung to the Lord" and he'd sing *Praise the Lord the King of Heaven* one way through and then he'd sing the other song.'

He performed a couple of songs at a small gig and that went fine, which gave him more confidence than it should have. Then his mother-in-law asked him to play at the Minneapolis Women's Association, which he accepted. Miss Sue felt that was asking for trouble. They turned up, were ushered to their table and waited. The house band had little intention of giving up the stage until interval when everyone rushed outside for a smoke or a toilet stop until Tiny approached the mike, which caused everyone to rush back. When he started singing *Tiptoe Through the Tulips*, Miss Sue knew something was wrong. She rushed to his side onstage. Big Tiny leaned on little Miss Sue and slowly slid to the ground. He was pronounced dead three hours later. [42]

The *Christmas Album* had been released one week before Tiny died. Martin and Tiny had their last phone chat just two days earlier. On 4 December 1996 the Basilica of Saint Mary Minneapolis held the Christian burial rite.

In Sydney the press got straight onto Martin. The headline read, 'Bound for Heaven, my Amazing Friend – Martin remembers Tiny Tim'. The article ran alongside *The Guardian* obituary. There were a lot of Obituaries in the world-wide press. [43]

About Tiny's passing, Martin stated, 'It's been a huge effort but it's been worth every bit of it'. He added, 'Tiny is more alive than ever!' [44]

# 11.
# THE GOSPEL ACCORDING TO MARTIN

*There was a good deal of chaos at Wirian,*
*A kind of cosmic circus in which Martin acted as ringmaster.*
Robert Tilley

Tiny's death did not diminish Martin's enthusiasm one skerrick. In some ways, it fired him up. It certainly reaffirmed the connections amongst the 'Tiny Tim people' worldwide, especially Bucks Burnett in Texas, David Tibet in London, webmaster Ernie Clark in Michigan and Martin & Dave in Sydney.

David Tibet collaborated with Bucks on Tiny's CD Songs From An Impotent Troubadour CD. And he collaborated with Martin on the UK release of Tiny's Christmas Album. Martin and Bucks did a swap: Martin designed the CD cover for Bucks' band The Volares, swapping original artwork for a 1970 Parker Bros Tiny Tim's Game of Beautiful Things. It was a win-win. Martin got a rare piece of Tiny Tim memorabilia and Bucks got a Martin Sharp album cover. Bucks was rapt, 'How the hell could I afford to hire Martin!' [1]

Two days after Tiny's passing Martin told the press that Tiny was 'Heaven-bound' adding, 'I thank God for bringing us together'. [2] Tiny was the crux, the cornerstone, of Martin's religious thought. In the wake of Tiny's passing, Martin reaffirmed his conviction that he was sent by God into the world of show business that 'wouldn't let him in'. [3]

'We knew the man - and now he's going to become a myth. I think it's a heroic life. You couldn't script a more perfect death. He died doing it 100 per cent. Tiny never stopped being famous. There are headline obituaries here, in America, in England. He was famous for being a failure! I think he was the King of American

Music but they couldn't admit it. Tiny is such a modern artist that I don't think a lot of people can understand him. He was too strange for them. Once they realised he was for real, they couldn't handle it, they were frightened by him. American show business didn't like what he was on about so they turfed him out. I understood him as an artist. That was my advantage. It doesn't seem as if he's died to me. Not at all. It's like the spirit is still here. He's so present still - in the singing. I'm doing a big tidy-up at the moment, getting all the files in order - Tiny's musical estate for his exiles here'. [4]

Joel Tarling had spent a week doing high school work experience at Wirian back in 1991. After this, he called in and maintained the relationship. Describing Wirian circa 1997, Joel said, 'Wirian was a collage of people all mixed in and I was part of that. Martin wanted a Greg Weight, a Garry Shead, a Willy de la Vega and a Joel-Nobody there as well. Finding that contact was something Martin did really well - drawing odd connections. Then the Bible started to dominate more and more.

'I saw things silently - more critical and in a different way. I felt Willy de la Vega and Wendy were a dangerous mixture for Martin because they were 'oh wow', 'amazing' - in awe of everything. Willy de la Vega would dive straight into the Bible and bring up a conspiracy theory!' [5]

Religion was another of Martin's collages. There was no consistent pattern of opinion amongst his friends.

Richard Neville affirmed the existence of a God on the Great Debate TV show. Richard and Julie were recovering from a car crash in Majorca. She suffered a fractured sternum, which has plagued her ever after. Richard too suffered a fractured sternum and several broken ribs. In his 1996 book *Out Of My Mind* Richard tastes every fruit the New Age had on offer. [6]

Yensoon was Taoist.
Jenny Kee was Buddhist.
Toto was a high-ranking Freemason.
Willy de la Vega attended Canon Jim Glennon's Healing Ministry at St Andrews Cathedral in the city. [7]
Garry Shead had alchemical sympathies. [8]
George Gittoes was a mystic. [9]
Roger Foley concluded, 'all beliefs are true'. [10]
Stephen Darmody moved in and out of religious circles.
Jesus Adam – the name speaks for itself.
Victoria Cobden had Seventh-day Adventist sympathies and loved Lindy Chamberlain's book.
Angelica attended an Anglican church in Auburn and a Baptist church in Sans Souci.
Rev Gary Shearston was an Anglican priest serving in the Diocese of the Riverina.

University (Melbourne) with a doctorate in Sociology.
Father Austin Day of Christ Church of St Lawrence was in regular contact with Martin – visiting him in hospital - as did Father James Murray, the Anglican priest a regular Sydney Morning Herald columnist. Martin read *Jews for Jesus* handouts and had meetings with Jehovah's Witnesses when they called.

Susan Jensen, Martin's former assistant, came as close as anyone in understanding Martin's faith when she said, 'I think all denominations have something to offer and everyone needs to feel part of a community, so I don't think any denomination is "right" or "wrong". The thing that matters is that people who call themselves Christians truly love Jesus and try to follow his example'. [11]

Former owner of the Yellow House premises, Ian Reid, was unimpressed. He said, 'Martin was very obsessed in certain ways. He was looking at a little bit of the cosmos but the cosmos is very extensive. There was no point in telling Martin anything like that. Martin was well and truly tracked. My move was towards the East.' [12]

While broadly tolerant of unorthodox, idiosyncratic and even eccentric variations of Christianity, Martin did not approve of unchristian and anti-Christian thinking. He openly criticised Neville Wran and Richard Walsh for their atheism.

Somehow their atheism didn't count against other friends like Jeannie and Mic. 'I never challenged him on his Christian beliefs, I just avoided it,' said Mic, who never felt distanced from Martin. [13] Although unashamedly atheist, Martin saw Jeannie as a type of medium, someone who 'brought things through'. [14] This had her completely baffled. Jeannie often dropped in to see Martin but neither party allowed religion to cast a shadow over the friendship. Said Jeannie, 'He went on about his religious stuff and I didn't necessarily disagree or agree'. [15]

Friends have puzzled about Martin's form of Christianity because it didn't fit conventional constructs, yet it was painfully conventional in other ways. For example, he partook of the Eucharist in Anglican and Catholic churches and was a fundamentalist in the sense that he took Bible texts at face value. (He played tapes of Bible readings or had someone read to him while he painted late into the night.) On one hand Martin was a Bible literalist. On the other, he was selective. He certainly didn't accept the section where God asks Abraham to sacrifice his son Isaac (ie. Genesis Ch 22). Martin dismissed that passage, 'God would never do that!' [16]

Martin also enjoyed listening to conventional hymns, some of which even Christians felt were past the use-by date. Tiny's hymns were always top of the list - *Put Your Hand In The Hand, When The Roll Is Called Up Yonder, When The Saints Go Marching In* and *He's Got the Whole World in His Hands.* Tiny's *Christmas Album* offered a different flavour of hymns. Visitors trapped in the Inner Sanctum were treated to *O Come All Ye Faithful, Hark The Herald Angels Sing, O Little Town* of Bethlehem, Amazing Grace, Throw Out the Lifeline, What A Friend We Have In Jesus* and *Silent Night*.

Even with Tiny, Martin took the bits he liked and passed on the rest. Tiny did the Rosary, Martin didn't. Tiny prayed earnestly in public, Martin didn't. Tiny prayed novenas, Martin didn't. Recalling Tiny in prayer (see the inside photo of the *Impotent Troubadour* CD), David Tibet said, 'I remember him doing the Rosary, he was invoking every single saint and saying little prayers to them. He also did Samael and Asrael – the angels of death. I said, "Tiny, it's very considerate of you to do the angels of death, but I don't think it's strictly called for by Christian orthodoxy, let's just stick with the main ones according to Christian belief – like Gabriel and Michael".' [17] David described Tiny as 'a weird type of Catholic'. Martin was Protestant in the sense that he did not invoke intermediaries.

Sometimes it became tricky to pick which religious line Martin might follow next. He didn't like people who dressed in black, yet Willy wore nothing but black. He picked and chose Popes he liked/disliked and brought Biblical characters to life in his day-to-day interactions. John Singleton, Martin described as the 'thief on the cross' – meaning that Singo would make a last-minute repentance. [18] The 'synagogue of Satan' in the Book of Revelation chapter 2, was a clear reference to Abe Saffron. And Vincent– of course – might as well have been Saint Vincent. Martin was offended by writers who questioned Vincent's sanity, insisting that he was 'patently sane' and pointing to his *Letters* as proof.

Jesus was Martin's No 1, Tiny made sure of that. Martin said, 'Tiny keeps referring one on. He doesn't let the buck stop with him'. [19] It was unclear what status Martin accorded to Jesus. A great teacher? A god or 'Very God of Very God, begotten not made'? (as stated in the Nicene Creed, which was familiar to him from school). Martin said, 'Truth is a characteristic of great leadership and Jesus always told the truth – that's what he based his teachings on, an expression of truth.' [20]

Maybe spurred on by the newly released Christmas Album, Martin began playing a lot of hymns – Little Richard (I Want Jesus to Walk With Me), Elvis (His Hand in Mine) as well as Tiny. Martin also enjoyed lesser-known gospel recordings. Robert Wolfgramm's song 'Emmaus' about two friends talking while walking down a road - then 'another joined in, they could not recognise…' reminded Martin of his late night musings with select friends, trying to get to grips with some religious obscurity. He was referencing the Gospel of Matthew 18:20, 'Where two or three are gathered together in my name, there I am with them'. [21]

When Robert sent Martin a transcript of his sermon 'The King's King of Kings' Martin was deeply impressed. Connecting Elvis - 'the King' - with Jesus, the 'King of Kings' was Martin's thinking exactly. Wolfgramm pointed out, 'Elvis won only three Grammys in his lifetime and they were all for his gospel albums – albums that his record company did not want recorded.' He pointed out that Elvis's favourite Scripture was the passage about love taken from 1 Corinthians 13. Wolfgramm said, 'This is what the King's King of Kings is all about – love. Thank you

Elvis for being a living testimony to our only hope'. Sixteen years later, Martin placed the transcript of Wolfgramm's sermon in the display cabinet of his last exhibition, 'Graceland'. [22]

Rev Gary Shearston's spiritual songs affected Martin too. Songs like, 'The Holy Spirit of Redemptive Love' from Gary's Aussie Blue CD (1989). Gary's decision to enter the Anglican priesthood was not welcomed amongst all his peers. 'Some friends of mine threw their hands up in horror when they learned I was going into the church. But I think you've put the thing in perspective. It's an instinctive feeling for a compassionate outreach to the underprivileged, the underdog, the people who are castigated in our society because they want to live a simple life, those who are suffering in any way, because our whole human condition is under a fair weight of suffering, especially in the present times. Given the climate of the times I have been a great admirer of the Catholic theologian Hans Kung'. [23]

Gary referenced Kung in a song, ('But as Mr Kung said, no peace will be had, til there's peace between all world religions…'). Martin liked that. He also pondered Gary's Aboriginal spiritual song, 'Baiame', about the Great Builder of All Things, the Great Spirit. [24]

Then Martin got a new gospel CD called *Straight Over the Moon* by Frances Greening (Angelica). Frances/Angelica was a back-up singer on Tiny's *Christmas album*, which is how she and Martin connected. 'Firstly, I want to thank Jesus for changing my life…' she wrote in her cover lines, 'Martin Sharp, this is your miracle'. Martin sometimes played her CD to guests on full volume when the Inner Sanctum was a waiting-for-Martin room. It was the last thing they expected to hear. [25]

Then – with plenty of encouragement from Willy – Martin started spotting pagan jewellery and imagery: pentacles, torcs, skulls, anything horned, the two-fingered 'Rock On' sign at concerts and No 13. These were deemed 'Satanic' even though Martin kept a large statue of a red Mephistopheles around the house (and you can't get much more Satanic than that!). He explained, 'One of the heaviest pieces in the Dream Museum is Mephistopheles. It doesn't matter how the Devil is portrayed, it's still a manifestation isn't it? Whether it's conscious or unconscious, it's still a manifestation.' [26] 'The Devil has a place. He's one of the characters. You don't avoid him.' [27]

Into this patchwork of religious thought came Robert Tilley who had studied these things. His qualifications were a BA, MA and a BD in philosophy and theology, all from the University of Sydney. At the time of meeting Martin, Robert was writing his PhD thesis. He was also writing an account of the Ghost Train fire titled 'Funhouse', subtitled 'Luna Park and the Ghost Train Fire and Martin Sharp'. [28] Robert explained, 'I used to meet with Martin before I moved into Wirian. I made a number of tapes with him where I got him to talk about the religious aspect of Luna Park. I used the tapes in the latter part of Funhouse when I discuss Martin's reading of the events that night'. [29]

Describing his own religious background, Robert said, 'I wasn't raised a Protestant/Calvinist in fact my parents were not particularly religious. However, for whatever reason, from a very young age I became a Calvinist on my own bat, but in my teens and early-20s I was more the hippy. I became a Catholic because I realised that Jesus Christ founded a visible Church with St Peter at its head and the only Church to answer this description is the Catholic Church'. [30] Robert moved into Paiwan's former quarters underneath Wirian. Being a lecturer in Biblical Studies at the Catholic Institute of Sydney, University of Notre Dame (Sydney) and a lecturer in theology and the arts for Catholic Adult Education, Robert added a scholarly voice to the discussions.

Martin had no systematic theology, which intrigued Robert, who came to the following conclusions, all of which he discussed with Martin, 'Martin very much saw himself in the role of the shaman. For a number of reasons, which I actually confronted Martin about and which he did not take issue with, Martin saw himself as a kind of Hermes-like figure (you might say that Hermes is the patron saint of those who think of themselves as "bridges" between worlds). That a good deal of chaos at Wirian was a means of rendering the borders between worlds permeable. A kind of cosmic circus in which Martin acted as the ringmaster.

'Martin found it difficult to submit himself to the teaching authority of the Church (any church for that matter) because he thought he knew better because he had experienced many things of a supernatural nature, especially at Wirian. He used dope as a means of creating this chaos and to aiding his shaman-like activities, as he did lack of sleep, drama, poor diet, incredibly strong coffee, mad people, and so on and so forth. Of course, he felt that all of this revolved around and devolved upon the events of the fire at Luna Park and the synchronicity served to confirm it for him.

'It is exactly this dimension to Martin that others do not get, cannot understand, indeed feel fearful of. And yet I would argue that it is exactly this dimension that tells the most about Martin; about the trajectory of his life; about his art; about his fascination with Tiny Tim; Luna Park; the way he ran Wirian; his manic episodes; his secrecy; his dabbling with people of many different and even strange religious and so-called spiritual backgrounds.' [31]

Willy reinvented himself and become what Martin called an 'Urban Monk'. He walked everywhere, wore black t-shirts, long black socks and black thongs and read nothing but Scripture, which stretched to include the Early Church Fathers, the Nag Hammadi library and forgotten gospels like the Gospel of Thomas and the Bible (naturally). That was what he read for several years. Robert and Willy's table discussions were wide-ranging. They might include subjects like the Council of Nicea, the stigmata or Willy's belief that the Papacy was 'full of Masons'. [32]. All this was quite interesting for Martin but challenging for a young woman caller Harmonie Downes who was flat out simply coming to grips with Tiny Tim!

Harmonie was a hippie child from Mullumbimby NSW. She had grown up in communes in northern NSW and came to Sydney to finish her education. She enrolled in Randwick TAFE and decided to call on Wirian because her mother knew people who knew Martin. With Luna Park memorabilia in the hall, posters, Popeye, Mickey Mouse, Kewpie dolls, Snugglepot & Cuddlepie, the Dream Museum, a room full of Tiny Tim memorabilia - and all the rest - Wirian was unlike any home Harmonie had ever seen. Despite a 35-year age difference, she fell in love with Martin. By May, Martin made it known that she was carrying his child and that they were 'on the edge of getting married'. [33]

This improbable marriage added a dimension that Martin had never encountered before. There was no wife to voice an opinion. He shared his finances with no one. Whether he could afford it or not, Martin hired recording studios, concert halls, framers, printers, film editors and – whether he knew how to use it or not – he kept buying state-of-the-art technology. People who knew how to use that equipment were on his payroll. Having a wife and child would require him to be a different type of 'Martin' and Wirian a different type of house. He'd had no constraints in his previous relationships. The birth of a son, due in October, would require a reordering of Martin's priorities. He worried about it, tried to think of a name and sought advice from friends.

Greg, Tim, Draff, Roger, Brett, all of them – they all had children. Not Martin. Not yet. It was the fulfilment of his mother Jo's hopes. [34] Several were critical of the age difference but Martin was way ahead of them. He visited Harmonie's family, who gave their consent to the union.

In the late 90s, social media was in its infancy. Google, Facebook, Twitter and YouTube had yet to be fully established. Most people had just switched from fax machines to email. Although he was well set up, Martin didn't even know how to use that. He often asked guests to check his emails. A hundred or so might come up and he'd dictate answers to some. Burning CDs had become a simple process that overtook the slower process of copying to cassette. Apple had released a range of film editing software that superseded the old-style cutting methods. Wirian's film editing room was equipped with all latest technologies. Visitors, students, nephews, callers would assist Martin with his computers.

Martin delegated the tape transfers to Dave and Wendy, and the film was sometimes being worked on by Marilyn or sometimes by young students who Martin would oversee though he would seldom get involved. He might ask an assistant to get onto a search engine and look someone up, like – say – Henry Burr, the Canadian singer Tiny had often referenced. Burr was a legend in his time but before search engines, getting information about him required a big effort. Other times Martin would ask someone to get onto Google Images and find – say - Georgio De Chirico's 1914 painting *The Song of Love*. Twenty or more images might come up. After studying the colours, Martin would pick one and ask for a printed copy.

Lots of callers dropped in, like Richard Neville – wearing a tie. Richard had ideas for a new book, which he discussed with Martin before heading home. Richard had co-established the Australian Futures Foundation with English businessman Oliver Freeman. He continued to write for the press, made regular media appearances and was on the speaking circuit. His 1991 novel *Playing Around* had gained scant attention. (35) In that same year Geoffrey Robertson fared better having written the TV drama *The Trials of OZ*. It was nominated for a BAFTA award. (36) Perhaps this inspired Richard to write his account of his London years.

Richard's new book *Hippie Hippie Shake* was the kind of memoir everyone liked, except those who were in it. It was self-critical, modest but indiscreet. On his own admission, Richard didn't allow the truth to overwhelm a good story. (37)

'I didn't like it much' said Martin, after scanning the book. 'I don't think Richard understood the 60s. I'm still living the 60s. He is too in a way, but obviously one trip wasn't enough'. Martin was offended by several sections including the claim that he slept with Richard's girlfriend Louise as payback for Richard sleeping with Martin's girlfriend Anou. 'Not true!' Martin exclaimed, ultimately blaming himself for not objecting sooner. He admitted that Richard gave him ample time to read it and make corrections. 'I could have changed it', he said. 'Richard gave me the opportunity but I was too sick at the time.' (38)

There are at least three different covers to Richard's book but Martin's was the most popular. Martin said, 'They put a lot of pressure to get a cover out of me. I had done a cover for Richard but he didn't like it. Then Marilyn suggested the Jimi Hendrix picture.' And that solved the problem. (39)

Sadly, Richard's older sister Jill died of uterine cancer in June. As *Hippie Hippie Shake* points out, Jill gave the travelling hippies - Martin and Richard – a toehold in London. Her house was where London OZ was conceived. Her contacts became Richard's contacts. Vale Jill Neville. (40)

Another death that rocked Martin was that of Lady Diana Spencer. He had always admired her. On 31 August, Diana was fatally injured in a car crash in the Pont de l'Alma road tunnel in Paris. Her funeral was one of the United Kingdom's most watched programs. Millions more watched it around the world, including Martin. 'The St Alma Tunnel where Diana died - or Ayers Rock where Azaria died - these are sacred sites,' Martin concluded,. 'Diana was a great leader in her way, especially when she did that *Panorama* interview'. (41)

*Panorama* was an hour long 1995 BBC interview in which Princess Diana spoke frankly of Prince Charles' extra-marital affairs, questioned his suitability to be King and said the monarchy was in desperate need of modernisation. She was frank about her depression, bulimia and she admitted her affair with James Hewitt. Martin admired her honesty, 'She called them into line and put her own head on the block. I think it's very interesting to have a family that has been there for so long and who have seen so many politicians come and go. They certainly do very beautiful religious services'. (42)

Death often comes in multiples. Anou Kissler, Martin's first girlfriend and inspiration for *Tales of Brave Ulysses*, died too. She died of an aneurysm and Martin attended her funeral. And then came the terrible news of Martin and Harmonie's stillborn son. For the last month of her pregnancy Harmonie moved from Wirian to her father's home in Burringbar, north of Mullumbimby NSW where she planned a home birth. Leaving the care of Wirian in Cousin Roslyn's capable hands, Martin travelled north to welcome his son into the world.

One morning Harmonie felt stomach had gone cold and she felt no movement. She and Martin rushed to Lismore Base Hospital where no heartbeat could be detected. Born 14 October, their stillborn son was named Marcello (Cello). The distraught couple broke down in tears. Martin was overwhelmed by a deep sense of failure.

Richard and Julie, and George Gittoes rushed to Lismore. Three days later Cello was buried in Mullumbimby Cemetery. George painted the word 'Eternity' in copperplate writing on the tiny blue coffin. Afterwards, Martin stayed in Bundeena with George and his family. George took him boating to childhood haunts around Port Hacking, which affected Martin deeply. He then returned to Wirian where he immediately took sick again and took more time out to recuperate. Martin was open about the circumstances surrounding Cello's death, to friends he said, 'Ask any questions you like'. Not many did. [43]

In September 1998, Martin's *Street of Dreams* film was televised on late night TV, which gave the film a sense of work-in-progress completion. The ABC screened the *Brighton Cut*. In this form the film later found its way onto youtube, even though Martin, Marilyn and others continued working on it. [44]

Miss Sue circulated her *Memories of My Husband* as a private publication. In this she suggests Tiny had a physical ailment from childhood that accounted for some of his behaviour. 'There is nothing wrong with Tiny!' Martin affirmed, as offended as when other writers questioned Vincent's sanity. [45]

In early 1998 Lin Utzon came to Sydney and stayed at Wirian. Martin arranged a kitchen table meeting between Lin and the chairperson of the Sydney Opera House Trust Joe Skrzynski. Skrzynski assured her that the Opera House Trust was sincere in wanting a rapprochement between her father Jorn and Sydney Opera House Trust. On her return to Europe, Lin discussed it with her father who was open to the idea.

Crediting Martin with providing the convivial environment that allowed the discussion to take place, writer Joyce Morgan describes the events that unfolded, 'Skrzynski and Sydney architect Richard Johnson flew to Denmark to meet Utzon. In collaboration with his architect son Jan Utzon and Johnson, Joern Utzon developed a set of design principles to guide the building's future. He also redesigned the Opera House's reception hall, to be renamed the Utzon Room, and designed a large tapestry to hang within it. Lin oversaw the tapestry's installation, and Martin was with her for its unveiling. Indeed he accompanied her to every milestone involving the architect and the Opera House.

'In the wake of the reconciliation, the world appeared to rediscover Jorn Utzon. He was awarded architecture's top honour, the Pritzker Prize, in 2003. Although he never saw his completed masterpiece, when Utzon died in 2008 his building was hailed by British architecture critic Deyan Sudjic as having "transformed the world's view not just of Sydney, but of Australia". Lin regards the meeting around Wirian's kitchen table as pivotal: "That first meeting with me and Joe Skrzynski and Martin ... was when everything started cooking."[46]

Bad news: Macleay Street Developments revealed its plans to pull down the Yellow House building to make way for a modern development. Worse news: in 1999 Yellow House painter, printmaker and sculptor Peter Wright died of cancer in Bathurst Hospital NSW. Peter and his wife Mandy lived in the Hill End artistic community in the Bathurst region. He was a good friend to all Yellow House artists, delivering the eulogy at Brett's funeral in 1992. Peter's work was well represented at the Yellow House Retrospective at the Art Gallery of New South Wales.

In August 1999, Barry Stern Gallery, Glenmore Road Paddington, held the official launch of Martin's 1992 drawing 'Thirroul'. Also on exhibit was a range of Martin's recent – and not so recent – works, including *Art Galaxy*, with Boofhead showing a drawing book to Rodin's Thinker. Hokusai's 'Great Wave' features on the picture with Vincent's Starry Starry Night swirling to the fore, along with the Southern Cross. Jim Anderson created a book of cut and paste collages he had made from the photographs he had taken of the crowd and of Martin's works from that opening. He titled it *Jim Anderson presents From Where to Eternity a Suite of Paper Collage Portraits provoked by Martin Sharp*. After the demise of London OZ in 1973, Jim spent 20 creative years in the alternative town of Bolinas California and was finally back in Sydney to renew old friendships and ease himself back into an Australian world. Not necessarily easy after such a long time away.

Jim mused later, 'That first collection of collages began my small career as a paparazzo taking quick shots of people at the openings, often taking photographs of the artist's work separately, in order for them to be collaged behind the faces and bodies. It made for greater emphasis on the artwork. I gave him a copy of the book and he liked it. I'd see Martin from time-to-time at Richard's place or at parties. Although I loved the idea of someone living in a big mansion rather than just a big house, I found the wonderful magnet that was Wirian also contained elements of the dark and the spooky. I certainly went there enough to get a good feeling for the important thing it meant to Martin.' [47]

After his Art School studies, 23-year old Luke Sciberras moved into Wirian. He started doing handyman jobs until he grew into the role of Martin's assistant. One of his ventures was to assist in the organising of a revisiting of the Yellow House at the Michael Nagy Gallery. The *Yellow House Now* was opened by Richard Neville and featured 37 works. The artists represented were Roger Foley, Juno Gemes,

George Gittoes, Mick Glasheen, Bruce Goold, Peter Kingston, Jon Lewis, Tim Lewis, Garry Shead, Antoinette Starkiewicz, Albie Thoms, Dick Weight, Greg Weight, Peter Wright and Martin, who exhibited *Thirroul* and *Art Galaxy*. With an asking price of $37,500, the most striking work was *Portrait of Van Gogh/Mickey Mouse* by Brett Whiteley and Martin Sharp. [48]

Fourteen years later, Martin's *Art Galaxy* would become the cover for Mic Conway's National Junk Band CD titled, 'Diagonally Parked in a Parallel Universe'. [49] But in 1999 it was his brother Jim and the Backsliders band who asked Martin if they could use his Pentecost picture on their *Poverty Deluxe* CD. There are two versions of Pentecost, the first is a reworking of Martin's Art Book collage. The second is enveloped in flames. Jim chose the latter. [50]

Then the *Disraeli Gears* cover made a comeback. It was the cover of Cream's 1997 *Those Were The Days* 4-CD boxed set, which included both Sharp/Clapton songs, *Tales of Brave Ulysses* and *Anyone for Tennis*.

# 12.
# WORLD'S GREATEST EDITOR

*Suddenly I felt a powerful call from the Lord to write 'Eternity'.*
*I had a piece of chalk in my pocket and I bent down and wrote it.*
**Arthur Stace**

Martin reckoned Arthur Stace was the world's greatest editor because he edited everything down to one word: Eternity.

Arthur Stace was born in an inner city Sydney slum in 1884. Both parents, both brothers and both sisters were drunks. His sisters also ran brothels and, like their brothers, spent a lot of time in jail. With no one sober enough to take care of him, little Arthur slept on canvas bags under the house and stole food or picked out garbage scraps. At the age of 12 he became a State ward and by the age of 14 he worked his first job. He spent his first pay cheque on booze and did his first jail stint at 15.

In his 20s he moved to Surry Hills, a seedy suburb at the time. His job was to carry liquor from the pubs to the brothels, especially his sister's brothel. He was also employed as a 'cockatoo' (lookout man) working for two-up schools and housebreakers. During World War 1 Arthur joined the Australian Imperial Forces, 19$^{th}$ Battalion, 5$^{th}$ brigade. Serving as a stretcher-bearer in France, Arthur came home gassed and partially blinded in one eye. He went straight back to old haunts, took to drinking with a vengeance and become a derelict alcoholic.

In 1930 he appeared in a Court House on Broadway (near Central Station). He was struck by the magistrate's words, 'Don't you know I have the power to put you in Long Bay Jail or the power to set you free?'

'Yes sir,' Arthur acquiesced, the word 'power' sticking in his mind. Power was what he needed to quit drinking.

Outside the Court House a group was heading to St Barnabas' Church. The church offered a free cup of tea and something to eat to all who sat through Archdeacon Hammond's sermon for an hour or so. There were about 300 attendees. Seated next to a well-known criminal, Arthur pointed to six spruce-looking men sitting down the front and asked, 'Who are they?' 'I reckon they'd be Christians', the crim replied. Arthur made an on-the-spot decision, 'Well look at them and look at us, I reckon I'm having a go at what they've got'. He quit drinking, cleaned up and got a job. In time he even got a wife, Pearl. They lived in Bulwarra Road Pyrmont.

Some months later, Arthur attended a sermon by evangelist Reverend John Ridley in the Burton Street Baptist Church at Darlinghurst. The preacher thundered, 'I wish I could shout "Eternity" through the streets of Sydney!' 'Eternity, eternity', Arthur kept repeating the word. He said, 'Suddenly I began crying and I felt a powerful call from the Lord to write "Eternity". I had a piece of chalk in my pocket and I bent down there and wrote it'. His usual scrawl was indecipherable but this one word – and only this word - came out in a beautiful copperplate hand. He said, 'I've tried and tried, but "Eternity" is the only word that comes out in copperplate'.

It is estimated that Arthur chalked 'Eternity' half a million times over the next 35 years. Several mornings a week, always before dawn, he wrote the word on Sydney pavements and entrances to railway stations from the city to Parramatta. Commuters would see the freshly written word but they'd never see the writer. Who could it be? The mystery was solved 24 years later when Arthur knelt to write on the pavement and Rev Lisle Thompson - who preached at the church where Arthur worked as a cleaner - saw him do it. In 1956 Thompson wrote a tract about Arthur's early life and *Sunday Telegraph* journalist, Tom Farrell, tracked Arthur down and interviewed him. Five years later a photographer cornered Arthur and asked to take a few pictures of him. He took four snaps of the little man in a suit and grey felt hat chalking 'Eternity' then ran out of film. He asked Arthur to stay put while he got more. When he returned Arthur was gone. [1]

As a child, Martin spotted Eternity in Cranbrook Road. It grabbed his interest, 'I'd never seen anything written on the pavement before!' [2] By the time Arthur Stace died in 1967 he had inspired a lot more people than he knew. In the early-60s Garry Shead used the Eternity motif in a cartoon published in the Bulletin, someone wrote a song about Mr Eternity for a university revue and poet Douglas Stewart provided a fitting epitaph in his poem 'Arthur Stace' - 'That shy mysterious poet Arthur Stace, whose work was just one single mighty stroke…'. [3]

Martin started appropriating "Eternity" too. The word appeared in major works like *Film Script, Portrait of Tiny Tim* and *Eternity Haymarket*. He didn't know much about the story of the man behind the word, no one did. Everything that was known was gleaned from a few newspaper articles until author Keith Dunstan included a chapter on Stace in his book about unconventional Australians like Bea Miles, King O'Malley, Percy Granger, Justus Jorgenson and Stace. Said Martin, 'Keith Dunstan's book *Ratbags* (1979) brought me in touch with the story behind it. I knew it was a guy called Arthur Stace. Ross Campbell found a poem about him.

'Arthur Stace is part of folklore. I feel these are very much a part of Sydney – Boofhead, Arthur Stace, Ginger Meggs. Pop Art gave them a chance to graduate – go into Art and keep them alive. And it turned out well with Mr Eternity. Someone sang a song about him at a university revue called *First No Pinky*, which must have been 1961 (which I did some work for). It was a great song about Mr Eternity. That would be the first resurfacing. Arthur Stace has certainly been honoured in aluminium in the replica of his calligraphy at Sydney Square by the architect Ridley Smith - who was named after the Reverend Ridley, the preacher who inspired him.' [4]

Remo Giuffré brought Eternity to Sydney's attention in 1990 when he commissioned Martin to paint the storefront picture for his *Remo* shop, from which he made prints and Eternity t-shirts. Mambo t-shirts, Billabong t-shirts, Ken Done t-shirts, now there was Remo, turning Eternity into streetwear. Eternity seemed to inspire lots of creative ideas. Conductor of the Tokyo String Quartet, Richard Gill, sported his Eternity t-shirt for a media photograph. Musician Dennis Aubrey was given one by his sister, which inspired him to write his 'Eternity' song. Author Maggie Hamilton wrote a kids book titled *Mister Eternity*. [5] The film *Eternity* - written and directed by Lawrence Johnston - was screened at Paddington's Academy Twin theatre. [6] Australian composer Jonathon Mills combined with novelist and poet Dorothy Porter to create an opera based on Arthur Stace's life. In 2008, director Julien Temple made that opera into a film titled *The Eternity Man*. [7] Martin launched artist David Lever's exhibition of 27 works, *Eternity: A Tribute to Arthur Stace* held at Macquarie University Library. And the Eternity Gallery was opened in the National Museum of Australia Canberra. The Museum published an A4-size book featuring a rare Arthur Stace original *Eternity* cover image written in white chalk on black cardboard, 450 x 180mm. It appears to be the only remaining original copy of his work. [8]

The Millennium New Year celebrations were a coordinated series of fireworks and events televised from major cities around the world, celebrating the end of the second millennium and the beginning of the third. Kiribati was the first land to see the millennium. Auckland was the first industrial nation to do so. Then Sydney where revellers hit midnight long before the great cities of Asia, Africa, Europe or the Americas. Celebrations were televised to two billion people around the world who watched a firework display climaxed by a spectacular fireball that temporarily hid the Harbour Bridge from view. When the smoke cleared Arthur Stace's distinctive 'Eternity' was seen 18 metres tall, right there on the Bridge. 'Let's Keep It For Eternity' responded one newspaper headline. [9]

Everyone recognised this as a big nod to Martin, though he never claimed credit, which was typical of Martin. When asked whether the idea was his, Martin deferred to the creative director Ignatius Jones and then Remo. [10] Said Roslyn, 'Martin often asked me to come over on New Years Eve. I spent New Years Eve 2000 at Wirian. I took three people over there, walked in and there was an Anglican Archbishop having tea with Martin. *Eternity?* He talked about it in the third person, he never pumped his own work up.' [11]

Just when it seemed 'Eternity' couldn't get any bigger, the eyes of the world – 3.6 billion people - again turned to the harbour city at the Opening Ceremony of Sydney's 2000 Olympic Games in mid-September. There was a prelude, welcome, anthem, a segment called Deep Sea Dreaming, The Awakening, Nature, Tin Symphony (about European settlement) and a celebration of muliculturalism directed by Lex Marinos, with Jenny Kee. As this piece peaked, performers from the other segments came out and joined the dancers, which climaxed with a huge representation of the Sydney Harbour Bridge composed of sparklers set off in the middle of the stadium with 'Eternity' again shown in the centre of the Bridge.

This was followed by Governor-General Sir William Deane's opening address. Deane was a Patron of Reconciliation Australia and also Patron of the Australian Indigenous Doctors Association. Martin admired that speech, 'Sir William Deane put the Aboriginal cause into a spiritual context and that is what I liked. He could bring the spiritual into the political. He gave meaning to that job, which I don't remember in anyone else fulfilling the role. He was unique.' [12]

The Opening Ceremony concluded when former Australian Olympic champion Herb Elliott ran the Olympic Flame into the stadium. Former Australian women Olympic champions and medalists, Betty Cuthbert, Raelene Boyle, Dawn Fraser, Shirley Strickland, Shane Gould and Debbie Flintoff-King brought the Flame through the stadium, handing it to Cathy Freeman who climbed the long set of stairs towards a circular pool of water. She walked into the middle of the water and ignited the cauldron around her feet in a ring of fire. The cauldron then rose out from the water, above her head and was transported up a long waterfall, where it reached its final resting place, high above the stadium.

Martin was transfixed! He bought the photographic book *Catherine: Intimate Portrait of a Champion* and left it on his table where guests could pick it up and read the inspirational quotes 'that give her strength and focus'. [13] Martin admired her, 'Cathy Freeman is very special. I like the way she runs and I like the way she talks.' [14]

Indigenous Australian issues had been on Martin's mind. The 60s folk movement - especially Gary, Jeannie and Black Allen Murawalla - alerted thinking Australians about pro-Indigenous issues. [15] He praised Paul Keating's 'Redfern Speech' adding, 'Some Aboriginal leaders have been great – Eddie Mabo'. Martin loved the secular mysticism of Jimmy Little's *Messenger* CD - covers of alternative and classic Australian Rock songs from the 80s. As a teenager, Martin attended Jimmy Little's performances at the Sydney Stadium. He said, 'Jimmy Little kept himself completely modern. He is the Aussie King really – certainly as big as Slim Dusty, if not bigger - a broader artist and deeper'. [16]

Broad enough to offer compromise as a solution to the indigenous concerns that bothered Martin. Jimmy Little said, 'In blunt terms it means: we've survived without you so we can do it again. We've got the space. We've got the land. This is the hard cold facts - Black Australians are going to say to White Australians, "You've done it overnight while we were sleeping, you've built on the land. We don't want to push you away, we want you here, but compensation comes into play: a compromise".' [17]

Eddie Mabo, Paul Keating, Sir William Deane, Cathy Freeman, Jimmy Little, all these coalesced and changed Martin from a quiet sympathiser to an art activist on indigenous rights. A milestone was reached in the process of reconciliation when 250,000 people turned out for the Walk for Reconciliation across Sydney's Harbour Bridge, making it the largest political demonstration ever to be held in Australian history. Martin took part in it. He explained, 'The first thing to work out is the situation with the original inhabitants. I think a lot of prejudice is formed by guilt not by reality. Guilt and shame is the "best" reason for not talking'. [18] At times he gave away money he didn't have. 'Just paying the rent,' he'd say.

Actor David Gulpilil was a Yolngu man from Arnhem Land. Gulpilil played didge and clap-sticks on Tiny's *Chameleon* album. Martin knew him since then, but they'd met before that. Gulpilil's first acting role was in the Nicolas Roeg survival film *Walkabout* (1971) set in the outback. Roeg had co-directed *Performance* with Donald Cammell the previous year. Gulpilil's next film was Philippe Mora's *Mad Dog Morgan* (1976), which was released the same year as *Storm Boy* in which he played Fingerbone Bill, which earned him an AACTA Award for Best Actor. In the 1980s and 90s he had played major roles in eight feature films including *The Last Wave, Croc Dundee* and *Crocodile Dundee 2*. In 2000-2001 he was work-ing on *The Tracker*. Sometimes with fellow actor Jack Thompson for company, Gulpilil would call on Wirian where he was always welcome to stay when he was in Sydney. When Martin enthused about his glorious acting career, Gulpilil re-plied, 'Yeah, but I haven't got a house'. It needled Martin that this prince of actors didn't have a regular dwelling place in his own country. Martin decided to paint Gulpilil's portrait.

Based on a Polaroid taken by Jonny, Martin sketched Gulpilil's face onto a 180 x 120 cm canvas on which Martin developed the portrait. Like most of Martin's pictures, it went through several transmutations - the eye was moved slightly more left, the green changed to blue, etc, until it settled into a basic image that Martin would overpaint then overpaint some more. 'The Thousand Dollar Bill', was so named because Gulpilil joked about his face appearing on Australia's banknotes - like the indigenous preacher, inventor and writer David Unaipon, the face of the $50 note. Fifty dollars wasn't big enough for Martin who made a $1000 'banknote' as a way of honouring this great actor who didn't even have a house. [19]

Martin also began a work based on a cartoon originally published in an 1888 issue of the *Bulletin* magazine. 'A Curiosity in Her Own Country' started as a straight take of Phil May's cartoon and over the next decade it gradually evolved into a nativity scene that Martin circulated as a Christmas card and eventually a contender for the 2011 Blake Prize.

Martin wasn't the only one who suffered from kidney stones, Dave did too. After a severe bout, Dave absented himself for several months. When he came back several projects needed completing with some urgency because technology had taken another turn. The buying public no longer required anything in physical format to listen to music. Cyber-space meant buying music online and downloading it. Listeners didn't even need to purchase a whole album, individual tracks could be bought for around $1.50 each (at a time when CDs cost around $30). Dave knew all about that, so did Satoshi. To release *Chameleon*, Satoshi began negotiating with Japanese company, Zero Communications. The success of the Japanese release of *God Bless Tiny Tim* proved there was a market for Tiny in Japan and Zero saw that niche. To make *Chameleon* product-ready, the original LP needed remastering. Welcome back Dave.

While Dave was away, he did some useful work for BMG Records who launched their 'Legendary' series with a 3-CD pack of Harry Belafonte's hits. Dave explained, 'We had big change in the industry. A lot of knowledgeable people, the old timers, were being turfed out and replaced with young blond-haired kids. The guy that had been doing the *Legendary* was one of the old knowledge people. I got a call from some young kid saying, did I know Harry Belafonte? Of course, I know Harry Belafonte! "Would you be able to complete this…?"' Of course Dave could, because he also knew the difference between the artist's hits and their B-sides, which was a bit of a fog to the young up-and-comers. Cover lines were another mystery because, in updating, the record companies had dispensed with the original album covers. Here Dave again proved invaluable because (after Glenn A Baker) he had one of the most comprehensive record collections in the country, therefore having the original cover lines at his disposal.

The *Legendary Belafonte* did really well so they asked Dave to take over the whole series. His job was to create 3-CD 'Best-Of' Legendary packages for artists like Hank Snow, Perry Como, Della Reece and Eartha Kitt. His involvement continued over the course of the next five years, a period when Dave also worked for Martin. Martin enjoyed the musical trip down memory lane. Said Dave, 'Martin was very impressed with the *Legendary* series. I made sure I gave him one, whenever a new one was released.' [20]

'Maybe there's stirring of the spirit,' wrote Martin, 'Dave Rowe has got involved again which is great. The film is being developed, taking it right back to the original rushes, eg. the whole of Miss Natasha....then making a long film containing everything that is interesting, which most of it is. I really feel Tiny brought a completely new dimension to The Performer. It's amazing how alive he sounds on his tapes. Art is the only way to go. Wouldn't it be a sad world if someone somewhere didn't acknowledge Tiny Tim'. [21]

Since the early-60s, Martin had been a popular personality for magazine interviews. His accompanying photo-portraits usually depicted him with whatever picture he was working on in the background, but the interview subject matter didn't show much variation. Journalists usually started with OZ, then Swinging London, how he met Eric, the 'written on a serviette' story about *Tales of Brave Ulysses*, followed by Tiny Tim, Luna Park, and usually including something about Martin being 'reclusive'. No one was immune from Martin's ire when misquoted, not even Australia's most respected journalists. Martin often complained that they 'made up' their quotes. That was probably because they usually jotted down on a pad what they thought Martin said instead of using exact quotes. After they'd left he would sit with Dave – or one of the Wirian crew – and analyse what that journo was 'really' up to. Dave described Martin as 'constantly suspicious', which was true, especially around journalists from the Murdoch and Packer press. [22]

With students, he was the exact opposite, as 16-year old Electra Foley – Roger's daughter – found out when doing her high school art assignment. Martin couldn't have been more cooperative. The picture she chose for her art essay was *Ginger in Japan* originally a collage using the images of Japanese 19th Century artist Hiro-shige and Australian cartoonist of the 1930s, Jimmy Bancks the creator of Ginger Meggs. From the collage came the picture, with Tim again painting alongside Martin. The picture was completed in 1996 and part of the Albie Thoms collec-tion. Electra wrote, 'Sharp's works are generally about reconciliation and peace between cultures. *Ginger in Japan* could be seen as reconciliation as Ginger Meggs is regarded as "the average Australian boy" and Hiroshige was a well-known highly respected Japanese Artist'. [23]

Martin wrote back and thanked her, 'Dear Electra, you have written some excellent words'. With the letter, Martin enclosed a photocopy of the Biblical passage, 1 John Chapter 4, 'Beloved, believe not every spirit but try the spirits whether they are of God; because many false prophets are gone out into the world. Hereby know ye the Spirit of God: Every spirit that confesseth that Jesus Christ is come in the flesh is of God: And every spirit that confesseth not that Jesus Christ is come in the flesh is not of God'. That page was addressed 'Dear Fogg and Electra'.

Electra asked lots of questions giving Martin the opportunity to explain his earlier Ginger Meggs poster (for the Nimrod Theatre) in which Ginger is wearing the politically incorrect blackface. He wrote, 'in about 1976 I found some old Ginger Meggs Annuals (of collected strips) and there was a story of Ginger and his school friends at the School Concert. Ginger was going to perform the poem "If" by Rudyard Kipling. One of his rivals, Eddie Coogan, lured him over to a hole in the wall and squirted ink all over his face. Determined to perform, Ginger took advantage of his black face and went on stage to sing "Mammy" and "Sonny Boy", two hit songs of Al Jolson who was the singing star of the 20s. He sang in the costume of a negro-minstrel.

'The Actor's Benevolent Fund asked me for a postcard design. I suggested Ginger Meggs sings "Mammy" at the School Concert. Here he has a dark blue face. There was a Chinese person on the committee of the Actor's B Fund who thought I was poking fun at negroes…of course this wasn't the case but in these days of political correctness and hyper-sensitivity to such matters I solved the problem by painting Ginger's face white like a clown and retitling the picture "Bring On The Clowns". [24]

Greg Weight was another productive Wirian resident during this period. He photographed and catalogued Martin's pictures and produced commercial work - like the *1997 Australian Yoga Calendar*. He also wrote magazine articles and photographed artists George Gittoes, Peter Kingston, Cressida Campbell, Garry Shead and other artists for *Australian Artist* magazine. [25] Greg played a weekly game of tennis with Garry at the tennis centre at Cooper Park Woollahra. Other friends joined them too, like Luke Sciberras who was fresh out of art school.

'I met Luke through Dad,' said Gria Shead, who later married him. 'Dad said, "You should learn tennis" so I went down there, played a game and Luke was there. (He'd been assisting Dad or Greg.) We still joke that it was like an Arranged Marriage. I wasn't with anyone at the time and Dad said, "you should meet this guy". I thought, "Oh god no, I don't want to meet any of your friends thanks – I'm not getting set up". And so Luke and I met. We got on straight away. That was at Cooper Park.' [26]

Gria and Luke had a mutual friend in Martin because they had both lived at Wirian before meeting each other. Gria lived there for most of 1990 and Terry Stanton had invited Luke to visit Wirian after speaking to him on the phone. So Luke had camped at Wirian on-and-off. At the time of meeting Luke was living at Palm Beach.

The relationship started in 1997. Gria said, 'We got together one night after tennis. We visited Martin afterwards and Martin asked us to stay. We both moved in briefly but we didn't moved stuff in, we camped there, in Jo's flat. We got the Royal Suite - but only briefly, possibly because Luke was doing work for Martin at that time - cleaning, housekeeping kind of stuff, also in the studio. Martin would ask Luke to sort out papers or put the prints away in drawers or organise the library.'

Gria and Luke's daughter Stella was born in 2000. Martin was her godfather. At this time they were living with Gria's mother Merle in Vaucluse. Luke was employed by Martin as his artist's assistant, 'which got us through that initial couple of years' said Gria. 'I was painting the whole time but painting seriously by the time Stella was about 18 months old. Luke was working for Martin for about a year, then he got a studio at Kingo's for about a year.' (27)

Adrian Rawlins died in September, aged 62. That poet, raconteur and scamp, died of cancer. Martin did the black-and-white poster for a celebration of Adrian's life held at Paddo Markets Church Hall. Titled: 'Mr Fogg's Music Hall Proudly Present Adrian – the Cabaret', acts included Jeannie Lewis, Jim Anderson, Austen Tayshus, Edwina Blush, Kavisha Mazella, Al Jones and Nic Lyon. The meaning of the 1994 statue of Adrian in Brunswick Street Fitzroy Melbourne changed from a celebration to a memorial.

Shortly after Adrian's passing, Arkie Whiteley – an accomplished actor, living between Sydney and London – went to hospital in Sydney and discovered she had cancer in both lungs and her liver. The doctors did not initially detect the primary cancer in her adrenal gland. Arkie had an operation, underwent chemotherapy treatment and married her intended, Jim Elliott. Two weeks later, a week before Christmas 2001, she died in their Palm Beach house aged just 37. The sweet little Yellow House girl who came up with the name Spookyland for Peter Wright's room was gone. (28)

'Death…' said Martin ruefully, '…I have known death'.

Towards the close of the same year a developer was told to redraft an application to demolish the rear of the Yellow House in Macleay Street. David Katon of architects Burnley Katon Halliday said there was an application to demolish the rear of the 1890s Queen Anne terrace house to make way for a four-storey building. The terrace was subject to heritage protection and a local law preserving cheap accommodation. South Sydney Council gave the architects six weeks to supply additional information about their proposed development. (29)

# 13.
# TELFORD, TRAVEL AND THE TINY TIM STAGE SHOW

*Performers want to be loved. I'm sure Tiny was like that.*
Mic Conway

The film editing room was brimming with memorabilia and tapes. It was like watching a museum grow. Rare singles, figurines of Tiny, books like Rudy Vallee's biography and pictures - some just photocopies taped to the wall – awaiting their moment. Miss Sue (Sue Khaury) sent Martin a dozen Tiny Tim Head Knockers (wobble-head) figurines. He kept some and gave away the others. [1] She also sent him video news footage of Tiny's onstage heart attack, death and funeral. That too was studied and filed in the film editing room.

Elsewhere in America, some guy had Tiny's handwritten 1963 Diary for sale. Martin and Dave hummed and hawed about that. How would they know it was genuine? The vendor mailed them photocopied samples and Martin set Dave a $3000 limit. Martin's ailing stepmother Dorothy had paid off the mortgage over Wirian, which gave Martin some much needed financial breathing space. [2]

Pilot Pete still called, though not allowed inside. He'd talk at the door, put the bite on Martin and off he'd go $50 richer. Peter Royles moved to Goulburn and quit drinking. Dave Sanderson was on medication. Mad Robyn had killed herself. Roger Foley visited occasionally, as did Sue Weight, Richard Neville, Mika (Lin Utzon's son) and many many many many more.

One evening Margaret Fink called in with a t-shirt on which she wanted Martin to write 'Eternity' in texta. A friend had died and the Eternity t-shirt was her burial gown. Friends brought food, frogs and crucifix orchids. Martin was also given two mightly aggressive chickens. If the French doors were left open, the chickens wandered into the Inner Sanctum and attacked. Guests had no guarantee of protection.

Martin loved the soundtrack of *The Tracker*, played tapes of Bible readings and edged his portrait of David Gulpilil with the colours of the Aboriginal flag. He didn't go out much, though he faithfully attended friends' art show openings. He bought a woodblock at Cressida Campbell's exhibition at the Rex Irwin Gallery and gave it to Dorothy as thanks for her support. Martin occasionally strolled to the Double Bay newsagency. Sometimes he bought a fabulous book from the bookshop. When given a choice of Double Bay eateries, Martin favoured *Arte e Cucino*, the venue for Garry's *Erotic Muse* book launch. Martin sometimes ran into Garry there, dining with poet Rudy Kaufman or owner of Australian Galleries Paddington, Stuart Purves.

In March, Garry and Judit made the *Sydney Morning Herald* front page when their 50-metre Harris Street mural was listed for demolition to make way for a development. Stuart Purves thought the developers were a bunch of philistines. He told the press, 'If you found a very early Picasso on the side of a building, would you pull it down? If it was an exhibition of ours, and if it was on canvas, the panels would be worth $60,000-$100,000 each!' [3]

A young Asian girl – Chaudry - was Wirian's cleaner now. Terry was the live-in handyman. Luke didn't live at Wirian but continued as Martin's assistant, sometimes his personal secretary. Robert Tilly lived outside downstairs and Willy lived inside upstairs. Robert and Willy sometimes bickered over topics like 'healing as a true gift of the Spirit'. In the film editing room, Wendy worked on the tape transfers until Dave came back, which he always did.

In 2002, Michael Wilkinson sold his Melbourne-based publishing house, Information Australia, to UK conglomerate Crown Content, a listed company that owned golf courses, gymnasiums and a publishing wing in England. As a condition of sale, Michael signed a restraint clause, meaning he couldn't compete in the publishing market for two years. The upside was that he was paid a lot of money. The restraint clause clipped his publishing wings, so he mused outside his regular comfort zone. Buying Melbourne's Comedy Theatre was an interesting option.

The Comedy Theatre is in Exhibition Street, in Melbourne's theatre district. Built in 1928, it seats 1000 people and is a perfect setting for nostalgic music. If he bought it, Michael wondered what he might stage there? More than 25 years had passed since he had interviewed Tiny for the *Melbourne Sun*. He was a cadet journalist then. 'Miss Vicky's gone and the tulips have faded,' wrote Michael in a 1975 piece titled, 'Tim's Just a Tiny Bit Broke'. Might a Tiny Tim stage show work? The foyer gloriously decorated with Martin Sharp pictures would be a helluva drawcard! [4]

Information Australia's flagship titles were the *Margaret Gee Media Guide* and *Australia's Who's Who*. It had also published Michael Chamberlain's book, *Beyond Azariah,* [5] which made Martin pleasantly disposed towards Michael when they met. Michael said he was confident the Marinner Group would sell him the theatre. They came to an 'in principle' agreement to move forward with a show. 'I enjoyed talking to Michael very much,' said Martin, 'We'll take this as a serious project'. [6] After he left Martin played Tiny singing 'Michael Row the Boat Ashore'.

Michael booked flights to America for himself and an assistant who interviewed Tiny's friends and family – cousins Bernie and Hal; daughter Tulip; producer of *God Bless Tiny Tim*, Richard Perry; the friend who was with Tiny the night of his first heart attack, Mark Mitchell; Tiny's webmaster, Ernie Clark; David Tibet, who released the *Christmas Album* from London, and Miss Sue who was totally obliging. After meeting her, Michael saw the show as a love story, with Tiny's 'Sue songs' as the finale – *Have You Seen My Little Sue? Sioux City Sue, If You Knew Suzie*.

Michael returned to Melbourne leaving Martin to contemplate stage design and who should play Tiny? Said Martin, 'The essence of theatre is making a few pots of paint, a bit of glitter, some lights, a few people and some music – turn into magic. This show could play Broadway, no worries. Melbourne's Comedy - that's the perfect theatre. If Michael's got it, let's go for that. Finding the right person to play Tiny is the essential thing. If you could get someone to talk like him, that would be something. Pure Tiny dialogue. I would have a person miming the singing with Tiny's voice, and once you've got Tiny onstage, you could have girls singing with him – you could have all sorts of things – but you should start with one person. You could do it in a theatrical way. You could start with the song *Welcome to My Dream*.' [7]

Michael wanted Barry Humphries to take the role. Michael knew Barry's writer, Paul Taylor, who felt the nostalgic songs would appeal to Barry.

'I know Barry - he won't do it,' snapped Martin. Martin wanted Mic Conway. Mic came over for a discussion but had doubts about taking the role, especially singing falsetto.

'The sound person can fix that.'

'I doubt it.'

'You might be able to direct it?'

'I would not be able to direct it', Mic replied (who thought Paul Capsis should play Tiny). 'I'm happy to collaborate with anyone who's writing it or not do anything at all. I'm happy to be whatever. I think you should do the set though.' [8]

Mic came up with the following draft, followed by two Acts:

Tiny Tim Show Fantasy

Outside the theatre, TINY and in smaller lettering 'A Beautiful Dreamer'. The generous foyer is an extravaganza of Martin's Tiny Tim images. Posters like Paddo, Opera House, Kinselas and Rock are on display as well as the portrait held by Macquarie University and Film Script. The music is from the Chameleon, Keeping My Troubles to Myself and Wonderful World of Romance CDs, which are for sale. Having taken all this in, theatre goers might stroll to one of the bars to sip and chat.

The prelim music stops, house lights are dimmed and the curtains part, revealing the inside of a huge circus tent arching over the entire stage. Within that tent is a two-storey stage evoking a Gnostic duality. Tiny's personality is torn between Heaven and Earth (not Hell). The stage props and imagery point to the conflict that is about to take place between Earthly Tiny – his lower self – and Heavenly Tiny – his higher self. Being already in heaven, Heavenly Tiny Tim is innocence and romance and not at all ambitious.. Earthly Tiny is ambitious and scared of sinning. The opening song, Welcome to My Dream, invites the audience into his world.

The stage show idea was an exciting idea for at least six months. The taped interviews with Tiny's cousins and friends gave Martin new depths to explore. 'Martin seems really nice,' Miss Tulip purred, 'I haven't really talked to him and I feel awful because he seems like such a nice person. He sends me books and things about my Dad and I feel bad because I never send anything back to him.' [11] Contact between Tiny Tim people in America and Australia was strong. Martin wanted to fly Tulip to Sydney and put her up at Wirian. Richard Perry offered to arrange an introduction to Tiny's first manager, Mo Ostin, if the Aussies would return to LA where he was recording *Great American Songbook Vol 1* with Rod Stewart.

Then the Marinner Group backed off on the sale of the Comedy Theatre. The deal fell over. Without the theatre, the show was just a might-have-been. Michael cancelled his LA flight. Martin did the overseas travelling instead. He had fallen in love with an Irish Rose that he nicknamed 'Min' (after Ginger Meggs' girlfriend). He wanted to marry her. He started playing Irish music, like John McCormack or the Fureys. Min didn't particularly like those artists, so he switched to Gram Parsons and Emmy Lou Harris. Martin held a big Wirian birthday bash for Min, attended by all Martin's short-notice crowd – Kingo, Roslyn, Russell, Philip, Greg, Denny & Clare, Tim & Bernadette, Alistair, Nathan, Dave, Jon, Victoria, etc. Happy birthday Min.

Then came another gathering, a family reunion from his mother's side - where Martin had only second cousins, no firsts. He explained, 'The Ritchie family branched out into the Hudson family and the Hoskins family, which goes into the Ashton and the Loveridge family. They were early successful railway people – builders, Scottish engineers. They had a family reunion and I went, which was great.'

Andrew Hudson now ran Telford as an Anglican Youthworks Conference Centre. He asked Martin to contribute a piece for their little magazine. Triggered by memories of George sailing him around Port Hacking when he was convalescing with the Gittoes' family in Bundeena, Martin wrote a 1000-word recollection. He titled it 'Memories of Telford'. Visions of his lost innocence came flooding back.

'George took me down there after I'd been sick. He knew the places,' Martin explained. 'I had a great experience with George. We got stuck in the sand bank in the houseboat. It was absolutely calm and we had to wait for the tide to come in. George had a rest and I got up on the reef and fed the fish, throwing bread in the water and seeing them swim up and take it on the sand bank. Suddenly the beauty of the place overwhelmed me. It said, "Martin where have you been? So good to see you again!" Suddenly it wasn't the house that had got me there but the place itself was my sacred site, the whole of the Port Hacking River, every young thing I had learned there.' (12)

Martin's written account starts with his childhood visits and friendship with the caretaker's kids, Ian and Jan Skinner. Martin reminisced about sharing a cigarette with Jan and nearly holding her hand. He wrote that the Skinner family home evoked a sense of love that his family lacked. They lost it when his parents headed for divorce. (13)

Rev Gary Shearston came to Sydney from Tenterfield to attend a different Anglican conference, one in the city. Gary did his Anglican stuff by day and spent his evenings with Martin. The Anglican clergy seemed oblivious that in Gary they had someone who got Aussie Folk music onto the music charts. The folk community were just as indifferent. Being a Christian priest did Gary's singing career no good. One problem was that he talked like an Anglican priest. He said things like, 'We need to remember the fanaticism that has occurred - and continues to occur in our own faith - and give thanks for the fact that in the middle of all this, the great theological minds of all these faith-backgrounds are continuing to dialogue and talk together and try and further understanding and appreciation of each other.' That's how he talked. (14)

Not everyone had forgotten Gary though. One evening, Celtic musician Carrl Myriad called on Wirian to arrange a concert to promote Gary's new CD, *Only Love Survives*. Carrl and Martin last saw each other 40 years ago, when Carrl had performed at the Yellow House in a duo called Carrl & Janie, (ie. Janie Conway, Mic and Jim's sister.) Carrl had the Druidic Awen symbol stuck on the headstock of his guitar, which at first didn't suit Willy. The meeting was strained until Gary arrived. Then it became perfect.

Gary and Carrl played a medley of Irish songs while Martin got out his brushes and daubed an updated version of his high school picture, *The Toff*. They switched to Scottish songs. Martin requested *Flower of Scotland*. They peaked when Carrl started strumming *Dingo* and Gary joined on vocals. 'Dingo, there's a hunter coming, run dingo run…'. Carrl understood *Dingo* as being about bushrangers, Martin read it as being about Azaria. It was joyous evening and a concert was booked with Carrl's band – the Ragged Band – as Gary's support and backing band. 'I'll do the poster!' Martin enthused, which he would have done had he not taken sick. (15)

This burst of interest in all things Irish reminded Martin that he was a double-Ritchie from both the Scottish and Irish sides of his family. The Irish Ritchies fascinated Martin. They hailed from County Tyrone, Northern Ireland. He wanted to see it for himself, meet Min's parents and do his courting in a traditional manner. At the end of July, Martin left for Ireland, England and Europe. It was meant as a two months trip but it took four. Robert, Marilyn, Terry and Luke 'held the fort' and Dave faithfully turned up five days a week to work on a new concept – Tiny's *Pop* album. Recorded in Sydney on Tiny's previous tour, the songs included *Rainbow on the River, My Girl, Satisfaction, House of the Rising Sun* and *I Am I Said*.

In Ireland, it didn't work out between Martin and Min, so Martin looked up old friends instead. He stayed with Marianne Faithfull before heading for Stockholm where his 60s girlfriend, assistant and inspiration, model Eija Vehka-aho put him up. Martin also looked up Lin Utzon and husband Count Hugues de Montalembert on the Spanish isle of Majorca. Then he returned to London where Peter Ledeboer of Big O Posters threw a big 'welcome back' party and discussed further reproductions. Simple ideas, like a pack of 10 Martin Sharp 60s posters-as-postcards to be sold at the Liverpool Biennial Festival of Contemporary Art and also the Tate. For the 2004 Biennial, the curator wanted to exhibit an exhibition of Martin's posters in a big space and Martin was as keen as his health permitted. (Unlike most bienalles, the Liverpool Biennial calls itself 'biennial' not 'bienialle'.)

Martin also stayed with Eric Clapton and wife Melia at Hurtwood Edge. While there, Martin's health started running down. Sometimes he was too sick to leave his bed, Melia brought him hot drinks and bowls of soup. So did Eric when he wasn't rehearsing for a memorial concert to be held at the Royal Albert Hall to celebrate Beatle George Harrison's music. George died in November 2001, his widow Olivia and son Dhani organised the concert with Eric co-directing and performing. Artists included Beatles Paul and Ringo, Monty Python, Tom Petty and the Heartbreakers, Billy Preston and other name acts. [16]

Shortly before coming home Martin attended *Concert for George* (later released to DVD). Paul McCartney recognised him, 'I'd forgotten how tall he was!' Martin chuckled. About Eric he said, 'I thought he was in his prime – magnificent, gone from strength to strength – his playing, singing, his organising of the concert, giving directions. He's made a wonderful marriage lately – children – living a very straight life and running that anti-addiction place. Remarkable, I think.' [17]

As a romantic quest, the trip was hardly a triumph. But it did remind Martin's London friends that his London art years were a 60s phenomenon worth celebrating. Said Dave, 'Martin told us about the trip but it was all about HER. You would have thought nothing else had happened other than that girl. But he stayed with Eric because he got sick and he did say to me that Eric had really looked after him. Marianne as well, I think.' [18]

While Martin was gone the Yellow House premises was converted from low-cost accommodation into up-market residential apartments. Restored by Philip Bartlett and Dr Ron White, two apartments in the rear of the building had an asking price of $825,000 each. Martin's Yellow House mural *Phantoma* was relocated to the foyer where could be seen by people strolling the pavement. At street level, the restaurant was named *Yellow*. None of the original Yellow House artists complained that it was they who had given the premises the provenance on which the developers $traded. [19]

Back home, apart from another bout of kidney stones, it was business as usual for Martin. The band Cold Chisel asked him to do the cover of their live *Ringside* CD. He liked that kind of commission because he liked the guys. [20] Indigenous-Australian, Kay Cook, moved into Wirian. Philippe looked Martin up while in the country. Harmonie visited when she came to Sydney. One of Martin's regular outings was taking his stepmother Dorothy to dinner. Although she didn't understand Martin's artistic vision, sometimes she helped financially, which was much appreciated. Roslyn often joined those luncheons. [21]

Dave divided his working life between Wirian and the Legendary Series. Dave prepared the Lou Reed and Hank Snow compilations for the Australian market. His work impressed BMG headquarters enough to hire him to compile the international release of *Legendary Jim Reeves*. He said, 'BMG-UK contacted me because I was doing those others for Australia. Would I be interested in helping them out with a project about Jim Reeves? They were in the process of releasing all the original albums to CD and needed to know all the information, cover lines, everything. That took me away from Wirian and there were times I'd explain my situation, "I've got to live Martin, I've got to earn my money".' [22]

And Richard Neville often popped in. Richard the Futurist was on the speaker's circuit. 'Steel workers last night,' he bemoaned. 'Advertising people today. It's an invention, my life. I am impudent enough to put the word "futurist" on my business card and I try to help people engage the future. I don't see that as any different to when I was publishing OZ. OZ magazine was essentially about social change and being alert to the signals of that change. I'm still looking for those signals of change.'

Don't see it as any different to publishing OZ???

Go on…!

'I'm just a futurist who wears bright shirts and jumps up and down a bit. When I go to a conference, I might be addressing franchise holders, advertising groups, TAFE students or people on local councils. At the end of the day these people have got to improve their material wellbeing so they can bring up their children and pay their mortgage. So how to you address that reality at the same time as catering to an idealistic impulse? You can't cost-cut your way to a sustainable future. Some of the older corporate heavies that I get to meet ask, "Is it too late for me to get stoned?" They're really expressing a recognition of their own existential vacuum. They've been so busy making the loot that their inner life was wasting away. What's that John Lennon line? "Life is what happens to you while you're busy making other plans".' [23]

Willy openly scoffs Richard's new book, *Footprints for the Future*. 'We don't need any more books! There are too many books already!' Martin was more concerned about Hippie Hippie Shake that he found plain indiscreet. [24] Richard was trying to sell *Hippie Hippie Shake* as a film concept, which is what Willy and Martin were worried about. There really wasn't much to complain about in *Footprints of the Future*. It was a grab-bag of facts, stats and thought-provoking Nevillisms like, 'Future pleasures will colonise the whole body, expand into cyberspace, download from a storehouse of digitized sensations and draw on a range of fleshy electro accessories which stimulate every nerve. The tyranny of the genitals is over!' [25]

Marianne Faithfull contacted Martin to let him know she wanted to catch up when she toured Australia in February 2003. Bob Dylan was in Sydney at the same time. Upon arrival Marianne spotted the billboards announcing Dylan's concert, so she organised to catch up with him through his road manager and was given tickets for herself, her boyfriend Francois Ravand, Martin and Dave for the Sydney Entertainment Centre concert on 17 February.

Said Dave, 'Marianne was to meet up with Dylan before the concert and from memory we needed to be at the back stage of the Entertainment Centre around 7.00pm. Marianne and Francois met up at Wirian prior to the meet-up time and Francois drove us there. Marianne went in on her own to meet up with Dylan. Francois, Martin and I went to grab some dinner before the show. We met up with Marianne just before show time and we had great seats.

'The show was amazing with Dylan in fine form. Whilst we and the packed Entertainment Centre were cheering for the encore we were interrupted by a torch shining down on us and at first I thought it was security and Martin had lit up a smoke or something, as he was prone to do anytime, anywhere. It was in fact Dylan's road manager asking us to come with him to the back stage area where we were all escorted up to the side stage area in time to see Dylan's encores of *Blowin' In The Wind* and *All Along The Watchtower*. Marianne was truly in awe and dutifully stood out in front of us on the stage to watch. As Dylan and band walked off stage after the encore, Marianne raced over to Dylan with us in tow. He gave her a hug, shook my hand while Martin stood back. In reflection, Martin's mood the following couple of days, he either regretted not coming over to speak to Dylan or he truly thought Dylan would recognise him and acknowledge him!' [26]

*

When cousin Sandy Sharp came up with the idea of a group exhibition of Sharps, Martin took to it instantly. Called '4 Sharps On A Flat Wall' the four exhibiting Sharps were cousins Martin, Roslyn, Sandy and Sandy's wife Yoli Salmona Sharp. Musician/cousin Kate Reid (Sandy's sister) composed a piece in the key of E Minor (four sharps). So it was really '5 Sharps'. Martin loved being part of a family, 'It's amazing how all these threads come together because it was like a tidal wave of Sharps!' (27)

Sandy was a program classifier for ABC television and photographer, Roslyn worked as a commercial photographer and radiographer, and Yoli had moved from fashion design to painting. 'All our fathers were doctors,' Sandy told the press. 'Martin's father was a Macquarie Street dermatologist, Sandy and Kate's father was a heart surgeon and Roslyn's was a radiologist.' Sandy felt it was their unconventional mothers who brought creativity into their lives.

One day Sandy said to Yoli, 'If ever I die before having an exhibition of photographs, would you organise an exhibition?' She replied, 'Why don't you do it now and have a group show?'

Roslyn joked, 'We weren't sure if we wanted Martin in the show and he asked to be in'.

Martin said, 'They were a bit tentative about asking me because they thought I might say no. I said yes. It's nice working with family.'

Sandy and Roslyn's photographs were well represented, as were Yoli's paintings. Martin exhibited cells from Sarah Weybourne's Scrapbook that he had collaged in 1974 for the film *Picnic at Hanging Rock*. ('God is Love'). The exhibition was held at The Depot Gallery, Waterloo, Sydney. (28)

There was a new CD project at Wirian too. While flicking through Arthur Rackman's illustrations for *Cinderella* (1919), Martin found a silhouette image of a King that resembled Tiny wearing a crown. Martin had the image blown up poster-size and came up with the thought that 'Elvis was the King, Tiny was the King-for-a-Day'. This became the concept behind the unfinished *King For a Day* CD. (29)

Said Dave, 'In that house there were many compilations and projects that we were going to do that never surfaced. *King for a Day* was one that Martin was really keen on. Martin took 'king' to mean Jesus but the project never saw the light of day.' (30)

Greg Weight won the 2003 Australian Photographic Portrait Prize with 'Railway Blues' a portrait of Jim Conway, in a wheelchair, on the railway track, harmonica in hand, ready-for-music.

At the New Theatre Newtown, towards the close of 2003, Jeannie launched *Southheart*, her new double CD. Inside, she thanked Martin, 'for constant creative pointers and poetry'. (31) Martin was present at the launch but Dave wasn't. Despite having worked with Jeannie on the mastering, Dave copped another kidney stone, which put him out of circulation for quite a while. Wendy left too, so all of a sudden the film editing room had no one working in it. No more *King for a Day*, no more film. Maybe it was time for change, the Liverpool Biennal and Big O Posters, got Martin mulling over his past. Ginger Baker, Jack Bruce and Eric were back on speaking terms and they were speaking about Cream.

'London' simply would not go away. *Art Monthly Australia* featured Philippe Mora's article 'Culture Shock: Australians in London in the Sixties' about his Pheasantry days. Philippe wrote, 'My role in all of this as a young artist was not particularly important, but I was a witness and a participant, and I had a productive time'. He looked back on living with Martin and Eric at the Pheasantry, George Harrison dropping in, exhibitions at Clytie Jessop's gallery in Kings Road Chelsea, meeting Peter Sellars – a real trip down memory lane with some previously unpublished photos. [32]

With OZ magazine celebrating its 40th anniversary, Nick Waterlow, curator Ivan Dougherty Gallery, put together an exhibition called *Larrikins in London* featuring people with an Aussie creative presence in London in the 60s. Waterlow made a generous list of creative Aussies in London, comprising a Who's Who that stretched the definition of 'Australian' to the max. For example, he included John Lennon because John wrote a song called *God Save OZ*. [33] And Yoko too, because she wrote *Do The OZ*. David Hockney because he drew nude full frontal sketches of the naughty OZ trio Richard, Jim and Felix. And Felix, because he worked with the Aussies.

The Larrikins were: Phillip Adams, Jim Anderson, Bruce Beresford, Ace Bourke, Clem Browne, Caroline Coon, Tom Cowan, Cream, John Crittle, Felix Dennis, Kerry Dundas, The Easybeats, Louise Ferrier, Andrew Fisher, Nicholas Garland, Juno Gemes, Germaine Greer, Barbara Hanrahan, Rolf Harris, David Hockney, Laurence Hope, Danne Emerson Hughes, Robert Hughes, Barry Humphries, Clive James, Clytie Jessop, Bronwyn Stevens Jones, Jenny Kee, Vern Lambert, Colin Lanceley, Kay Lanceley, John Lennon, Freya Matthews, Master's Apprentices, Mike Molloy, Philippe Mora, Lewis Morley, John Mortimer, Jill Neville, Richard Neville, Mike Newman, Sidney Nolan, Jane Norris, Jane Oehr, Yoko Ono, Michael Ramsden, John Rendall, Geoffrey Robertson, Marsha Rowe, Normie Rowe, Lilian Roxon, The Seekers, Martin Sharp, Garry Shead, Peter Smalley, Albie Thoms, Noel Tovey, The Twilights, Richard Walsh, Robert Whitaker, Brett and Wendy Whiteley.

Clive James' closing footnote in the accompanying booklet read, 'Dear Nick Waterlow – I am definitely not interested in being included in the Larrikin exhibition, which I think is a thoroughly bad idea.' [34]

# 14.
# CHANGING
# DIMENSIONS

*For some time I had been thinking about a reunion of Cream and given the fact that we were all still capable of playing together, I thought it would be fitting to pay tribute to ourselves while we still could.*
Eric Clapton

With 2003-2004 came a surge of interest in Martin's late-60s art, partly because his return to London had stoked old sparks and partly – maybe mostly – because Cream was reforming after 25 years apart. The cover of their Martin-designed second album *Disraeli Gears* came up again and again: book cover, CD cover, 4-CD boxed set, DVD and eventually a print. [1]

Swinging London! Big O Posters wanted to reissue Sharp product in London and Liverpool. The 2004 Liverpool Biennial wanted to exhibit his London years. A TV camera crew was sent from BBC in England to Australia to interview him about that period. [2] And Belgian radio personality, Johann Rai, flew to Sydney and interviewed Martin about – yep - those London years. In each retelling, Martin never lost his spontaneity, making it sound fresh each time. [3]

At last, Martin conceded what he'd previously tried not to admit - that *Disraeli Gears* was indisputably his best-known work. He likened it to the way the image of *Demoiselles d'Avignon* flashes to mind whenever Picasso's name gets mentioned. [4]

As usual, Martin was more interested in his current works than in revisiting his past. Either way, he was certainly not in any shape to catch a flight if required in Liverpool or London. Health issues were in the background of everything that happened to Martin over the next two years, indeed for the rest of his life. He hadn't even kept his Medicare card up-to-date, and he needed it when he suffered a perennial abscess. Richard helped out with the forms and got him a new card. That abscess required a brief stint at the Prince of Wales Hospital where the doctor insisted Martin quit smoking, which he did for a time. 'I felt it gave me up. I was dedicated to it or it was dedicated to me, I just didn't need to smoke any more'. (5)

Martin spent New Year's Day 2004 sketching a 'toon for the front page of the next morning's *Sydney Morning Herald*. The city councillors wanted to disguise their smelly cross-city tunnel with a work of art. That was their news peg. The editor commissioned Martin and two other artists to contribute whimsical or satirical impressions. Martin drew a b/w chimneystack with the word 'Eternity' wrapped around it and named it *Smokestack Eternity*. He faxed it to the editor, who faxed back that he wanted it coloured. Martin simply made 'Eternity' yellow and that was that. (6)

Like Cranbrook School, there was always a new hassle with Luna Park. Martin wrangled with the committee and, to their credit, they didn't write him off and he didn't write them off. Martin returned all the memorabilia rescued from the tip after the 1981 auction and sold back the items he'd bought, like the Joy Wheel and the Turkey Trot. (7) There was a general agreement that a memorial should be placed on the site and Martin submitted the Eternity motif as his contribution. He said, 'I felt right at the beginning - eternity was there. Just set a plaque into Eternity. Eternity would be the best one.' Martin had originally favoured a green park, 'Maybe seven years ago, I thought the park should become gardens, I still think that's more valuable than an amusement park.' (8)

Six weeks later a dutiful-looking memorial was dedicated on the site. Set against a red wall, the plaque read, 'This building stands on the site of the Ghost Train, destroyed by fire on the night of Saturday 9 June 1979 with the loss of seven lives. John Godson, Damien Godson, Craig Godson, Richard Carroll, Michael Johnson, Jonathan Billings and Seamus Rahilly. They are remembered.' A more attractive memorial was dedicated in August 2007. The sculpture was located in Art Barton Park, near Cliff Street Milsons Point and designed by Peter Kingston and Michael Leunig. It read, 'To all those who take refuge in this place to make a small commitment to the protection of children as they play.'

Martin continued his concerns about indigenous Australians. He played a cassette of 'Aboriginal Prophets', watched a DVD that celebrated the life and ministry of Auntie Ella Gordon and read a biography of Pemulwuy, the leader of the Eora people who lived in the area occupied by the city of Sydney.' (9) Martin conferred with Kay Cook on indigenous issues arising from the book and he reworked Gulpilil's portrait. (Gulpilil was the subject of the winner of the 2004 Archibald Prize, Craig Ruddy.)

There was also a surge of interest coming from England, Martin was asked to write about those years. He muttered, 'I'm trying to get together something for the Biennal in Liverpool next year – that's 2004...' As usual, he spent a long time ordering his thoughts. A two-page letter might take three days to complete. He'd write a bit, paint a bit, smoke a bit and come back to the writing.

Martin began this account with a false memory. For some misguided reason he thought late-50s boy-singer Laurie London hailed from Liverpool. (Laurie London came from Bethnal Green, East London.) Martin got an assistant to track Laurie London on Google Images. He printed off his picture and taped it to the wall. Martin started this memoir with, 'The first time I ever heard of Liverpool was in 1958 when Laurie London, a 13-year old black kid from Liverpool, had a hit with *He's Got the Whole World in His Hands*. I'd like to do a multi-media exhibition tracing my interest in Liverpool from Laurie London. Five years later the Beatles erupt out of Liverpool, break the domination of America on the popular music scene. The Beatles had something to do with Tiny being in England – that show at the Albert Hall was for a big charity called Cornerstone, like a showbiz charity gala night, and boy it was packed!' [10]

Martin surely must have foreseen that the Liverpool exhibition was never going to come off. The original curator wanted a Martin Sharp show only, no Tiny. Then the curator's marriage fell apart and so did he. Someone else took over, someone with even less interest in Tiny.

3 April - Harold the Kangaroo died. And Les? She was doing well running her own cleaning business. She was no longer known as Les Bean.

In August Gary Shearston's CD launch concert was held at Almost Acoustic, a folk music venue in Rozelle - the concert planned with Carrl Myriad, the one for which Martin had intended to do a poster. Martin was looking forward to attending. Instead he did well to stay home. He woke up feeling strange. It was a sensation he had previously experienced but on a lesser scale. There were other people in the house but none within earshot. Should he call for help? Or, should he ring 000? He thought not. He feared a worse attack if he moved. He didn't want to go downstairs, open the door and let the ambos in.

Instead he went back to sleep, woke up and felt okay. Next morning, he saw a GP. Roslyn explained, 'Martin got dropped off at Dr Hansen in Oxford Street, who must have done an ECG and told him he had to go straight to St Vincent's Hospital. He'd a small heart attack.' [11] Martin picked up the story, 'I went down to Emergency but it had moved. That's when I felt really bad - it was hard to get back up the hill to find Emergency. In Emergency they have a great big room, beds all around, anything and everything comes in the door. It's a fascinating place, all sorts of drama going on. They all rush. You're suddenly very impressed. One of the nurses said, "It's good you came here, this is God's own hospital". Someone else said, "Your heart rate's gone through the roof. This is going to hurt when we inject this into your heart." Then I went up to some ward upstairs. It was a new kind of social life made up of patients in extremis, doctors, nurses, tea-ladies, wardsmen - a whole other world. I was their guest.

'They do an exploratory. You're not unconscious. They stick a machine up your groin, going up an artery to your heart and they pump stuff in that they can film – quite a bizarre experience. They can see the state of your heart arteries. Then they decide what they're going to do. If you're lucky they put in a stent. Apparently I needed more attention than that. The Registrar said, "We've got to do a triple by-pass. We cut you open here, put you on this heart/lung machine while we operate on your heart…"

'He told me it would take 12 hours. I wasn't feeling up to going through that sort of operation. I said, "Oh? I think I'll go home," and his face looked so sad – sad that all he had to offer was being rejected. They let me stay for a few days to think about it. My cousin Philip (ie. Dr Philip Sharp) who's a surgeon, said it was a good operation and I should seriously consider going through with it. There was a lovely Chinese doctor with a long plait, very attractive. She was the one who talked me into it.

'The operation pushes you right to the edge of existence. On one level I thought I might go – pass away – or whatever it's called. I thought I might change dimension. You shift into a space with a different set of priorities. I didn't worry about the work or leaving a big mess behind - it's not the problem of the dying or the sick. I didn't have any ego or ambition towards finishing because I'd done what I could. I'd done my best. I thought it's not my concern any more. Then I slowly started to come back to life and I groaned inwardly because I thought, "Oh god, I've got to get back to all those problems again". I'm glad I'm back but at the time I wasn't so pleased. It's very uncomfortable and you really want to get away from the discomfort.

'They have to do it all in one go. It's very intrusive. They take arteries out of your leg, your breastbone - spliced into your heart. You are disconnected from your heart and lungs and put onto a machine. That's when they said you might have some dreams, surreal experiences. They said, "You might see things" so I thought, "Oh? I'll keep my eyes open if anything crops up". And I did. I took some notes. I did a few little sketches. I did a drawing for one of the nurses.' (12)

Roslyn added, 'Martin wrote extensively about how he felt about the heart attack. He was very interested because he had terrible hallucinations, which is a common occurrence with people who've had triple by-passes.' [13] Martin always took hallucinations seriously.

Martin eased back into Wirian. He seemed weak but well. He quit smoking again and proudly showed off the 18-inch cut on his left leg. George's film *Soundtrack to War* was televised and well received. Greg's *Portrait of George* was hung in the National Portrait Gallery Canberra. Garry and Luke dropped in with baguettes, camembert and conversation. And Martin's fisherman friend, Allan Broadhurst came to Sydney from Bermagui and presented Martin with a tiny abalone shell that Martin wanted embedded into the bottom of his *Abalone Diver* picture frame.

They got chatting about heart attacks. (Allan had one shortly before Martin.) Martin drained every detail of the subject, which was certainly not what Allan had expected. He expected something about Art. Allan said, 'It's amazing how people from such diverse fields suddenly find something in common through calamity. "Let's talk heart attacks - what sort of tablets are you on?"' (14)

Since Tiny's passing there had been a worldwide surge of interest in the ukulele instrument. It seemed that every community had its own uke-group - Newcastle had its Ukestra, the Blue MUGS were the Blue Mountains Uke Group, Mandurah had Manuleles, Melbourne had their Ukulele Kollective, etc. Such groups were peppered all over Australia, England and America. Greg Weight and Carol Ruff ran Gallery East, East Clovelly, exhibiting many fine artists. With 'Coral Reef' as her charming stage name, Carol was a uke player too. She and Greg decided on a uke-themed exhibition with ukuleles painted by 50 artists including Martin, Greg, Mic, Garry, Reg Mombassa, Bruce Goold, etc.

It was a welcome success. Along with Phil Donnison and Cazzbo Johns, Mic and Jim Conway performed on an outside stage, joined by uke virtuoso Azo Bell. Carol performed a few songs too. There was a festive air. The crowd spilled onto the road and blocked traffic. The Police eased everyone back to the pavement. Kate Ceberano, The Sandman, H G Nelson were there too. Martin was expected. His painted uke was hung (with tulips) and he had posed for publicity shorts with Greg and Carol. So where was he tonight?

Later in the evening Kingo announced that Martin had suffered a stroke and was back in hospital. It had happened at midnight the previous Saturday night, after Martin had taken leave of a party. He was walking up the driveway and attempted to say something to the people with him, but the words didn't come out right. Martin surmised that they probably thought he was alcohol-affected and offered to drive him home. They saw no improvement in him when he got out of the car, so they took him straight to St Vincent's Hospital. Martin said, 'I could understand what they were saying, but what I thought I was going to say and what I actually said were not combining. And I understood that when people look at you like you're a bit weird, you know that they're thinking things aren't right.' Martin had had a small stroke which he felt was related to his triple bypass operation, 'some little clots drifting around inside get stuck somewhere. It was like having a slightly defective video machine in one's brain - sticking and picking up the correct speed again.' (15)

The doctors asked a few questions. Martin got his name right and correctly stated that he lived in Wirian with the Cranbrook School next door. But for his address he wrote, '3 Coyagbictricovyn'. They checked him in immediately. He said, 'They put me on this strong de-coagulant which worked pretty fast.' (16) Roslyn explained, 'He was one of the first patients to be given the clot-dissolving drug that you have to give within three hours of a stroke. He was given it and he made a complete recovery.' (17) With a window view, Martin was okay about this hospital stint. He hated the food first time around, this time he looked forward to meals. He stayed in his room, read a John La Carré novel and sketched.

When he got home, Martin felt slightly impaired – not that anyone noticed. 'I think I'm a little bit disabled, sometimes when I walk I veer to the left a bit.' (18) Martin painted a bit and watched TV a lot. He watched the new Azaria film, with Miranda Otto as Lindy and Craig McLachlan as Michael. He watched tennis and he always watched the news. His music of choice was Archie Roach and Ruby Hunter's Opera House concert. In the film editing room, Wendy was gone and there was no sign of Dave. Marilyn was back as Martin's assistant, followed by Sam Reid, a cousin's son. Sam won the 2003 Justin O'Brien Art Prize in his final Cranbrook year.

Chaudry, Steven Darmody and Robert Tilley were around the house. Martin was back to eating at *Arte e Cucino* with Kay and Luke and a wall was constructed outside the kitchen window just beyond the *porte cochère*. It was built to accommodate a 'thank you' by Lin Utzon. First the wall was erected. Next the ceramic tiles arrived from Europe. Then they then had to wait for Lin to return to affix the tiles. Willy was living there at the time, Lin's wall was built shortly before he lost faith in the Healing Ministry. Canon Glennon – the healer - died 11 June 2005.

Robert explained, 'Willy was involved in Canon Jim Glennon's healing ministry. Glennon's brand of healing was akin to a kind of Christian Science/New Age idea that if one believed one was well then one would become well. He lost his faith in that ministry not because of Glennon's death (which I think was related to his asthma, but he was old). It was because a couple of people who had cancer and were involved in the ministry showed what appeared to be great faith but nevertheless died. Willy later joined his older brother José who was and is a very big developer of real estate programs. Willy and José are based in Argentina.' (19)

\*

Thirteen years after their induction into the Rock n Roll Hall of Fame, Eric decided to reunite Cream because – as Martin explained, 'They're one of the bands that can – because they're all still living!' (20) Jack gave everyone a scare when he underwent liver transplant surgery the previous year. That crisis behind him, he was back on bass. In his autobiography Eric wrote, 'For some time I had been thinking about a reunion of Cream. It had been almost forty years since the creation of the band, and given the fact that we were all still capable of playing together, I thought it would be fitting to pay tribute to ourselves while we still could. I was also very aware that I had always been the reluctant one on this score so, cap in hand, I made some delicate enquiries as to whether Jack and Ginger would be interested.' (21)

Would Martin be attending the Cream reunion concert? 'If my health's good enough I'd love to go. It's great that they're getting back together again. It's really going to be something because they're very comfortable in the Albert Hall – it's their venue. I saw Tiny there – so there's a bit of an echo.' (22)

Cream booked three weeks of rehearsals. If the rehearsals went badly, they would cancel. The opposite happened, it came together so quickly that they didn't need the whole three weeks. Their four Albert Hall concerts sold out within two hours. Fans came from America and Japan, some paying over $2000 on eBay to see the band. Later Cream played Madison Square Garden, which is when Ginger and Jack got back to arguing just like old times.

The concert was released as a double-CD and a double-DVD. Caps, t-shirts, limited edition screen posters and other merchandise were sold at venues and online, many of them featured Martin's images. A biography of the band was published in 2005, acknowledging Martin's valued contribution. [23]

Having gloriously survived – or endured – the revival, Ginger and Jack weren't required to play together again. The type of thing they argued about was – say - the rhythmic phrasing of a song. They didn't have to do that any more, they could just reminisce to camera crews about the good times. They didn't even need to be in the same room to do that.

British TV documentary series *Classic Albums* created the *Disraeli Gears Story* for MTV and DVD formats. *Tales of Brave Ulysses* appeared twice on that DVD. The filmmakers interviewed a wide group of contributors - the band members of course, and others like lyricist/poet Pete Brown. They flew a film crew to Australia to interview Martin. In his Inner Sanctum, seated in front of his paintings of Hendrix, Gulpilil, and a print of *Disraeli Gears*, Martin retold his story for the camera. Martin and Eric's accounts were later spliced together.

'I was at the Speakeasy one night, just hanging out,' said Eric. 'I was dating this girl Charlotte Martin, a very beautiful French lady and I think she knew Martin. She introduced me to him. We started talking and we hit it off. He was a designer and an artist. He painted and drew pictures for a magazine called OZ. Martin had written these lyrics on this sheet of paper and Jack found a way to sing them over this riff.'

Martin teased, '*Strange Brew* was the A-side. I was a bit disappointed *Tales of Brave Ulysses* was on the B-side!' As for the cover Martin dismissed it as '…quite simple really. I'm glad they liked it'. [24]

A box of Martin's newly printed Big O postcards arrived from London. Martin was mostly pleased but not totally. Unhappily one of the cards was a poster he did for Cream. Martin ripped it up calling it 'the ugliest thing I've ever done!' The rest was fine. [25]

Again from London, Felix Dennis launched a poetry and pictures magazine, *The Illustrated Ape*, in which he featured eight of Martin's images, mostly as full-page illustrations. Martin shared cover lines with John Lennon, David Hockney, WB Yeats and Rudyard Kipling. [26] He painted a big red heart for the cover of Felix's *Lives and Rhymes* poetry CD that came with the magazine. [27] Felix, that bearded scamp from London OZ trials, had reinvented himself first as a hugely successful businessman and now as a poet. With a publishing empire worth $750 million, who was going to argue? Felix arrived at poetry readings in a helicopter and served only the finest wines. His tour was called 'And Did I Mention the Free Wine?'

Martin must have been flavour of the month because, writing for the London *Guardian*, even Robert Hughes had a piece of Martin, 'Where is Martin Sharp whose weird drawings used briefly to lighten the images of the long-defunct OZ magazine? (Answer: back in Australia, an acid casualty, still said to be pursuing his 20-year fantasy of making a film about the justly forgotten entertainer, Tiny Tim with his greasy ringlets and stupid little plastic ukulele, wherever he may now be).' [28] Martin chuckled about Hughes over the phone to Richard. 'I don't think he ever forgave me for beating him in Chess!' Martin laughed.

As part of the 2005 Queen's Birthday Honours, Martin was awarded the Order of Australia medal. The Old Establishment guys didn't nominate Martin - it was Luke. Disinclined to accept, Martin told the press, 'When the letter came, my postie could tell what it was. He insisted I take it. He's a wonderful postie so I felt I should.' [29]

Privately he explained his hesitation, 'I'd always thought it was wrong for artists to have Orders of Australia or knighthoods. Bureaucrats can't really judge those things. They give it - not for the things I consider most important I guess - just the things you'd do normally. Maybe for not dying! I said to the postie, "I don't know if I should take it". Anyway, the postie said, "You've got to take it for your grandfather". The Order of Australia is most commonly presented to artists and writers. There's three different degrees - this is the least honourable of the honours. I think they gave it to me for the Yellow House. Pop Art was one of the things mentioned - and maybe for encouraging young artists. Now I've got to encourage young artists!' [30]

In September, Martin attended the launch of Margaret Olley's new biography at the Art Gallery of New South Wales – *Far From A Still Life* by Meg Stewart. Barry Humphries launched it. Martin parked along Mrs Macquarie's Chair Road, a short walk from the gallery. He arrived exhausted. One of his lungs was playing up. The two Richards – Neville and Walsh - stayed in touch with Martin during this period of ill health.

Abe Saffron too was on the decline. Ritchie Walsh wrote an article in which he affirmed, 'there are two Abe Saffrons'. Ritchie depicted Abe One as the notorious owner of strip joints and other dubious enterprises. Abe Two, he wrote, was a part-time philanthropist, which is how Abe would like to be remembered. Martin read it to guests. As for Richard Neville? Martin chuckled when he told Martin that he'd figured out that he was descended from Shakespeare. 'Richard likes Shakespeare,' laughed Martin. 'When we were in Asia he used to recite Shakespeare to all these bewildered children!' [31]

Martin visited Braidwood NSW where he stayed with an old school friend, also called Martin. They were trying to save a church and – unusually for Martin – he made a public speech for the cause. (32) Martin turned his attention to church art. Religious themes combined with Indigenous themes in his new pictures, like the cross Martin painted in the colours of the Aboriginal flag. It was one of the few sculptures Martin ever made. Steve Darmody did the carpentry. He said, 'I had an idea of doing the Aboriginal colours on the cross – a bit like a Mondrian.' (33) Father Ted Kennedy was the priest of Redfern, some of the Aboriginal ladies from his church took Martin's cross to Rome at the beatification of Mary McKillop. Did they remain at the Vatican? Martin didn't know, 'I don't know what happened to those crosses. I'm sure they're doing okay. Vincent said, "A good picture does good wherever it is" – I love that line.' (34)

Built in 1885, St Saviour's Anglican Church Redfern was an innovative church, keen on community outreach. Cartoonist Reg Lynch organised an art exhibition there and contacted Martin. Martin agreed to lend his big Eternity canvas as a centrepiece. The newspaper reported, 'St Saviours Church is open for prayer and meditation during the week and no doubt many people will find Martin Sharp's painting an inspiration'. (35)

In America, Ernie Clark kept interest in Tiny alive via his website. He attracted filmmakers who were interested in making a biopic. Ernie was initially asked to write it, before being switched to 'adviser to the writer'. Jeff Goldblum was reported to have an interest in playing Tiny. (Then he wasn't.) Casting around for someone else, some thought John Turturro would be perfect.

The film project remained in the air for most of the year, with Ernie and Martin swapping ideas over the phone. One of the things Martin told Ernie was that it peeved him that Tiny was not inducted into the Rock N Roll Hall of Fame nor ever likely to be. Ernie thought the Ukulele Hall of Fame seemed more realistic and worked that front. After all, when people thought 'uke', sooner or later they thought 'Tiny'. Ukulele magazines featured articles about the type of uke he played and how unusual the instrument was in the 60s and 70s. Tiny was given a good spread in a recent book, *The Ukulele, A Visual History* by Jim Beloff. (36) All this revitalisation of Tiny stimulated Martin, 'I must get something out,' he said, 'not as a response to the movie but as a duty'. (37)

At this stage, the most efficient way of 'getting something out' was Satoshi's idea. On behalf of Martin, he entered into negotiations with Japanese company, Zero Communications. The initial interest was in releasing the *Chameleon* CD only. (Satoshi had his own online company too, Mojo Associates Fine Art, from which he sold a range of Martin's prints and posters.) Before the year was out, Zero compiled a limited edition 7-track demo of selections from *Chameleon, Wonderful World of Romance* and the *Pop* Album. The planned release date for the three albums was to coincide with the 10$^{th}$ Anniversary of Tiny's passing. (38)

*

Martin was precisely three days older than Roger Foley (Ellis D Fogg). And Luke approached Roger with a plan, 'Foggy - you've got to have a *When I'm 64* party!' Not keen at first, Roger softened when Luke suggested a combined Martin-Roger birthday event. Martin was happy to share his birthday with Roger but he didn't want to do the inviting because he feared leaving anybody out. Luke wasn't sure whom to invite either, so Roger stepped in and said, 'I know who your real friends are Martin... I'll take the flak!' Martin said, 'O good Foggy, I'll leave it up to you'.

For the venue, Roger suggested the old harbourmasters' cottage at Green Point, which was ideal. Along with his wife Francesca, Roger invited Jeannie Lewis, Tim Lewis, Albie Thoms, Louise Ferrier, Richard Neville, Peter Kingston, Luke Sciberras and Jim Anderson, who photographed the occasion. Roger said, 'We had a great party. A lot of the people who are Martin's friends influenced my life from an early age.' [39]

More than 30 years after opening the main building, Queen Elizabeth II returned to the Sydney Opera House to open a new colonnade addition. Martin was there with Lin and Jan Utzon (architect Jorn Utzon's children). He was 'very impressed' with the Queen who said it was fitting that the world-famous structure was now being considered for world heritage listing. Jan Utzon told the Opera House crowd that his 88-year old architect father who designed the building was disappointed he was unable to attend but sent his warmest regards. His father was pleased to have reconciled the differences over the building and to have the opportunity to work on it again, 'He (Jorn Utzon) is too old by now to take the long flight to Australia. But he lives and breathes the Opera House and as its creator he just has to close his eyes to see it. He also wishes to thank the many people who have supported him over the years, notably the famous Sydney architect Harry Seidler, who sadly passed away a few days ago'. [40]

Wednesday 10 May 2006: fire destroyed St Barnabas Church Ultimo. Built in 1859, St Barnabas' Anglican Church was famous as the church where Arthur Stace converted to the Christian faith. The landmark church burned down in less than three hours. Firefighters were called at 3.30am but could do nothing to save it. [41]

Greg Weight married artist Carol Ruff in Central Australia and Martin took the trip to Alice Springs and was Best Man. While in the centre, Martin visited the grave of the pioneer of indigenous art, Albert Namatjira. Greg and Carol also took Martin to Hermannsberg Lutheran Mission where Namatjira started to paint seriously at the age of 32 in 1934.

In September-November, Martin and Kingo held a joint installation at the Art Gallery of New South Wales. Titled, *Notes from the River Caves*, it was a collaborative cupboard of curiosities, a mini-museum of Luna Park memorabilia and other kitsch collectibles. It featured Kingo's England V Australia chess set (ie. Dame Edna, Ned Kelly, Norman Gunston, etc) V the Royal Family + corgis. Martin's pictures include some of his earliest works as well as *Abalone Diver, Miss World, Al Jolson, Swanee/Ginge, Donovan* and *Snow Job*.

As her health deteriorated, Martin's stepmother Dorothy moved from her Neutral Bay home to Lulworth in Elizabeth Bay. During this time Martin often consulted Roslyn. She said, 'It started with phone calls to talk about Dorothy before she died and when she went into Lulworth and it all centred about how he should care for her.' After Dorothy died, celebrity chef, Kylie Kwong cooked at the wake. For this kindness, Martin gave her the *Courage My Friend* print. [42] Dorothy left an unacceptable will that would entangle Martin in legal matters over the next two years.

Abe Saffron was also fading. Speaking in her role as a radiographer, Roslyn said, 'I started x-raying Abe Saffron at St Vincent's when he was really sick. I took his chest x-ray the day before he died. I told Martin.' [43] Abe Saffron died 15 September 2006.

In October the City of Sydney held its *Art & About* festivities, with displays of art and photography at Customs House, Circular Quay, many galleries and various locations. Especially interesting this year was 'The Face of Sydney' theme. Martin's face of Gulpilil was commissioned for street banners, posters, invitations, newspaper ads as well cover of the *Art & About* booklet, of which thousands were printed. The original portrait was also on display. [44]

Marianne Faithfull and Martin stayed in regular touch over the phone. He described the conversations as 'very loving'. One night Marianne phoned in a state of high anxiety. Test results showed she had breast cancer and her response was to undergo surgery. The press didn't know yet, only Martin and a few close friends. She spoke to Martin at length about her fears. She wasn't ready to 'change dimension' (as Martin put it) yet. Marianne got through the surgery and made a complete recovery. When she was ready, she went public and told the press about her ordeal, 'I didn't realise how many true friends I had. I feel so lucky and loved.' [45]

She sent Martin a demo copy of her newest CD *Before the Poison*. Someone else sent Martin a copy of Bob Dylan's 'Theme Time Radio Hour' a one-hour radio program in which Dylan introduced a selection of obscure and not-so-obscure songs. Dylan called this selection 'Flowers' and it got sent to Martin because Dylan selected *Tiptoe* as one of the featured songs. It came too late…Martin was through liking Dylan. In his Memoirs Dylan wrote about his Greenwich Village period and described one venue as full of 'Tiny Tim-type people', which Martin interpreted as a sneer. He said Dylan was 'mean-spirited' and stopped listening to him. [46]

After an intense career as a public sculptor, Tom Bass was holding a retrospective exhibition and the *Daily Telegraph* revisited the famous OZ cover where a youthful Martin, Richard and Ritchie supposedly pissed into Bass's water feature. To help publicise the exhibition they agreed to reprise the shot with Bass in the foreground, which was how Martin, Richard and Ritchie understood it would appear. But the editor cut Bass out of the picture and turned into an OZ story instead. Martin was furious, 'I was upset for Tom. He was a witness in our favour in the trial, so when we got called to help him with some publicity, we agreed to do it. We were publicising his exhibition.' [47]

Albie's films were screened, as was Tiny's marathon at Martin's next exhibition at Ivan Dougherty Gallery. The catalog was an impressive booklet with an introduction by Richard and an interview by curator Nick Waterlow. Martin exhibited his earliest pictures from childhood and high school days and brought viewers right up to date. New works included *The Toff 2, Abalone Diver, Babylon the Great is Fallen* and *Reprise of Giorgio de Chirico's Song of Love*. The face in the latter would gradually evolve into Elvis over the succeeding years. Titled 'Love Me Tender' in this exhibition and it was finally retitled 'Graceland'. [48]

# 15.
# HIPPIE HIPPIE SHOCK

*Martin: I'm in 55 scenes and none of them happened.*
*Richard: But Mart, it reads well…*

In November 2004, Aboriginal Palm Island resident Cameron Doomadgee was allegedly causing a public nuisance and died within one hour of being picked up by the Police. He had a ruptured liver, which suggests that he copped a severe beating. The autopsy report did not state cause of death and a riot erupted when this was made public. The local courthouse, police station and police barracks were burned down. Eighteen local police and their families were forced to flee and barricade themselves in the hospital. Eighty police from Townsville and Cairns were flown in to restore order.

In response to the riot, the Premier of Queensland, Peter Beattie, established the Palm Island Select Committee to investigate the issues. In December 2006 the Director of Public Prosecution (DPP) announced that no charges would be laid against an arresting officer whose punches were thought to be the cause of death.

Four weeks after that verdict, Bwgcolman woman, Maggie Walsh and teenage daughter Lorraine, left Palm Island and arrived in Sydney. On Gulpilil's recommendation, they came to Wirian. Lorraine stayed a short time, Maggie stayed longer. Maggie was born in Townsville in 1964. She was separated from her mother from the age of two when her mother was sent away to work. Maggie was raised by her mother's friends, they were women sent to Palm Island, away from their homes and families.

Maggie played guitar, sang and wrote poetry that she recited with conviction. She wrote about things she knew, like clubs, pokies and domestic issues. Maggie soon got to know other Indigenous Australians from The Block in Redfern. Some came to Wirian to visit her. Martin got to know them too. Sometimes he gave them money. Martin had a soft spot for Redfern. As a founding Member of the Australian Labor Party (ALP) in 1891, Martin's great-grandfather William Henry Sharp won the Seat of Redfern, which he held for three years on a Labor-Protectionist platform. [1]

Sticking with Indigenous themes, Martin's kept reworking Phil May's *A Curiosity in Her Own Country* (*The Bulletin*, 1888). May's black-and-white cartoon depicts an Indigenous mother and her child dressed in European-style clothes and seated in a city street. They are surrounded by rudely staring well-dressed onlookers, including a Chinese man. Martin titled this curious and troubling nativity scene *What Next?* This slowly evolving picture would re-emerge three years later in a blaze of colour as the cover of Sydney Morning Herald's *Spectrum* magazine (2009) and as a Christmas card sent to friends. Martin added a wild Starry Starry night sky, spinning prisms and halos on the Aboriginal Madonna-and-child. [2]

Martin was low on energy. Painting was okay because everything was set up in the Inner Sanctum and he only had to pick up a brush. He could do that while talking to visitors. The film and the *King for a Day* CD required more energy, and Martin took a break from them. He daubed a few canvasses, took short walks, drank herbal drinks and smoked the occasional cigar because he had quit cigarettes.

Late one morning a package arrived from Zero Communications Japan. It was packs of three new Tiny Tim CD releases – about to be made available in selected stores and via the Internet. Martin and Dave had battled to negotiate a CD release of *Chameleon* for ages and Satoshi made it happen. Not just *Chameleon,* but *Wonderful World of Romance* too, with bonus tracks. The third was a new concept called *Stardust.* Its 26 tracks were a mixture of studio recordings, informal minidisk recordings and a track sung in Luna Park's Floating Palace, 12 January 1979, the day of the marathon. Smartly packaged, each CD included a 16-page booklet in which Martin retold his story - from *Tales of Brave Ulysses* to Tiny's performance at an Australian worker's club - via the Royal Albert Hall. Martin's art was well represented in the booklets – *Hokusai's Wave, Boofhead Thinker, Eternity*, the *Chameleon* poster as well as a profile of Tiny wearing a crown, appropriated from Arthur Rackman. [3] Martin described Tiny as, 'The one singer who is all singers, the Spirit of Popular music made flesh'. [4]

The CDs sounded livelier because Dave remastered the original disks and in some instances, changed the mix. For example, he restored Gulpilil's clapping sticks and didge on the *Stayin' Alive* track. They were inaudible on the record. Dave and Satoshi were happy with all that but Martin wanted to do even more production work on *Chameleon*. He wanted to delay release and when he couldn't do that, he talked about it as if it was just a demo. Of course it was much more than that. *Chameleon* was the Tiny Tim record that Martin's friends had genuinely enjoyed, unlike the Brighton tapes that nobody played. [5]

After a year as Martin's assistant, Luke became a father. Said Gria, 'We were living in a tiny 2-bedroom flat with a baby. One of the rooms had been Luke's studio but when we had Stella there was no more studio. Two weeks before I had Stella I had my first show at Eva Breuer Gallery (Woollahra). I was painting until I gave birth. Luke's career took off the moment Stella was born so he had to have a studio. It was a tiny little section of Kingo's house where Luke was able to go and paint.' [6]

Later, Luke and Gria moved to Hill End, near Bathurst NSW, a former gold mining town that was a haven for artists ever since Russell Drysdale and Donald Friend discovered its charm in the 1940s. Hill End was home to several of Martin's creative collaborators in uni days - Peter Doring, the late Peter Wright, Mandy Wright and John Firth-Smith. Said Luke, 'I didn't move to Hill End to be surrounded by other artists or because of the town's reputation with previous artists. I moved here because I fell in love with the community'. [7]

Gria said, 'We bought Hill End together because Sydney rent was going out of control. We'd go back and forth because the place in Hill End had no running water and no toilet. We built it over years. Stella had to go to daycare in order for me to paint, so we straddled between the two places. We weren't staying in Wirian but Luke was still doing a bit of work for Martin here and there.' After 12 years together, Gria and Luke broke up. She moved to Woollahra and Luke continued to divide his time between Hill End and Sydney. [8]

Eric Clapton and his band returned to Australia for another tour and Eric called on Martin as part of his 2-day Sydney stopover. It was a quiet affair. Robert Tilley swept the verandah and Angelica snapped photos while Eric and Martin chatted like a couple of battle worn veterans. Peter Royles travelled from Goulburn – probably a six hour round trip - to play his rendition of *Wonderful Tonight* to Eric and get his autograph. Puzzled, Eric asked Martin, 'Why would anybody do that?' ('Because you're Eric Clapton' was the answer, I guess.) Eric was pleasant to everyone and everyone was calm, unlike his 1985 visit.

The royalty cheques from *Tales of Brave Ulysses* never missed a beat, as each new generation learned to enjoy Cream. But Dorothy's Will came as a shock, not just to Martin, but his friends and cousins too, with whom he openly discussed these matters. 'She's been got at' was the going phrase when it became known that Cranbrook School and St Paul's College were left bequests of $300,000 each. There were genuine grounds to suggest that Dorothy had been unduly influenced because the lawyer who drew up her Will was also the lawyer for Cranbrook School. Martin started procedures to contest the Will. It was a protracted legal struggle, putting Martin under considerable financial stress when he was physically at his weakest.

Said Roslyn, 'Dorothy paid off the mortgage in exchange that Martin would not get anything else. Martin told me she said that but he didn't think she would give everything away. Martin fought tooth and nail to get the Will drawn back at great expense. He fought it for the moral obligation. I went to the mediation court with him. I can't say what happened in there but he carved it back two Wills.' [9]

Judit Shead died nine months after being diagnosed with a virulent form of pancreatic cancer. Terrible.

Judit and Garry lived in Wirian while painting the Harris Street mural in the mid-80s. They moved to Bundeena where Judit helped Garry focus on his art. It paid off. Garry had become one of the nation's most respected figurative artists. Martin attended the opening of a combined Garry & Judit exhibition at Australian Galleries, commemorating Judit by featuring her beautiful sculptures and Garry's moving tributes. [10]

Back when Garry and Judit lived in Wirian, no major newspaper would touch Martin's theories about Abe Saffron and Luna Park. It was a surprise to all when the *Sydney Morning Herald* front-page featured an interview with Abe Saffron's niece, Anne Buckingham, who confirmed that her uncle was behind the Ghost Train fire. 'I don't think people were meant to be killed,' she told the news reporter. [11] The same writer followed her previous story in The (Sydney) Magazine. This article linked Saffron to the disappearance of Juanita Nielsen and reaffirmed the claim that Abe was the secret owner of Luna Park at the time of the fire.

In the years leading to his death, Abe Saffron had fought hard to clean up his shady reputation. He successfully won a defamation case against a Gold Coast newspaper that published a crossword clue: 'Sydney Underworld figure nicknamed Mr Sin' with Saffron as its answer. That didn't deter the *Sydney Morning Herald* running the headline, 'The sordid legacy of Abe "Mr Sin" Saffron'. [12]

*Gentle Satan* was the titled of Abe's son's biography about his father. That's quite a title, coming from someone trying to clear his father's name. Alan Saffron's tone was candid. He linked the murder of Juanita Nielsen to one of his father's associates (Big Jim) - nothing to do with Abe - and admitted owning over 100 machines at Luna Park at the time of the fire, but denied that his father had anything to do with subsequent events. He wrote, 'Any suggestion my father was involved in the tragic fire had already been contradicted by the police and fire department reports at the time. Sadly, on 25 May 2007, after my father's death, *The Sydney Morning Herald* revisited these horrible events with front-page headlines based on allegations from my cousin Anne Buckingham who accused my father of being behind the tragedy. She provided no corroborating facts and later recanted the story, saying it was taken out of context.' [13]

Anne Buckingham got people talking about the Ghost Train fire again. Interviewed on ABC Radio, Martin moderated his position about Saffron. He laid the ultimate blame on the city of Sydney itself, 'Look at the organisations that have been tested by it. Government – fail. Law courts – fail. Police – fail. Church

– they're still not talking to me about the fire. It couldn't have happened unless the city had been in a position to have it happen – meaning there was enough corruption and enough control of Police – enough to make it appear that it was kids mucking up, not big businessmen!' (14)

Roslyn had more to do with Saffron than anyone else in Martin's crowd. When she photographed him, her Sharp surname must have connected her to Martin in his mind? On one occasion, Roslyn attended a venue accompanied by another cousin, Andrew. There were only six tables in the room. One had a card 'reserved for Sharp' and beside it 'reserved for Saffron'. Did Saffron not notice?

Roslyn said, 'I met Abe Saffron about five times because I became friendly with Christine Knight, a character in the Cross. And I was photographing "characters" in the Cross. She would get a box of French champagne every week from Abe. She lived in Darling Point and when I was visiting to photograph her, Abe rang up when I was there and she put Abe on the phone. She said, "Tell him to come over and meet you."

'I met him again when we did this fantastic little film of the community centre and Edwin Duff - the Be-Bop jazz singer - interviewed Abe Saffron. He had worked for Abe for years as a singer. There was some fantastic footage. I'd been hassling the Community Centre to get all the rushes transcribed digitally because it was only on videotape and would deteriorate. We had a small screening of it at the Mansions Hotel. Abe came to that and I photographed him with Mandy Sayers. He was an old man then. Martin told me to watch out if anyone knew I was related to him. He said I could be at risk and he didn't want to put me at risk.' (15)

Richard's *Hippie Hippie Shake* had received mixed reviews – many critics loved it. The *Independent on Sunday* called it 'the perfect Sixties book'. The *Book Depository* described it as a 'hilarious, colourful and provocative memoir'. The *Sunday Times* reckoned it was 'utterly unputdownable'.

Jenny Diski, *London Review of Books*, wrote, '*Hippie Hippie Shake* (what a title, for goodness sake) includes a multitude of photographs of Richard Neville in his twenties, but none of him in middle age; the writing, too, tells of his adventures then, even his hesitations, but there's no sense of having moved on intellectually or emotionally, of the man reassessing the boy. The present is barely referred to beyond the fact that he lives back in Australia and has a wife and two children. Of course, what he's up to and thinking now isn't necessarily any of our business, and he may have actually intended to write a book that merely described the events that brought him to the dock of the Old Bailey rather than a thoroughgoing analysis of the period, but the time warped effect contributes to the slightness of the enterprise. A lot of grand thoughts were rolling around – counter-culture, revolution, alternative reality – but when all is said and done in Neville's recollection, it appears it was little more than a hiatus, an overextended gap year between school and real life.' (16)

Richard was reputed to have sold the film rights for a six-figure sum. A film company put $A32 million into it and hired first class young British actors. Sienna Miller played Louise and Cillian Murphy played Richard. Martin and others depicted in the film were unsettled that their lives were being sensationalised to suit whatever the screenwriter wanted the plot to do. The draft script also offended them because they saw themselves as artists not hippies, whereas the film was a thumbnail sketch of clichéd hippie behaviour. Scriptwriter Lee Hall (known for *Billy Elliot*) did whatever he liked with the personal lives of the characters. Germaine was portrayed as a joint-smoking nymphomaniac and Martin had sex with people he never had sex with. [17]

'They call it dramatic licence! I was involved in 55 scenes in this film and none of them happened!' Martin protested.'

'But Mart, it reads well,' Richard replied. [18]

Germaine was not happy. She slammed Richard as 'one of the least talented people of the London scene in the 60s' and described his book as a 'continuing search of the fame and fortune that continue to elude him'. She disapproved of the actress chosen to portray her - Emma Booth. [19]

Not as blunt as Germaine, Martin too was genuinely nervous about who was going to play him. The film people told him he was being 'difficult' but he swears he wasn't. Martin, and others, didn't want to sell out their identities at any price. Max Minghella was the young actor picked to play Martin. Born in 1985, Minghella made his debut in *Bee Season* (2005) before starring in *Art School Confidentia*l in 2006, which drew reasonable reviews. Nice guy, rising star, but it was inconceivable that he knew the 60s in depth. 'It's a theft of one's life,' Martin told the press, 'and it's a very uncomfortable feeling'. [20]

Philippe didn't like it either. From his Los Angeles home he wrote, 'if real names are being used, why not keep it factual? The script I read is a clichéd attack on artists and hippies.' More dissatisfaction arose when it was noted that (1) the film was funded by General Electric and (2) Australian actors were not used to play the Australians. Philippe continued, 'I don't think you can be against the war on terror, as Richard has continued to write, then go and sell your life story to General Electric'. [21]

To assuage the tension, film director Beeban Kidron flew to Sydney for meetings with Louise Ferrier, Jenny Kee, Jim Anderson and Martin. Martin accepted no money from the film company and came to no agreement, even though they would have written him a $25,000 cheque on the spot for a 'yes'. On her return to London, Kidron amended the script once again not to anyone's complete satisfaction. So it was amended again until it began to resemble a sieve patched with Band-Aids. The film was eventually shot in 2009. Director Kidron and husband-writer Lee Hall, left during post-production, citing artistic differences with the producers.

Martin felt he'd been trashed. He scoffed the clichéd hippie content, 'Obviously you can't be at a love-in if you're working hard.' (22) Talking to Felix Dennis on the phone, Martin complained, 'No research - not even based on Richard's book!' He told Felix that he hated being treated like a Chess piece in the film. 'In life, all you've got is your name!' (23)

Once Felix got involved, that was the end of the film. Felix, who started out as a London OZ street-seller, was on Britain's rich list. (No 64 – something like that.) He agreed with Martin, Philippe and Germaine. His net worth of $750 million ensured that he had the legal clout to ensure the film was dead in the water if that's what he wanted.

OZ was about personal freedoms and social consciousness. Felix 'got' that. He was a philanthropist, he was good to friends and he poured profits into planting one million trees on 20.000 acres of forest. The world was a better place for having Felix Dennis. When Judge Argyle pronounced Felix 'less intelligent' than his cohorts in the OZ trials, that old fogey could not see beyond Felix's long hair and beard. Dennis Publishing made Felix wealthy enough to proudly indulge whatever he wanted. He made no bones about his libertine ways, drug use and penchant for fine wines. And he said no to the film.

Another film was released around this time, one about the art of Luna Park, exactly the angle that suited the artists. *The Art of Fun* was a 45-minute documentary film about the Park funded by the North Sydney Heritage Centre/Stanton Library and directed, written and produced by Helen McGrath and Cris Parker. *The Art of Fun* explores the people who created the Park and features interviews with artists Martin, Kingo and Leigh Hobbs all of whom celebrated Arthur Barton's legacy. (24)

Jason Holman spent his first night at Wirian at the start of December. Martin went out that night, so Jason accompanied Maggie to a karaoke night at the Redfern RSL. As a 5$^{th}$ form schoolboy, Jason was seated in the carriage that was about enter the Ghost Train, but was stopped when the fire was detected. The four Waverley College boys who died - Richard Carroll, Michael Johnson, Jonathan Billings and Seamus Rahilly – were his schoolmates. They were in the carriage before Jason, the one that was not stopped. Jason shared his story with Martin and in his capacity as a film director, Jason was hoping to convey his version of events at some point. Martin was eager to help and he appreciated Jason's positive energy.

After all these years, Robert Tilley still lived downstairs at Wirian. Never quite in sync, Martin and Robert continued their discussions on religion. Pope Benedict XVI was an unpopular Pope. Robert defended him by writing a book titled *Benedict XVI and the Search for Truth*. It was the first thematic and popular overview in English of the theology of Pope Benedict. Martin brushed that project aside. (25)

Robert Wolfgramm was another 'religious Robert' who called in. Martin had enjoyed his gospel songs over the years. He was appointed a member of the translation team for the *New Fijian Translation* (NFT) Bible project. Martin was so impressed: an actual Bible translator! (26) Not only that, Robert Wolfgramm came with information about someone who sang hymns non-stop for 30 hours straight. Regrettably, he told Martin, *The Guinness Book of Records* didn't acknowledge him. 'Like Tiny,' sighed Martin, mindful that neither of Tiny's 'Non-stop Singing Records (for a professional singer)' had been listed.

Robert Wolfgramm describes an encounter with Martin, 'I was sitting in the kitchen with him having a lunchtime coffee (with Marilyn in the background) and I asked him what he believed. He smiled and ah, grinned, and ah, "Believe, yeah, ah, (still grinning) - Lord I believe, help thou mine unbelief - is that how it goes?" I said yes and realised he was a person of genuine faith, because only people like that admit that belief and unbelief lie side-by-side. Pious hypocrites preach the myth of singularity. None of us are consistent. We all mute certain beliefs. We hide back-stage what we don't want to make front-stage.

'The other occasion that stands out in my conversations with Martin (they always came back to religion by the way) was when I asked him where he stood in relation to Tiny. He rambled a bit then said smiling, ah, grinning, ah, yeah, 'He must increase, I must decrease'. I was in awe that he should think like that - but summing up their relationship like that was deep and insightful.

'Martin's faith was like his house - chock-full of symbols. An array of collectible beliefs discarded from every religious tradition he came across, all thrown in there together, rooms cluttered with art and artefacts, belief and unbelief side-by-side, wow, it was jaw-dropping. A logician's nightmare - the enemy of religious rationalism. You couldn't talk religion, spirituality, faith, belief with Martin in anything like a straight line. He had Escherian loops that led everywhere. That was Martin's faith right there; a fundamentalist today, a mystic tomorrow. Existentialism in the morning - Jehovah's Witnesses in the afternoon - Zoroastrianism in the evening - and a smoke after dinner - without ever becoming any of these. What I loved about him was you could change the channel anytime you liked and he was still with you.' [27]

In mid-2006 David Gulpilil was in trouble with the law. He was charged with carrying an offensive weapon and found not guilty as his machete was deemed to be of cultural use. Gulpilil did not fare so well in March 2007 when a Darwin magistrate imposed a 12-month domestic violence order on him and told him to stay away from his wife when drinking. In December 2007 Gulpilil was hospitalised in Sydney and was in poor shape.

One night (perhaps with Maggie's assistance) Gulpilil absconded from hospital and showed up at Wirian still wearing the tag around his wrist. Maggie and a friend brought him over because he wanted to show Martin his latest short film *Crocodile Dreaming*. Jack Thompson was there too. Gulpilil was introspective that night. He sat in an armchair, watched the film quietly and occasionally pointed things out to Martin. Everyone fussed over him, even Jack. [28]

Over the years, Martin met a few of Tiny's family: mother Tillie in New York, second wife Miss Jan in London, and he had some email contact with Tiny's cousin Hal Stein and wife Sherry who announced that they were visiting Sydney for a stopover on their around-the-world cruise. Their ship, MS Statendam, moored at Circular Quay across the harbour from Luna Park, which Hal noted as the venue for Tiny's 1979 marathon. He and Sherry visited the Opera House, admired the harbour and called on Wirian.

Martin wanted the visit to be perfect. He described it as a visit from a member of the Royal Family of Popular Song. Being an only child, Hal was the closest that Tiny (or 'Herbie' to Hal) came to having a brother. They were playmates and confidants during the 30s and 40s when they lived in the same apartment block in Washington Heights NY. They attended the same school. Then Herbie became Tiny Tim and Hal became promotional manager for Radio WKTU. 'He got a better position than you!' is how Tiny's mother ribbed him on camera in 1981. [29]

Hal knew Herbie better than anyone – it was the 'Tiny Tim' persona that had him proudly bemused. And Sherry was amazed to find herself in a living museum to her husband's cousin! They couldn't look anywhere without seeing something of Tiny: records, his ukulele, the Tiny Tim game, a Wobblehead figurine, a painting of Tiny by a friend, a figurine of Tiny by Kingo, photos by William, press clippings, 1000 cassette tapes, Martin's ever-evolving *Film Script* painting and posters of Tiny at Luna Park, Paddo, Opera House, Kinsela's, Brighton and the *Rock* CD poster. Martin loaded Hal and Sherry up with all the best prints, which must have been awkward to carry while touring, but worth it when they got home to Bensalem Pennsylvania.

Martin screened the film footage on two iMac 21.5 computers – one showed the unedited marathon, the other the Brighton Cut. Wendy was Martin's assistant at the time. She organised a smoked salmon platter for lunch and took snapshots. Robert Tilley popped in and out - and Martin played lots of Tiny Tim music, including *Courage My Friend,* outtakes from *Chameleon* and Wirian kitchen recordings. Martin gave Hal and Sherry a full Tiny Tim experience. Privately, Sherry whispered, 'This is good for Hal. He never forgets Tiny's birthday'. [30]

Meanwhile, life progressed quietly at Wirian. Quite a few handyman jobs required attention. The gate was hung at last but the plumbing was deteriorating. One evening the downstairs toilet wouldn't stop flushing. Water spilled under the doorway until the entire hallway was under an inch of water. Everything had to be lifted off the floor and everyone in Wirian helped. Carpets, pictures, toys, anything made of paper or cardboard...an emergency that could not be fixed until morning. Martin stabilised the situation and went to bed instead of staying awake all night like old times. He frequently took afternoon naps too. He went walking when he remembered his doctor's orders, and started-and-stopped smoking according to his moods, sometimes quitting for weeks at a time.

Someone sent Martin a 1991 bootleg recording of Tiny performing at Hollywood High School. Half the set was about America (*California Here I Come, America the Beautiful, God Bless America, Yankee Doodle Dandy, I'm Coming Back to California*). Martin felt the song selection contained an important message. Another CD that caught Martin's interest was *The Last Ghost Train Home* by Perry Keyes, which John Barker brought it to his attention. Martin read a whole lot into that Perry said he never meant. Yet he was pleased that Martin had found a deeper meaning in his song, affirming that the essence of a song can be negotiable, according to performer, audience and circumstance. [31]

The Australian Songwriters Association (ASA) is a national organization founded in Melbourne in 1979. It holds an Awards Night every year, rewarding the best songwriters in their category and saluting some of Australia's best songwriters. In 2007 Brian Cadd was inducted into the Hall of Fame, in 2008 – the year Martin attended - it was the Angels. Held at the spacious West Ashfield Leagues Club, the evening was organised by events manager, Clare Burgess.

Said Clare, 'We always play a category winning song, but if the person's not there to perform it, we do something interesting on stage instead. This time we thought, why don't we have someone create a 3-minute painting on stage? We rang Martin to ask if he knew somebody who would do it? He didn't but said he'd like to come to the awards.' [32]

Martin was seated at Glenn A Baker's table. Accompanying him were Wendy, Angelica and Maggie. The evening was attended by pioneers of Aussie Rock - Little Pattie, Dinah Lee, Lonnie Lee - the writer of *I've Been Everywhere*, Geoff Mack, was present too. [33]

Maggie went to the Smokers' Room during intermission. She got everybody's attention by reciting an impressive stream of poems – which seemed like song lyrics, given the context of the night. Having stunned that audience, Maggie rejoined her table and heard Martin's name mentioned from the stage. It was Denny - acknowledging Martin's international contribution to Australian songwriting through co-writing *Tales of Brave Ulysses*. Said Denny, 'It was such an honour to have him come along!' Martin reciprocated by donating a poster as an auction item. [34]

When working directly under Director Curatorial Tony Bond, Wayne Tunnicliffe had expressed interest in the Art Gallery of New South Wales running a major Pop Art exhibition, featuring international artists as well as Australian content. To run a major exhibition, art galleries require a long lead-time, perhaps five years. In 2008 Tunnicliffe was promoted into a position where he could influence the decision to run a Pop exhibition for the general public, so plans were laid for the future event.

Tony Bond explained, 'It had been around as something Wayne wanted to do for 4-5 years I suppose. Wayne was very committed to doing an Australian component. If you were going to have Rauschenburg and Johns you probably need to look at Annandale Realists for example. That Australian component was very much Wayne's idea. The closest thing to Pop (as such) would be Martin - in terms of image in the public's mind and his interest in popular culture. It's something that Wayne was inevitably left to do.' [35]

The *Pop to Popism* exhibition was held for three months at the Gallery at the close of 2014. The banners featured Martin's 'Blowing in the Mind' Dylan poster, alongside Andy Warhol, Keith Haring, David Hockney and Roy Lichtenstein. But 2008 was when all the groundwork was being laid.

# 16.
# POVERTY DELUX

*Martin, God put you here for us to look at these things and contemplate the spiritual and sinister dimensions, and to not be blind to them and unconcerned.*
Rachel Kohn

Dorothy's Will was the catastrophe that ruled Martin's life until April 2010 and beyond. In contesting the Will, the legal fees drained his finances to breaking point. Cranbrook School was among the beneficiaries, which was particularly galling, given that Martin was bullied and beaten in his student days and later pressured from the school as a neighbour.

The school honoured Martin while the Will was being contested, which made him uneasy, 'I was suspicious when they made me Old Boy of the Year at Cranbrook. It was completely unlikely, so I was suspicious of it. That was when my stepmother's Will was being brought down in favour of the school to a large degree, so it's like I've got to look like a sap because I was so very unlikely to be an Old Boy of the Year. I had been nominated by someone who is a nice person and it was a bone fide nomination but I can't stand that official level at school. They have come to tolerate me because I've endured. It's been a long hard haul to get an artist in there!' [1]

Said Roslyn, 'Martin was in a bit of a slump. He didn't know how he was going to work his future. Dorothy's Will - where he expected he was going to get his father's inheritance – really shook him. It definitely took years off his life. He became an expert on the law. He looked for things that people would have given up on a long time before. Like anything he got into, he really delved deeply – religion, Aborigines, law, health, crime, Abe Saffron....!' [2]

Roslyn accompanied Martin to court when the verdict was delivered. She described it as a 'moral victory'. He called it a 'pyrrhic victory'. The magistrate ruled in favour of going back two Wills. Cousins were now included as beneficiaries. Contesting this verdict would have meant mustering the energy for another battle, re-structuring his finances and cancelling a major retrospective exhibition at Sydney Museum.

Said Roslyn, 'He was incredibly short of money, that's when I became more involved. He kept asking me to come over and was very concerned with what he should do with everything he had and trying to work out what was the best thing. He pealed back two Wills which meant all the cousins got an inheritance from Dorothy which they didn't get from the last Will she wrote. Martin did not benefit financially from that at all, he did it for a moral reason. He was passing a kidney stone at the time. He could hardly walk when he left, he was in so much pain.' (3)

Said Martin, 'I initially thought I could beat these lawyers over my stepmother's Will and then you realise that you can't unless you want to re-mortgage Wirian. I thought it was probably wiser to hang onto the house, get on with the show and luckily I did have that exhibition (Sydney Museum Retrospective) because I wouldn't have won anyway if I'd put that extra attention in. I did a lot of work on it – three years worth, studying law and lawyers.' (4)

Although Dorothy had no children of her own, she gave $20,000-$50,000 to 20 members of her extended family which allowed for a bequest for the writing of a Sharp family history, a gift to the emerging generation, the children of Martin's cousins. (5) Reading the accounts of each of his 15 cousins' lives gave Martin a sense of family, 'The effect of our family was like a bomb exploding and we – my cousins and me - were the shrapnel of this powerful collision. And we spun off further. Now we're trying to swim backwards and pick up some of the pieces from the explosion.' (6)

Speculatively, Martin and his cousins may well be descendents of passionate slave abolitionist, Granville Sharp (1735-1813). If so, the painting titled 'The Sharp Family' by Johan Zoffany in London's National Portrait Gallery features 13 of Martin's antecedents. Knowing none of this when growing up, Martin was filling in the gaps, 'No one ever said to me, "you come from a great family who did all these things". I only found out when this family history was written. It gave me a sense of my own history'. (7)

\*

Go back to the mid-60s when Martin placed an ad: 'Wanted Nude Model for a Martin Sharp collage'. A girl called Linda applied, did the shoot, got paid $40, got taken to lunch and that was that.

Not quite.

Linda became a lawyer and married Roland Gumbert, another lawyer. They lived in Oxford Falls, raised a family and after living in Sydney for 40 years they decided to move to a country town. They saw an ad for an early-19th Century homestead for sale in Goulburn NSW. Two days later they won the bidding, bought the property but what to do the place? They weren't farmers. They didn't want to run a bed and breakfast place. And - although the place seemed to suit a gallery - they didn't have a background in the arts.

'Maybe we should speak to Martin Sharp about how to open a fine art gallery,' Linda surmised, remembering the photo shoot. Too shy to phone, Linda wrote him, '…you wouldn't remember me but we're starting a gallery…' etc. Martin rang back and said, 'I remember you really well and still have the photos – come over'. And that's how South Hill Gallery started.

South Hill Gallery is a big homestead with a barn, shearing shed and heritage-listed chookyard. The homestead spills into a 4-room gallery, one of which the Gumberts turned into a museum celebrating Martin's art. With the Gulpilil street banners as the curtains, posters and prints hang on all walls, OZ magazines are on display and another glass cabinet is full of Martin's badges, postcards, illustrated books, LP and CD covers, letters and lots of Tiny Tim stuff. [8]

Martin accepted the Gumbert's request to become Gallery's patron. He reckoned it was a great role – 'you don't have to do anything' although Martin contributed a good deal more than just lending his name. He drew the gallery's logo, contributed museum items, signed beautiful fulsome autographs and encouraged other Yellow Housers to support the gallery too. In time, Dick Weight, Reg Mombassa, Max Cullen, Jon Lewis, Roger Foley, William Yang and Jim Anderson would exhibit in the gallery. Sandy Gutman would perform there as Austen Tayshus. Peter Royles – an original Yellow Houser who lived in Goulburn - was resident muso at the Yellow House get-togethers, which essentially comprised the Class of '72 - Tim Lewis, Jon Lewis, Roger Foley, Greg Weight, Michael Bell, Michael Glasheen, Garry Shead and others.

After spending six months traveling through the atolls of Kiribati, Jon presented 46 photographic images portraying the vibrant culture of these islands being devastated by storm surges and freakish waves. In October 2010 Martin launched Jon's exhibition *Portraits from the Edge, Kiribati* at the South Hill Gallery. Gary Shearston sang and Jon responded with a generous speech. He summed up the experience, 'There was a Yellow House feel to it'. Guests suggested that if anywhere had continued the Yellow House spirit, it was this place. On his return Martin checked straight into hospital where he was admitted for pneumonia. Horrified this happened immediately after his opening, Jon said, 'Martin was ill again and I hope it wasn't because of me wanting his endorsement! The day, as I recall, was cold.' [9]

Martin saw the upside, 'Pneumonia had a silver lining - being able to keep people away a bit, not go out and stuff like that. I'd rather just stay here and get on with my work because either it's worth something or it's not worth anything. And when you're not feeling good it doesn't seem that it's worth anything.' (10)

Justin Martell was a young filmmaker from Connecticut USA who contacted Martin because he wanted to write a biography of Tiny Tim. He was young – too young to remember Tiny during the 60s. Who was this guy? He came out of nowhere. There had always been a regular string of writers trying to get to Martin by feigning interest in Tiny. Was Justin just one of those? Dave checked, but webmaster Ernie Clark didn't know him, neither did Bucks Burnett. Dave couldn't find out much either, except that Justin was in his early-20s, had never met Tiny and claimed to be fascinated by everything he'd heard.

Over the next six months everyone hemmed and hawed whenever Justin's project was mentioned, then suddenly it was all go. Justin convinced Martin that he wanted to write a proper biography, not just a quickie. Martin agreed to a taped telephone interview and, in a moment of excitement, he even wanted to fly Justin to Sydney, put him up in Wirian and grant him access to the tapes, press clippings, the lot. Justin interviewed Martin and Dave. Writing the bio was a long project, his book *Eternbal Troubadour, the Improbable Life of Tiny Tim* was published in 2016. Along with the author's mother, the bio was dedicated to Martin and Ernie, neither of whom lived to see the final product. (11)

While Martin's health held out, life at Wirian continued much as before. Robert Tilley lived downstairs and continued lecturing at tertiary institutions. Terry Stanton and Stephen Darmody lived in the house and helped fix the place up. Martin attending opening nights, continued his own projects and bought a few more books. A facsimile edition of Vincent van Gogh's handwritten letters (in French) of 485 hand-numbered copies was for sale ($300) in a secondhand bookshop in Hornsby. Martin got someone to buy it for him. 'It brings you one step closer to the artist,' he explained. Maggie moved into Jack Thompson's Gearins Hotel Katoomba for six weeks before coming back. Wendy also left around this time and Dave came back and compiled what he and Martin dubbed Tiny's *New York Apartment Tapes*. Martin said, 'I'm just progressing with Tiny. I keep holding these things together, growing them. It's good *Chameleon* got out. Satoshi did his best but it was quite painful getting the CDs out. I don't think they've gone out far enough!' The royalty statement from Zero Records listed sales as: *Chameleon* - 418, *Wonderful World of Romance* – 352 and *Stardust* - 374. (12)

Julien Temple's *The Eternity Man* is a one-hour film/opera about Arthur Stace. Composed in 2004 it was released to DVD and general viewing five years later. Poet, Dorothy Porter's libretto was set to music and played by a grand 25-piece orchestra, which evoked the opposite of Stace's humble background. (13) Martin disliked opera as the chosen medium, 'I didn't see Arthur as an operatic character,' he said. 'I don't think that's the form for him. There's something to be said for a popular song as opposed to operatic. I think (actor) Christa Hughes was very good but I don't think they've actually "got" Arthur. It was a quite dramatic piece but it didn't have a Christian viewpoint - although it showed a lot of stuff from Luna Park.' [14]

Martin had his own opportunity to make a statement when a retrospective exhibition of his pictures was held at the Museum of Sydney in the heart of the city. There were at least 120 works displayed in chronological order from left to right. A grand piano was in the room for anyone to play and the Tiny Tim film was on constant screening. It came across as a kinetic art piece and, as such, was well received. Former Premier Neville Wran launched the show, giving a summary his involvement in the first trial of OZ. Wran's wife, businesswoman, Jill Hickson also made a speech. And Maggie recited some poems. Then it was all on. Like all Martin's openings, 'everyone' was there - scrunched against the walls, checking out pictures and posters from his earliest to his most recent. Martin sat quietly near the entrance, sipping wine and chatting to a queue of guests waiting to shake his hand and tell him how much they'd enjoyed his work.

*Sydney Morning Herald* reviewer, John Macdonald wrote about it, 'With the current show, Ace Bourke is credited as the exhibition coordinator, but can anybody coordinate Sharp? The show gives the impression it is largely self-curated – a rambling visual autobiography on shocking blue walls that takes us from the artist's days at Cranbrook, through the swinging 60s in Sydney and London and finally to the seclusion of the family home in Bellevue Hill where all Sharp's fondest obsessions have been incubated'. [15]

After the grand opening, Martin attended the exhibition as often as he could, usually sitting in the outside coffee shop area and greeting people on their way in. Martin reckoned, 'The Sydney Museum exhibition did a lot of good. I guess it did the trick – did the job. I almost cancelled. The people there were excellent. They weren't scared of any images. They were very supportive. There was enough there to baffle most people. My framer was a great help. I didn't have a bean at the time. I was hoping to get some money in from the settlement of the estate but they held that off for as long as they good.' [16]

**A terrible November day**: Nick Waterlow and daughter 37-year old Cloe Heuston were found dead of multiple stab wounds in her Randwick home. Waterlow had curated *Larrikins of London* and helped research Martin's Museum of Sydney exhibition. In a bid to repair their fractured relationship, Chloe invited her brother Anthony to a dinner at her house. Their father Nick was there too, as well as Chloe's three children. The meal had barely started when Anthony, a paranoid schizophrenic with a history of violent behaviour, took a carving knife from the kitchen and killed his father and sister. He then walked out of the front door and along Clovelly Road, his shirt covered with blood. Anthony was on the run for three weeks. In 2011 he was found not guilty of murder by reason of mental illness. Martin kept the press clippings and pinned a picture of Nick on his noticeboard. [17]

'How'd you like to spend Christmas on Christmas Island?' were the words to one of the songs on *Christmas in the Heart*, a Dylan album of hymns, carols and popular Christmas songs. News: December 2010, 48 asylum-seekers died off the coast in what became known as the 'Christmas Island boat disaster' when the boat they were in smashed against nearby cliffs. Martin saw Dylan's song as a pointer to that event. Although Martin had gone right off Dylan, Dylan's earnest rendition of *Little Town of Bethlehem* brought him back, though not enough to buy tickets when Dylan came out in 2011. Asked if he'd be going to the concert, Martin replied, 'This time he can come and see me'. (18)

Martin was interested in other singers too. One day he reckoned he had 'cracked' the mystery of Susan Boyle, a star contestant on the TV show Britain's Got Talent. He said, 'Susan Boyle was a major encouragement. She's like the voice of the Magdalene in the modern world. I wouldn't have thought of that if I hadn't been through all the experiences of Luna Park, the boys and the Magdalene Church. Her name is Susan Magdalene Boyle – a saint's name. I pricked up my ears at that. Through the name comes the connection. Initially Magdalene becomes the first disciple, the first Christian, though she's not generally attributed to that position. I've got Susan Boyle's first CD. I bought it at the Post Office and began to listen to it. Also there was a very good interview where she comes out with a statement that her sister was trying to stop her going in the singing competition, "you'll ruin the reputation of the family..." and "you'll bring disgrace on us all...!" Anyway, through hearing that her name is Magdalene and how serious she is about her faith, I started to listen to the album and – to me, at any rate – I felt that album was like Magdalene was speaking through her in the present day. She was telling her story from the inside, using the language of popular song, songs you wouldn't expect. I didn't think of it until I realised her name was Magdalene and then I started to listen to it.

'When she made that performance, which went round the world like a tidal wave of some sort – I watched it and was very impressed. And the back story - the courage she had, the promise to her mother to make something of her singing, and the battle with her sister and others trying to stop her from making a fool of herself. She made terrible mistakes, she couldn't find the venue, she was late, she fell over when she got there and it was only by the skin of her teeth that she managed to get out there and sing. Something happened as soon as she opened her mouth and sang those first lines. I read in that Joseph Campbell book "where the world turns" – she turned the world when she opened her mouth. And out of nowhere! Incredible! *I Dreamed a Dream* – she dreamed a dream!'

'Susan Boyle was stopped from singing *Perfect Day* to the Pope and the Queen. It was the first time the Pope had had an official tour of England for 600 years or something. She was going to sing that (and maybe *St Francis' Prayer* was the other song she was going to sing). She was ready to go with it and Lou Reed was attributed to stopping her. I listened to it in the light that she was going to sing it to the Pope and the Queen: "You're going to reap just what you sow…" for everyone, even the Queen! Apparently she was devastated that permission was refused her to sing *Perfect Day*. Maybe the protocol stopped her singing it to them - Lou Reed might have been the excuse. I think she sang *I Dreamed a Dream* for the Queen and the Pope. I thought she was very courageous. And through Luna Park comes the connection to the Magdalene Church Rose Bay where they had the Memorial Mass for the four boys in the fire. It's the only Magdalene Church in Sydney. It's a rare name. So it's a powerful, more romantic presence in the Christian story. [19]

After 40 years in Walker Lane Paddington, Clive Evatt closed the Hogarth Galleries and consigned its contents for auction. He opened the gallery in 1972 and after 40 years he and his wife no longer had the energy to oversee day-to-day operations. Among the pictures being auctioned was Martin's *Eternity Haymarket*. The Australian newspaper photographed Martin touching up the original. [20]

Rachel Kohn did a radio interview with Martin titled 'The Spiritual Vision of Martin Sharp'. She handled the interview sensitively, which encouraged Martin to open up on pet subjects. About Luna Park he said, 'I loved Luna Park but it was a Moloch Temple disguised as a funfair. You can expand it to include Hollywood and Las Vegas and places like this. The Beast rules these places. You see it for instance in the roulette wheels which are central to casinos. The numbers of the roulette wheel add up to 666, the number of the Beast in the Book of Revelation. These patterns are there.'

About Tiny, 'He wasn't a churchgoing person but he certainly kept the Bible very handy. He taught me a lot about religion. He did teach me about Christianity. I wondered why he had such a great attitude even though he was dropped from the peak of show business. I wondered where his good cheer came from. He was quoting scriptures often.'

And about Aboriginal matters, 'I think God put Aboriginal people here first - for a reason. It makes sense to me but we should try to understand what that reason is and treat them with the respect they deserve.' To which Rachel Kohn replied, 'Well Martin, I think God put you here for a reason – for us to look at these things and contemplate the spiritual and all the sinister dimensions, the underbelly of Sydney and to not be blind to them and not be unconcerned about them'. [21]

\*

At the start of 2011, Marianne Faithfull slipped quietly in-and-out of Australia with no concerts and no media. She came for a holiday during the course of which she shared the demo tracks of her forthcoming album 'Horses and High Heels' with Martin. The song titled *Eternity* is one of her own compositions. Martin's *Remo Eternity* print hung in her Paris apartment and although she never dedicated the song to Martin and he never claimed it, his print was surely an inspiration behind the song.

Robert Tilley was still living at Wirian as well as Steve Darmody. Maggie was around. Shane (from Broome) and Lisa his assistant took photos of Maggie for screen tests and they also photographed Martin painting *Curiosity in Her Own Country*. Richard got Martin to sign a small stack of OZ prints for a forthcoming exhibition. Willy de la Vega still called in, so did his niece Chi. Louise Ferrier and Albie Thoms called in too, reminiscing the Museum of Sydney exhibition, for which Martin had sometimes turned to them for advice. Garry and his new partner Rose called in with gozlemé. Marilyn was handling Martin's bookkeeping. Harmonie's sister Anna stayed at Wirian with her friend Heidi. It was not unusual to find indigenous people from The Block in the Inner Sanctum, often sitting silently. Carol Barossa from South America was in-and-out, cleaning, helping, bringing drinks. Dave worked on *The Kitchen Tapes* – tapes of Tiny singing in the Wirian kitchen circa 1974. He reckoned he could hear Martin straining for breath after the shortest exertion. There was a new Tiny Tim release, a CD called *I've Never Seen A Straight Banana*. [22] With Tiny's new music playing in the background, Martin happily remarked that the place was running like an internal Yellow House.

Martin always had an ever-changing group of confidants. Up to the mid-90s it was always the late night drop-in crowd. This changed when Martin started getting sick. There were no more all night sessions, in fact Martin often had an afternoon kip, leaving guests alone in his Inner Sanctum to flick through some book left on the table, like a history of Steinway pianos because Martin had been approached to paint one. He didn't do it because they wanted something that resembled *Disraeli Gears* whereas he had something else in mind.

Richard and Martin talked through plans for the future of Wirian, which seemed to be a 'museum' of sorts. When Martin stopped eating, Richard asked Dave to keep him informed, 'But I don't live there…!' Dave complained. Richard often visited Wirian, invariably with interesting gossip. Like, having had supper with Geoffrey Robertson whom he described as 'getting pompous, like a high court judge'. He also told Martin about Julian Assange. He reckoned he was great on technology but unable to handle the public sex stuff. After getting Martin to sign a Mick Jagger OZ print, Richard offered to go out and get some food. Martin reluctantly considered eating fried prawns. When Richard returned, he settled in with Martin and watched all three hours and 38 minutes of Prince William's wedding to Kate Middleton.

Martin's health declined even further. He stopped accepting calls, and visitors were kept away. Russell organised a Japanese girl to work as his cleaner and when that didn't work out he got him Andrea (Andy) Warrell who had worked for their Aunt Elizabeth. Roslyn said, 'Martin was impossible to look after. One cleaner got sacked because he didn't like the noise of a vacuum cleaner. But Andy is very strong-minded, she organises people's lives but she has to do it her way. Martin and her would argue all the time about how things were done. She was working out a strategy to keep him fed.' [23]

Despite declining health, Martin continued producing new works, like the poster for *World AIDS Day*, which became a t-shirt produced by Josef Lebovic Gallery. He also encouraged young artists. One afternoon three Year 12 Cranbrook students - Steven, George and Joe (the son of Todd Hunter, bass player for the band Dragon) - called in to show Martin their visual diaries. Martin stopped what he was doing and gave them as much time as they needed.

OZ that Never Was

*Mojo* is a popular music magazine published monthly in the United Kingdom with a circulation of around 75,000 and available from all newsagencies. The periodical features Classic Rock acts and regularly includes CDs that tie in with a magazine article or theme. In covering the 60s phenomenon, the editors decided to run a feature about the underground 60s press. They contacted Richard and proposed an OZ magazine insert inside the regular magazine. This was to be a 16-page 'Best Of' centrepiece combined with new material.

Jim Anderson and Richard met in Martin's Inner Sanctum where OZ to create one final OZ, with Martin on hand to assist. 'I'm keeping out of it', said Martin, who had other things on his mind. He'd been invited to participate in a panel discussion for artist Robert Crumb's Australian tour, though he didn't feel well enough to accept. (The tour was cancelled.) Jim had other things on his mind too. He was moving his current Redfern exhibition to South Hill Gallery. Richard was enthusiastic. He and Jim covered the table with blank pages, which they proceeded to fill up with ideas. Felix wouldn't (or 'couldn't') be involved but gave them permission for them to publish his poems. Martin contributed *A Curiosity in her Own Country* and his 'Give us this day our daily bread' b/w anti-pokies OZ-toon of money pouring from a one-armed bandit into a punter's gullet.

After working all afternoon, Martin got testy with Jim, so he and Richard withdrew. Jim said, 'When we were doing mini-OZ/Mojo and Martin was ill. We decided we'd go to my place where we'd work for the rest of the day.' [24] Richard and Julie were staying in Bondi at the time, where Richard planned to work an all-nighter. Jim did the same. They finished around midnight.

Richard and Julie hurried home with some urgency because the lead story on the TV News was 100kph winds in Blackheath, which did a lot of damage, but Happy Daze was okay. Trees and branches were down everywhere, so Richard loaded up his vehicle and delivered a load of ironbark to Wirian so that Martin could light the fire in the Inner Sanctum. When mini-OZ hadn't been published by November, Richard checked with the editors who said they'd postponed it until May of the following year. But it never happened. Martin didn't care. Said Dave, 'Martin wasn't keen on the project in the first place. It was like he was be-ing pushed into doing something he didn't want to do and you couldn't do that with Martin.' [25]

Getting Martin to sign anything was always easy, except contracts. He autographed everything put in front of him, the Yellow House *Catalog*, Tiny Tim records, posters, old copies of Peter Draffin's *Pop*, and Craig Macgregor's *People, Politics and Pop*. One afternoon Martin signed a stack of prints for Richard. He just sat, smoked and signed as Richard placed each one in front of him and replaced it with another. With contracts though, Martin was cautious. One day he said, 'You should never take a publisher's advance – because then you've got to deliver the book!' With contracts Martin usually had the same objection, the subsidiary rights – the add-ons.

There were always plenty of offers. Like a well-respected Rock journalist who approached Martin with an offer to release a boxed set of Tiny Tim CDs, but the small print included a promotional documentary. Martin reckoned the boxed set was the 'bait' - the doco was what they really wanted, 'but they don't realise the amount of disruption the presence of a film crew causes to one's work'. [26] Martin was always wary of feigned interest in Tiny as a way of getting to him.

Blue Pie Records is a multi-national digital music company with a presence in Australia, USA, UK, Ireland, China and Canada. Dave had been negotiating Tiny's music with Damien from Blue Pie and Damien had been coming over in the evenings and cooking meals for Martin. The original agreement was straightforward, then Martin gained the impression that Blue Pie was getting a stranglehold on Tiny from all his material, plus they were negotiating with Justin Martell to publish the Tiny Tim biography. 'Does Justin know that Blue Pie has never pub-lished a book before?' Martin questioned. However, Dave's negotiations meant Martin would get a few cents off each track whereas at the moment, he was getting zip. Martin wanted to revert to the original agreement, which was the Chameleon album only. He felt the add-ons in the contract had grown with time - Disraeli Gears t-shirt rights, 10 more points like that. Plus he was unhappy with the ac-companying booklet because he felt the writer had gleaned the information about both Tiny and Martin from nothing more than Wikipedia. Dave's great disap-pointment, after a lot of hard work putting together an online digital-download distribution deal, Martin pulled the plug on the Blue Pie deal.

Dave was incensed, 'Martin didn't want to go ahead with it. He was trying to pull out of this but we'd already struck a deal. We'd agreed to do the download. The project was ready to roll. So to appease Martin, Damien said, "Let's call it *Chameleon* but we'll change the track listing so it's not the original album. We'll put *I Love Rock N Roll* on it as well." So we changed the track listing and released it. It's set up in Martin's account. At least we got it out on iTunes!' Phew. [27]

One July night, Jason Holman whizzed Martin to hospital with a problem with his right side. Not pneumonia, not a stroke, not the lungs, not the heart – this time Martin was diagnosed with dehydration and malnutrition. Dehydration and malnutrition are sicknesses caused by neglect. Friends were concerned. They started discussing some sort of system to keep Martin fed.

Then came news of two deaths. Following a long illness, Martin's *Disraeli Gears* collaborator, photographer Robert Whitaker, died in England. Margaret Olley was closer to home. Greg was the last of Martin's friends to see her. He was photographing her latest canvases for her next show. As he was loading the last painting into his car, she stopped him and said, 'Not that one. I want to do a bit more on it. Come back tomorrow at 2.00.' Next morning Greg received a phone call to say that she had died during the night. Greg hurried to her house and recorded her workspace before anything was moved. (Greg's 'Photographic Studies from the Studio of Margaret Olley' was exhibited at Australian Galleries in 2012.)

Knowing Martin had the facilities and an assistant (Dave) who could change recording formats, a friend of Margaret's, Philippa Drynan, called in with an ABC radio interview with Margaret, snippets of which she wanted extracted to play at her funeral service. [28] Martin and Dave helped Philippa choose the segments and Dave did the transfer. Martin suggested her saying, 'I'd liked to be remembered for helping people'. Margaret Olley's private funeral was held at Northern Suburbs Cemetery.

Sixty years after Justin O'Brien won the inaugural the Blake Prize, Martin's picture *Stranger in her Own Country* (renamed 'Madonna') was short-listed among the finalists for the Blake. Sadly, the judges' decision marked the triumph of conceptual art over Art. It ruined the hope of Martin winning on the anniversary of his art teacher's triumph. Instead, the winner was Khaled Sabsabi whose work was a 90-minute video presentation on three TV monitors, showing a group of Sufi Muslims practicing communal chants and prayers.

*Sydney Morning Herald* art critic John McDonald wrote, 'Around 1999 the prize went to a crypt and was reborn the following year as an award for "spiritual" rather than "religious" art. At this point the floodgates were thrown open. Soon the prize was full of dumb abstracts, dull landscapes, oblique photos, aimless videos and every other permutation of contemporary art'. [29] When Rachel Kohn featured art critic McDonald on her radio program he reiterated his thoughts that the Blake was no longer 'religious art', just art that the artist had decided to vaguely label as 'spiritual'. When asked which pieces deserved to be there, Martin's picture was the first that he named.

Martin's health continued to decline. Then his dog, Imelda, died, 'the only one who cared for me when I was sick' said Martin. He painted, re-read *The Territorial Imperative* by Robert Ardrey, because there were tensions in the Wirian kitchen, where Martin was feeling banished by his own tenants. By October Martin's health got worse and he was trying to keep quiet about it. He stopped smoking, this time for keeps. Russell stepped in and told guests that Martin wasn't well enough to take visitors. Angelica started helping in an official capacity. Roslyn made more frequent visits. She was on a high because her 'Breakfast at Sweethearts' photo (from her Kings Cross series) was blown up on the big screen at a Cold Chisel concert. Martin was pleased for her. He liked the boys from Cold Chisel.

By November, Martin ill health was common knowledge. There was no 'keeping it quiet'. Radio presenter Philip Adams talked about it on his radio program. In the same week Martin returned to hospital. Again he said he was 'okay' – whatever that meant. So he came home briefly, then went back for another fortnight. 'I took him to a lot of doctors and tests in those first six months', said Angelica. [30]

When Martin came back he was put on an oxygen mask and he could no longer go upstairs. A four-poster single bed was moved into the Inner Sanctum in the corner where the sound system used to be. Metal supports were installed in the downstairs toilet and Angelica, Roslyn, Gria and Fairlie Kingston were rostered to take care of Martin. [31]

# 17.
# STAYIN' ALIVE

*Tiny was a major inspiration to Martin and everyone
thought that was really funny.
But I thought no, the substance was Tiny -
and it always was.*
Dave Rowe

Martin was on a leash. He could go no further than the length of the oxygen tube that tethered him in his Inner Sanctum where he spent most of his time anyway. Martin had a form of blood cancer known as myeloma, which develops in white blood cells. Symptoms include bone pain, frequent infections, excessive thirst, nausea and weight loss. Although the recovery rate was higher than it had ever been, myeloma was not considered curable. [1]

Said Roslyn, 'It's a precursor to leukaemia - nothing to do with smoking. It was terrible. White blood cells stop infections and the red blood cells take the oxygen around. The oxygen being taken around Martin's body was compromised by emphysema and a bad heart. So the blood was not doing its job. That's why Martin had to have blood transfusions.' [2]

Every Wednesday, until he could no longer leave his bed, Martin was wheeled into St Vincent's Hospital where he would undergo a full blood transfusion. He often invited friends along for company. Tim was one, 'Martin was always glad to see me. I went there during his illness and this lovely lady walked down the driveway and said, "Who are you?" It was Lin Utzon. I was in tears. I said, "I'm Tim". She said, "He's having a transfusion in the hospital, come with me". So I went with her.' [3]

Martin would not engage professional healthcare. He preferred the assistance of friends and family who worked out a roster between themselves. That's how Martin wanted things to run. Angelica was rostered three days per week but was also on 24-hour call. She lived with husband Davy Alan in the Sydney suburb of Moorebank, a full 45-minute drive from Wirian, so Angelica had a big job. She also wheeled Martin around in his wheelchair when he went out, which was less and less.

'Angelica looked after him three days a week,' said Roslyn. 'She would come in the afternoon and stay until she was picked up. Angelica would also come if there was a special appointment that no one could take Martin to when he became sick. She would do the extra things and then at the end of his life she stayed more. Martin had his public life and he had his private life. He didn't have to put on a show with Angelica and I'm glad he had that comfort. Andrea would come in two days, look after him and clean the house. Fairlie Kingston would come in and Gria Shead would come in as well. I would do Sundays.' [4]

Other help came from Jubilee the cleaner, Ella Walker (Roma's daughter, ie. Martin's nanny when he was four) and lots of other friends, some of whom would bring food, sit around, talk or read to him. Luke was one of those. Jonny too. Sometimes Steve Darmody took over. Neighbour, Dr John Gregory Roberts was another regular. He had attended Cranbrook School with Martin and took Martin out to dinner once a month. When Martin could no longer go out, he brought the meals to Martin. [5]

Visitors came and went. They were vetted by Martin's respective 'gatekeepers' but at the start of his bedridden phase they called in unannounced, as they had always done. As Martin's mobility became restricted, certain 'friends' started helping themselves to items around the house, ('Oh, I lent Martin that, etc,') necessitating the closing of certain rooms.

Wirian was seeping around the edges. Tighter management was required, so Roslyn and cousin Sandy Sharp stepped in. 'Crazy things were happening,' said Roslyn. (Like a rumour that went around that Wirian was on the market. Cranbrook School picked up on it. Their lawyer contacted Martin's lawyer only to find it was untrue.) Roslyn continued, 'Some weird texts were going around offering Wirian for sale for $9 million. That's when we had to say, "enough's enough!" Martin asked me to do the Power of Attorney (POA). I said, "No, I reckon you should use Sandy and Marilyn..." because Marilyn had done his books and Sandy would be absolutely loyal to Martin. I took on his Guardianship. That was all set up 18 months before Martin died.' Martin's Will was dated 20 September 2012.

'Martin had the added anxiety about worrying about money on his deathbed. He was getting the interest of his stepmother's estate while he was alive - and it was a lot of money (after he died that went to Cranbrook and St Paul's College). I said, "How come you have no money Martin?" It turned out that they hadn't been sending the income. I said, "I'll ring up Hugh Massie..." (Hugh Massie was an executor of Dorothy's estate and would have been horrified.) Martin agreed with that. All I had to do was email Hugh Massie and say, "Hugh, if there's any money send it immediately".' [6]

Projecting into his own future, Martin's thoughts went straight to the Wirian. 'You think, "My god, how much am I going to get finished before Rookwood Cemetery?" Wirian is quite difficult to maintain, just to keep it good and let it hopefully flow on. It's a great old house. It's done some interesting things in its time. You don't know what happens in the future – the attitudes of the school or whatever. I see Wirian as quite a scholastic place in its way. But I realise what a controversial subject Tiny is and Luna Park. Boy! [7] I've felt at times - when I've seen it clearly - that the Wirian is the work of art, the whole place and all its ingredients make sense.' [8]

In the past, Martin had often projected that Wirian might be a Tiny Tim/Luna Park university. But before the year was out, it was Martin himself who received the honour. The University of Sydney conferred on him an honorary doctorate, making him Dr Martin Ritchie Sharp OA, Doctor of Visual Arts. At the graduation ceremony held in the Great Hall, the Chancellor Her Excellency Professor Marie Bashir (Governor of New South Wales) conferred the degree.

The opening words of the citation read, 'Chancellor, it gives me great pleasure to commend Martin Sharp to you for admission to the degree of Doctor of Visual Arts. As an artist, cartoonist, songwriter and film-maker he has distinguished himself through his outstanding contribution to the visual arts and his creative achievement in Australian and international culture since the early 60s and he is hailed as Australia's foremost Pop artist.' Clothed in a professorial hat and gown, Martin eased himself out of his wheelchair to accept the degree. [9]

Martin's condition worsened and he was readmitted to hospital. (He was admitted a total of 97 times.) His plight caught the attention of the Governor-General of Australia. With a film crew trailing her, Governor-General Quentin Bryce visited St Vincent's Hospital. There a Sister of Charity informed her that Martin was a patient. She had always wanted to meet Martin. This was organised and the meeting photographed. Lying in his bed and breathing from his oxygen unit, Martin showed Quentin Bryce a Hokusai sketchbook.

Christmas can be a tough time for people requiring healthcare, often with only emergency staff on deck. Australians party, cook BBQ prawns, sip wine, attend family gatherings and bestow gifts on eager grandkids. Most medics go on holiday. So Christmas Day was tough on Martin, who needed help. This alerted Roslyn and Angelica to the seriousness of looking after him at all times.

In January Roslyn wrote, 'Martin has been very sick but is making slow progress. It has been very difficult not having medical help available over the Christmas break. His medical people are around again now. Martin is still not answering the phone but he does listen to his messages when he's up to it. It has been a rough time having him so sick but he is a joy in so many ways to look after as he is determined to get better.' [10]

Martin turned 70 in January. The Aboriginal flag flying above St Vincent's Hospital was Martin's gift to them. He also gave a print of *Pentecost* to the West-mead Children's Hospital. In February, Martin wrote, 'As I sit here at my table in my studio at Wirian surrounded by the pieces of my life, in this physical feebleness at the beginning of my seventieth year I wonder about the mystery of life… not for the first time, and probably not the last, but there will be a last time. It is not too far away. I am feeble in my body so I very much live in this room, a tube brings me oxygen. My friends bring me food. In these words I hold on to life. I am not ready to leave. I have things to do before I go, God willing! 5.00am.' [11]

A segment on the ABC television program, the *7.30 Report*, left no doubt about the gravity of Martin's condition. He was skinnier than anyone had ever seen him, breathing through his oxygen machine and he appeared frightened. Martin was filmed lying in his bed in his Inner Sanctum with Garry sketching him in the style of Dr Gachet's drawing of Vincent on his deathbed. Garry had often sketched Martin but never like this. Having decided to paint Martin's portrait again (he did so in 1986) Garry entered his *Martin Sharp and His Magic Theatre* in the Archibald Prize. It was a picture of a white-bearded Martin with piercing eyes, Luna Park glowing in the background and figurines to the fore: Ginger Meggs, Popeye, Mo (Roy Rene), Jiminy Cricket, Mickey Mouse, Tiny Tim and Eadweard Muybridge's little running men.

Said Garry, 'I drew Martin when I decided to do the painting. When I heard that he was sick, I thought I needed to be there to see him. I didn't think he was going to last that long and the painting just flowed out. I did some studies and when I came back everything fell into place. Greg took a lot of photos I was able to use.' [12]

The Governor of New South Wales Marie Bashir saw that program and was startled by Martin's condition since she had last seen him. 'What can we do to help this national treasure?' she questioned. Bashir wanted to ensure Martin was getting the best health care, especially when told of the neglect that he experienced around Christmas. She organized a banquet at Government House for Martin and his retinue: Martin, Roslyn, their Aunt Elizabeth, Fairlie and Peter Kingston, Garry and Gria Shead, Luke Sciberras, Lin and Mika Utzon, Lucy Neville, Julie Clark, Angelica, Jenny Poidevin, Maggie Walsh, Lois Cook and King Des (Barnes), allegedly Edward VIII's illegitimate son. Angelica took a lot of photos and made a splendid album recording the occasion. Before dashing off to meet-and-greet the Israel ambassador, Bashir discussed Martin's estate with him, especially with regard to the future of continuing Wirian as an art place. [13]

When it got out that Martin was so ill he was inundated with phone calls. People just kept dropping in. Many were turned away because he didn't have the energy for them but some long-term friends got through. Dr Pepper (David Pepperall) visited from Melbourne. Victoria Cobden made contact. Martin tried to reach out too, to Miss Tulip, Michael Chamberlain and others.

Beating back bad health, Martin continued taking on new projects. With Natalie Pratt and Kingo's assistance, he started a boxed set of prints – the *Schoolbook*

*Series* - based on the portraits he painted as a schoolboy. The boxes were to be individually covered with extracts from his school reports. Martin entered the *Gulpilil* portrait in the Archibald Prize. It was named among the finalists, as was Garry's portrait of Martin. Then Martin started a new picture – a big one - the 'Hendrix' picture - an image he'd previously painted twice as a poster-print. One image had Jimi playing left-handed, the second had him playing right-handed. Hendrix was a left-handed guitarist who played an upside-down right-handed guitar, which Martin found difficult to grasp.

'What type of guitar is that?' Martin asked. Answer: a Fender Stratocaster. 'What it's like upside down?' Martin acquired a small figurine of the instrument, about four inches in size, which he referred to as a check point. Roslyn saw the new *Hendrix* picture develop, 'Hendrix was a photo of the painting that he'd already done, he was painting over the top of it but it didn't look right. He didn't finish it. The paint did not work on photographic paper.' [14]

Martin had always punctuated conversations with music – whatever caught his ear - and always Tiny of course. Although he didn't play much music any more, he enjoyed Paul McCartney's new studio album, the cheekily titled *Kisses on the Bottom*. 'Like Tiny...' Martin reflected. The record comprised a dozen good-natured covers of traditional hits that read like a set-list from one of Tiny's marathons. Songs like *Ac-Cent-Tchu-ate the Positive, Sit Right Down and Write Myself a Letter, Always, Bye Bye Blackbird*, etc. [15]

Although Dave Rowe had given Martin a copy of *Elvis 30 #1 Hits*, Martin didn't play many Elvis songs. He wasn't playing much Tiny either. 'I haven't done anything for Tiny,' Martin rued, 'I had to put down that load'. Dave added, 'Martin would listen to those rambling Tiny Tim tapes while he painted. Maybe it was a bit crazy but he needed it for inspiration. People write off the Tiny connection with Martin but I think it's more relevant than anyone could possibly know. He needed that. The substance was Tiny and it always was. He would quote Tiny when I'd arrive in the morning, "Dave, listen to this bit…" and you'd sit there thinking, "Why is he playing this?"' [16]

Tiny was definitely the heart of the matter. Martin explained the importance of Tiny to Lin Utzon and Roslyn too. Roslyn said, 'Tiny and Luna Park were the two major things he talked about. He explained how Luna Park was about good/evil/religion and the moral compass of the city. He was quite lonely then. There weren't a lot of people dropping in.'

Friends were no longer sure where they would find Martin. Was he in bed or in hospital? Said Roslyn, 'He was so patient in hospital. Everybody loved looking after him because he was so polite and he didn't push his weight around. When he was going to hospital every six weeks or so, I'd say to the head nurse, "I know your beds are full but he will improve very quickly if he is put next to a window". He hated the food but towards the end he was loving the food.' [17] Located with an outside view, Martin sketched what he saw from his window, some of which were his last prints.

The honour that moved Martin most was conferred by the National Art School (East Sydney Tech) where he had studied in the early-60s, along with the old gang. It was where he met Peter Powditch, Jenny Kee, Garry Shead and so many others, sometimes not even at art school – but where the art students hung out. Martin described picking up the award, 'I reckon it was one of the greatest nights of my life! They were so good to me, I felt very at home, I felt very moved. I spoke about being at my old alma mater. I stood up to do it with my oxygen machine. I was pretty feeble but I was moved to tears by the citation and the atmosphere. I started off saying, "I left school, I didn't know what to do but it was Justin O'Brien my art teacher who told me Why don't you go to the National Art School? So I did. And here I am…" - and it went from there…' [18]

At one memorable Wirian gathering, everyone sat around a spread laid out on a table on the back porch. (The oxygen man was present to ensure that Martin had a long enough line-extension.) Steven, Angelica and Maggie sat with Martin outside while Natalie was computerising Martin's pictures inside. Cousin Katie's son Rupert Reid called in and sparked Martin up. As writer and director, Rupert was a finalist in the Tropfest short film festival for his short film *Boo* – a sardonic comment about death. Greg gave Martin a smaller oxygen inhaler and Martin presented a possum skin cloak to Maggie. There is great significance around the making and wearing of possum skin cloaks, which Martin understood when he honoured Maggie that afternoon. She responded by reciting her poems from memory. Then she got out her book and kept reciting. Martin happily exclaimed. 'This is exactly what Wirian is about!'

One of Angelica's hospital patients had given her a photograph depicting Henry Lawson (or someone playing him) drunkenly holding forth at Speaker's Corner at Sydney's Domain. It was a picture no one had seen before and Martin wanted to verify its authenticity. If genuine, he wanted to make an official release via the Mitchell Library. The Library had recently taken down Martin's *Tapestry* for cleaning, with plans to re-hang it two floors down.

After a long illness, art critic and fellow 'Larrikin of London', Robert Hughes died in New York in August. His best selling books include *The Shock of the New* (1980), *The Fatal Shore* (1986) and *Goya* (2006). Martin and Richard used to frequent Vadim's coffee lounge in the early-60s where Robert held court to admirers who clung on his every word. While between digs, Martin lived with him briefly in London. He laughingly recalled his mother meeting Robert and telling him, 'I can't understand a word you are saying. You are far too clever for me'. [19]

Albie Thoms died too. Albie - the pioneer underground filmmaker and cornerstone of the original Yellow House. The years had passed but his colleagues' high esteem remained unchanged. Said Tim, 'Everyone loved Albie. Jonny took a great shot of Martin and Albie standing outside the Mitchell Library arm-in-arm. They went there for a function and they were both dying of cancer. They had a wake for Albie at Paddington Town Hall. He was a very good writer. He wrote the book shortly before he died. His last thing was to write his book, *My Generation*'. [20]

Albie's memoir gave an inside look at the period when he and his peers were at the epicentre of Sydney's creative happenings. In his Foreword, he wrote, 'This is an account of the Counter-Culture in Sydney in the Sixties as I experienced it. Beginning in 1960 at Sydney University, where some of its ideas first emerged, it ends in 1972 with the election of the Whitlam government, pledged to deliver much of its program. In between are the efforts of a diverse group of people, most of whom had some sort of contact with one another, though they rarely acted in unison. They were, however, united in their opposition to censorship, conscription, cultural conservatism, racism, sexual discrimination and Australia's role in the Vietnam War.' [21]

Jeannie was another strong 60s voice. She released her *So U Want Blood* album to CD and gave Martin a copy to enjoy - he did the 'So U Want Blood' poster for her 1983 show. Since then, Jeannie had never stopped looking Martin up. Sometimes she'd sing to him. Other times they'd talk, 'One day when he was sick, Kingo brought over a DVD of James Michener who wrote a book about Hokusai. I knew nothing about Michener but we watched the interview. The day we were there Martin had bought the eight books of Hokusai's drawings and he showed us that. I came home so inspired so I wrote him a letter. I said, "Even when you're not well you give me inspiration when I come to see you!"' [22]

In February 2013 the Damien Minton Gallery in Redfern, held an Eternity-themed exhibition with Martin's big painting as its crowning glory. Enthroned in his wheelchair with his oxygen pack, Martin was wheeled in by Angelica. Guests queued to say hi and to be photographed with him. Martin told those people how well he felt and that – at last – he was on good terms with the school.

Held annually in Katoomba NSW, the Blue Mountains Music Festival marked OZ Magazine's 50th Anniversary by having Richie Walsh and Richard Neville interviewed as one of the featured acts. Martin's health made it inconceivable that he should accompany them. Anyway, he didn't feel Richie and Richard needed him. They were a self-contained lively 2-person act. They didn't even need the ABC interviewer – they bounced ideas off each other and knew all the feed lines. Richard had sold his OZ files to Yale University for a good price. As for the general public, as if too much OZ was barely enough, *The Australian* newspaper commemorated its 50th anniversary with a celebratory 3-part article spread over four days. [23]

Afterwards, Richard checked out the other acts. He was terribly impressed by Arlo Guthrie playing the Big Tent. 'How long has this been going on?' he asked. *The Blue Mountains Music Festival was in its 19th year and only 15 minutes drive from Happy Daze. How could Richard ask such a question?* Whispers were spreading that Richard was suffering from Alzheimer's Disease. Martin would have none of it. 'What's Alzheimer's!' he snapped, as if it was all fiction. [24]

When the documentary *The Sharp Edge - The Art of Martin Sharp* was televised on ABC-TV's Artscape program. Martin reckoned it was like watching one's own obituary – 'it almost killed me!' he exclaimed. Directed by Rebecca Baillie, a regular producer of *Australian Story* and the *7.30 Report*, the documentary followed Martin's artistic journey through the eyes of friends Julie Clarke, Richard Neville, Jenny Kee and Peter Kingston. Martin was not pleased. He felt they had been edited the wrong way. He was also annoyed to see himself portrayed as a smoker, having not smoked for eight months. Martin believed the program was scheduled for screening two months earlier and that they expected him to be dead when they screened it. [25]

Angelica overheard all this, 'I had a lot of feedback about *The Sharp Edge*. They said, "Why did they make it like an obituary?" We thought it was going to be about Martin's art but it's not, it's all about Martin's friends. He's been very brave. He doesn't smoke. He can't have smoke around him. In his spirit he's a lot better. He's had some very tough days. It's been hard for me, because I had to be there, just to be a support. The hardest part for me was watching how hard Martin struggled. People didn't understand that. People would get really mad at me at times because when someone is really sick, they can't handle talking to people. More questioning, more turning up, it exhausted him. It's just that he couldn't cope with it as well as fighting his body. People would understand in some respect. If you say "Please, not today" you're not offending them, it's just saying, "I've got to fight for my life right now".' [26]

In his room, Martin re-stoked his interest in the Kopson side of his family – the Fijian connection – and Angelica assisted him to source his family documents. He also read the Bobbie Hardy book, *Their Work Was Australian: The History of the Hudson Family*, which linked to the railroad side of his family. [27] He also enjoyed flicking through old copies of the *National Geographic* magazine, where he found pictures of wild prehistoric men and saw a parallel between them and the Minotaur photo of the boys at Luna Park.

Gary Shearston suffered a stroke at the end of June. Knowing it was his time to say goodbye Gary's attempted to contact Martin. But Martin didn't answer the phone that night because, as Angelica put it, 'Martin had his own battles'. [28] By the time Martin found the strength to return the call, Gary was gone. Said Garry Shead, 'Martin told me he received a message but didn't answer the phone. He must have picked it up the next day. It was Gary Shearston saying, 'I'd just love to talk to you Martin' and then he died that night.' [29]

The Yellow House premises in Macleay Street had been earmarked for development for several years. Downstairs was a smart restaurant called *Yellow* which was the venue chosen for a Yellow House Reunion, a gathering of the remaining troops and a celebration of their past. Martin sat hunched in a corner, sometimes struggling for breath as he called each Yellow House artist by name and awarded each person a certificate from the 'Ginger Meggs School of Arts' – they each accepted their certificate from Martin - George, Kingo, Peter Royles (who filmed the whole thing)…and so on. Certificates were inscribed with a personal message - 'friendship' being included alongside artistic achievements.

Martin struggled through that speech, reminding everyone that the Yellow House premises had always been an art-place. He name-checked Russell Drysdale, John Coburn, Terry and Thelma Clune. He commended George's *Yellow House Jalalabad* project. Martin closed with special mention to departed Yellow House friends like Peter Wright and Albie Thoms. He lifted his glass of short black coffee and proposed a toast. Before leaving, Martin autographed a brick on the outside of the building. In texta pen he wrote, 'This is a brick – 28.7.13' which the new owners have endeavoured to preserve. Using Marcel Duchamp logic, in signing the building, Martin declared the building a Found Object art piece and he claimed it. [30]

Returning to his Inner Sanctum, Martin worked on his enlarged version of De Chirico's *Song of Love*, a picture he'd developed with Tim Lewis in 1973 and never stopped working on. It had been exhibited several times as a work-in-progress, most notably in the Ivan Dougherty Gallery exhibition in 2006. [31] In his darkened room, with a shaft of light striking the picture, Martin scratched away at the hair on the picture that he would soon retitle 'Gracelands' and – with Peter filming him – Martin told the camera that the face was redolent of Elvis. Said Roslyn, 'He was changing the De Chirico one to make the face look more like Elvis. His last picture was for the Elvis show.' [32]

Held at Damien Minton Gallery Redfern, the 'Gracelands' exhibition was the last that Martin would attend. Like the Eternity exhibition, guests queued to talk to him as he sat confined to his wheelchair. The 'Elvis' billboard collage was exhibited and Martin sought Robert Wolfgramm's permission to reproduce a long extract from his sermon 'The King's King of Kings' in his explanatory letter to contributing artists. It was about Elvis's favourite Scripture, 1 Corinthians 13, about love. [33] In the display cabinet, Martin exhibited a framed transcript of the sermon alongside Robert's *Refugee* CD.

Many friends called to see Martin at home. Pop people like Peewee and Carla, Denny & Clare too. Martin suggested to Denny and Clare that they release his Tiny Tim tapes – particularly the talking tapes - through their Regal Records. Denny recalled, 'Martin would tape everything Tiny did, even his talks. Martin specifically said that he wanted us to take the Tiny Tim tapes so we could get them all out. We said we'd do that. He was also talking about all the dialogue he had on tape. I was thinking - "Hmm, that'll take a while…"'

Clare picked up the thread, 'He called us in to talk about that a couple of weeks before he died. He said he couldn't rest easy knowing they're not out there. We emailed back after that meeting and said "You can put it out on Regal Records if you want to and we'll see what we can do about editing them down". He was happy with that.' It was later suggested that Martin's entire collection of 1000 Tiny Tim tapes should be donated to the Smithsonian Institute, which has 19 museums and galleries across America. [34]

For her final year school Art project, Mic Conway and Roey Cook's daughter Tango chose to paint a 4-panel tribute to four artists: Martin, Reg Mombassa, Greg Weight and herself. Mic said, 'At that time Jeannie was having much more contact with Martin than me, so I said to Jeannie, "How do you feel about us going down, having fun with Martin, me singing to Martin, you singing with me as well and Tango doing drawings?" So that's what we did. Martin really enjoyed us coming around. Sometimes he was in bed and sometimes sitting up. The Cranbrook headmaster came over a couple of times when I was there. Martin was certainly happy to have this headmaster guy in there. Martin gave me and Tango a print (*Art Galaxy*). When I looked at it I asked him, "Can we use it on the CD?' He said, "Certainly, I'd love you to."' [35]

Jeannie explained too, 'Tango wanted to do a drawing so Mic and I came over and sang. (I'd already been singing there.) Mic and I did *Over the Rainbow, Singing in the Rain, Cheek to Cheek*, even Tiny Tim songs like *The Old Front Porch*. Even if I didn't know them to play I'd still sing them. Some of the songs from God Bless, or even The Second Album - *Down Virginia Way* and of course *Street of Dreams*.' [36]

And the Cranbrook headmaster, Nicholas Samson was another regular caller. Said Roslyn, 'Martin felt terribly responsible for what happened to Wirian right up to the end. He tried to do another deal with Cranbrook, they put a proposal and he didn't accept it. So he was resolving his issues with Cranbrook, maybe for pragmatic reasons to save Wirian but they couldn't come up with a deal that suited him. The headmaster was constantly dropping in. Martin wanted him there. I think he gave Martin comfort. I remember he would come over Sundays. When they first got to know each other their relationship was quite formal but they did get very close.' [37]

Martin was asked to judge the 2012 and 2013 Cranbrook art awards. 'He also created a sculpture for the school to be placed in the Chapel. It was his gift of love and the last piece of art that he did,' said Angelica. [38]

Wirian was in shutdown for the last two months of Martin's life. Joni Nelson, who had a regional radio program in Sydney's inner west decided to call Martin right out of the blue. She said, 'I decided I would try to get in touch with Martin Sharp. I found his phone number in the White Pages and just rang him up. He answered and I was nervous as hell. I thanked him for his work and we chatted about Tiny for a while. "He was one of Elvis' generation, a great performer," Martin said. "I'm still working with him." Eventually I told Martin I'd love to organise a screening of *Street of Dreams*, which I had just seen for the first time that day, and asked him if he'd like to come and introduce it. He seemed receptive but hesitant - and asked me to put it all in an email. "At least we have goodwill," he said. He died a few weeks later.' [39]

Martin's health continued its downward spiral. Said Roslyn, 'The cardiologist registrar said, "Martin, when you've had these attacks – there's not much we can do. You can see the chemicals aren't really bringing it back. There's not much hope." So he knew and he thanked them. Martin had a bit of cry in hospital about his parents and life being so short. Also that he didn't show enough love to people and stuff like that.

'He talked extensively about Luna Park, Tiny Tim and Wirian. He was very sentimental about keeping things, even a spider's web. There's some graffiti on the wall near the patio saying "do not remove" and it's a spider's web. Towards the end of his life he moved into a different way of making posters - a photographic image on art paper. Natalie Pratt was working very closely with him and she was his last printer. She's very loyal to Martin and he was very fond of her. A lot of the last prints – like the *Schoolbook Series* that he was doing that he never finished - the painting has been photographed and he's reproduced it on photographic paper rather than on silk screens. Then he would put his stamp on it to make it individual. He was moving into the digital age. He wanted to learn how to work an iPad. Martin wasn't interested in his emails but he liked Google.' [40]

Martine kept a visual diary of drawings and notes to the end. He also contributed to Carol Ruff's bi-annual Ukulele Exhibition, which he could no longer attend.

Moana Olson of the Pinjarra tribe saw Martin four days before he died. He asked her represent the Aboriginal Nations at his funeral by carrying the Aboriginal Cross that he had painted. Said Angelica, 'The last thing Martin asked me to do the week before he died was send out Christmas Cards that were his drawings he gifted Cranbrook School to print and send them out to all his friends.' [41]

Many friends found it tricky getting past Martin's gatekeepers to say goodbye but Garry wangled a brief moment. 'The week before he died he really didn't want to be visited but I went in,' said Garry who stayed overnight in the eastern suburbs every week to play tennis with Greg, 'I'd sleep over then I'd spend the morning going to Martin, every Thursday. So I thought, "I'll just draw a little drawing" – I did a drawing of Vincent and Martin with angels wings sitting together.

'I had some sunflowers. I went there and was told, "You can't go in". I said, "I'll just put them on the end of his bed" and said "bye". He saw me, yes. I didn't wait for him to look at it - I just went.

'That was it.' [42]

That was it indeed, bringing this story to a close with the sad conclusion with which all biographies end.

# 18.
# WHY MARTIN MATTERS

*Martin was at a crossroad - whether to go to New York. He would have mixed in well there. But he chose to come back here and his life took a different turn. It would have been very different if he'd gone to New York. We're very glad he came back here.*
Peter Kingston

When Cream reunited in 2005 it became abundantly clear to everyone, including a reluctant Martin, that *Disraeli Gears* was his best-known work. Before 1967 no one was doing concept covers. Pre-1966 covers belonged to Marketing Departments. They'd find a promotional mug shot of the singer's face, or if it was a band, they'd line them up and someone would go click. That's how album covers were done: Beatles, Elvis, Beach Boys, Bob Dylan, Pink Floyd, The Who, Rolling Stones…click.

Then Eric asked Martin to do a cover for Cream. What he expected, we don't know. Maybe he wasn't sure himself. However, he'd seen Martin's posters, OZ artwork and paintings at the Pheasantry. Maybe Eric sensed the era of photo-covers was over (at least for a time). Maybe that's why he asked Martin…?

After *Disraeli Gears* the **concept cover** was unleashed. Some artists built a career out of it - Hipgnosis for example. Three of the best-known album cover artists were part of Martin's crowd. Matí Klarwein designed Santana's *Abraxas* and Miles Davis' *Bitches Brew* (both 1970). It was his wife Sophie who invited Martin to accompany her to a Salvadore & Gala Dalí soirée (and what a soirée that was!). Bob Seidemann designed the *Blind Faith* cover (1969) and Jerry Garcia's first solo album, *Garcia* (1972). When the Pheasantry got busted and the place was full of cops, Seidemann was the guy knocking to get in when everyone else was trying to get out. Most notorious of all was Bob Whitaker's *Butcher's Cover,* which is the Beatles 'meat' cover that was withdrawn in America. Whitaker was Martin's flatmate for a time and court-photographer to the Beatles. He and Martin did the *Beatles Calendar* together. It was Whitaker who did the Eric, Jack & Ginger photo shoot that Martin snipped up, combined with Albrecht Dürer wings and other images to create *Disraeli Gears*.

What would the cover have been without Martin? A Bob Whitaker photograph seems logical. Therefore, it would have been a band portrait of sorts. Cavorting on Ben Nevis if they wanted to look friendly - though Cream was a progressive blues band and serious musos liked to look surly, as if to enhance their musicianship by looking the opposite of smiley Pop stars. Martin's luminous colours made the cover an acid trip not a music lesson. And he made Cream look like artists not Rock stars.

Martin simply cut up the work of a 'famous' photographer, splashed a pink wash over the faces, overwhelmed the image with cut-ups and created what had never been done before and copied ever after. Where did he get that confidence? The sheer confidence of – not just Martin, all those larrikins in Sydney and London – was staggering. Even as 20-year olds, Martin, Richard Neville and Ritchie Walsh handled an obscenity trial in the Court of Criminal Appeal with aplomb. They chipped the Stipendiary Magistrate in the OZ magazines leading to the verdict and conducted themselves as if they regarded the whole matter as rather silly. Back in suburbia, everyone else's parents were hassling their teenagers for growing long hair. Yet here was a tribe of slightly older peer leaders who were way…way…beyond that!

Martin regarded his Psychedelic and Pop Art of that period as part of the flavour of the times. Art about Pop Music was everywhere. British Pop artist Peter Blake did the Beatles' *Sgt Peppers* and Richard Hamilton did their *White Album*. Normally, high art thumbed its nose at popular culture but during this brief late-60s hiatus the two art forms were forced to face off. It was enthralling to see the two styles complement each other until someone invented Baroque Rock and rendered the coupling absurd.

In his book *Cross-Overs – Art into Pop, Pop into Art*, John Walker writes, 'As art forms develop through time it becomes harder and harder to find something new to say; consequently there is a tendency to renew old art forms by appropriating material from other media and by recycling the art of the past. Transposing an image or idea from one context to another is often sufficient to alter its meaning or significance, or to recharge its shock value.' [1]

The word 'appropriation' has often been used to categorise Martin's art. He reckoned he didn't know what the word meant, but if it was a way of legitimising his *Art Book-Art Exhibition* period, he was pleased enough. Martin described the art world of the time as a car park with an empty space. He reckoned he slipped into that spot with his 1972 *Art Book*, which were cut-outs of classic paintings, with characters intermingling in each others' pictures. It was art about art. Martin depicted a Degas ballerina lilting through Vincent's cornfield, Lichtenstein's 'Whaam!' was set against Mondrian, Munch's nude was in Vincent's *Late Night Café* sitting on the pool table…

Martin said the first surfacing of that idea was Magritte's *Ready Made Bouquet* (1956), which is a figure in a black coat and bowler hat on which the artist has superimposed a glorious female figure from Botticelli's 15$^{th}$ Century painting *The Allegory of Spring*. The Botticelli image was cut-out and stuck on and what Martin called 'in its purest form'. Martin also said that *Art Book* was been deeply influenced by popular song. Other than Hamilton's Bing Crosby against a De Chirico streetscape, it's difficult to know what Martin meant. Did he see in his own montages a collage of song that would later become Tiny's marathons?

London publishers Mathews Miller Dunbar, published *Art Book* and Martin returned to Australia carrying those themes. In 1973 he decided to paint some of those pictures on canvas, and so – with Tim Lewis as his co-artist – they created *Art Exhibition*, a concept he never lost. Through the maze of film, posters and music that became Martin's life, it may be difficult to see that fine thread in Martin's later pictures, but *Pentecost* came out of *Art Book*, as did the concept of his final picture, De Chirico's *Song of Love* that he retitled *Gracelands*. And the Dream Museum - what was that if not an intermingling of different worlds? *Eternity* too, popping up in Haymarket, with Tiny, on the road to Tarascon, in 'Australia' (*Federation Tapestry*). Martin would say, 'I never create a new image when one already exists doing that job'.

Martin also impacted on some of Sydney's most significant buildings. The current face of **Luna Park**, since 1982, is a fibreglass mould of his 1973-1981 face, so in a distorted way, Martin's face still serves as the gateway. We probably wouldn't have Coney Island if not for the efforts of Martin, Kingo, Sam Marshall and other Friends of Luna Park. If not for the whole tribe of them, many valuable pieces of Arthur Barton's art would not have been preserved. First - they attended the auction, second - they bought everything they could afford, third – they rescued the pieces that didn't sell from the tip, fourth – they stored them, fifth – they restored them until they finally got them back into the Park. And the Memorial? Who knows if there would have been any memorial if the Friends - with the support of Jenny Poidevin - had not insisted?

After the Ghost Train fire, Martin pieced together a theory that Abe Saffron had deliberately orchestrated the conflagration as a way of getting control of the place and turning it into a development. Six children and one adult died, which no one wanted to happen. Martin reasoned his case from synchronicity rather than from empirical evidence, which made some people think his ideas were quite loopy. The years pass. Nobody ever records this period about Luna Park without tabling Martin's case, whether they agree with it or not. They laughed then but they're not laughing now.

Martin also impacted on the **Sydney Opera House** saga. In 1965 Jorn Utzon withdrew as Chief Architect and even though the Utzon name has always been synonymous with the Opera House in the minds of Sydneysiders, his name was omitted from speeches at official functions. For an architect deserving of the highest praise, the insult could not have been more palpable. Martin always backed Utzon. He had the Opera House blueprints framed and hanging in his hall. Along with Jorn's daughter Lin, Martin played a crucial role in affecting reconciliation between the architect and the Opera House committee. Utzon may not have travelled to see his masterpiece but his son and daughter did and he graciously accepted the committee's efforts to make peace and give him the credit that is his due.

Martin seldom claimed credit himself but in the Millennium New Year celebrations and Olympic Games 2000, the **Sydney Harbour Bridge** was ablaze with the word 'Eternity' for a worldwide audience of 3.6 billion. Asked whether this was his input, Martin usually credited Ignatius Jones, Remo Giuffré and Arthur Stace, even though everyone else associated the 'Eternity' revival with Martin. He used it to great effect in the *Haymarket* poster for the public rally that resulted in Paddy's Market's building facade being preserved. Another 'Eternity' features in Martin's big portrait of Tiny held by Macquarie University. 'Eternity' just kept going and going – at least three films, several books, lots of poems and songs, and often featured on the billboards outside Protestant churches.

Another building associated with Martin was 59 Macleay Street Potts Point, which became the **Yellow House**. It went through many phases and many changes but never lost its provenance as the site where Martin and crew created an exciting live-in art gallery that Sydneysiders have never forgotten. The effect of the Yellow House on one repeat visitor was that it taught him that you could live in Art, which he has attempted to do ever since. The Yellow House was always a Martin Sharp place. Maybe that's what he was acknowledging when he signed the building in 2013. After he left in 1972, Martin left his pictures, which is why it always seemed like a Martin Sharp place even after he was gone.

Given enough time, most of Martin's fascinations came good, even the little running men. Eaweard Muybridge is known for using multiple cameras to capture stop-motion photographs and is credited with being a pioneer of motion pictures. In 2015, a film was made about him directed by Canadian actor, writer and director Kyle Rideout with Michael Eklund (*Smallville, Bates Motel, Dirk Gentley's Holistic Detective Agency…*) taking the role of Muybridge.

Even the Dream Museum lives on. Surely the **Toy Museum** in Leura in the Blue Mountains was inspired by Martin and Richard Liney's Dream Museum?

Hokusai has gone from strength to strength too. In August 2017, the claim was made that Hokusai's 'Great Wave' is the most reproduced artwork in history. It's on t-shirts, canvas shoes, socks, laptop cases. It is also used in advertising and as a reference in films. *Hokusai's Wave* is also a pictogram or what is known as an emoji used on iPhones. It certainly did not enjoy that status when Martin started appropriating it.

Even Martin's most contentious subject found a comfortable place in music history. That Tiny had never been given a boxed set annoyed Martin for years. Ten years after Tiny's passing Rhino Entertainment, a division of Warner Bros, released the 3-CD boxed set of Tiny's complete Reprise recordings. And in 2000, Richard Perry released Tiny's inspirational Royal Albert Hall concert to CD. Nothing is obscure any more, thanks to the Internet. Tiny is there for everyone who wants him. The worldwide web has ensured that everyone, anywhere, can track Martin's pictures. His strike rate on Instagram exceeds many great Australian artists. Martin gets 700 hits to their seven. Like Toulouse-Lautrec, Martin's best-known works are his posters.

The building Martin treasured most was **Wirian**, his family home. Its status was described by the *Sydney Morning Herald* in these words: 'The dying wish of Australia's greatest Pop artist, Martin Sharp, was that his grand heritage home Wirian in Bellevue Hill be preserved and used for exhibiting and continuing his work. And he asked the Cranbrook school to stop using his name for its annual art prize, saying his permission was never sought or granted. His estate was valued at $11.25 million including $2.1 million of art, furniture and personal effects, most of which are inside Wirian. He envisaged the property to be a place for education in his work and that of other artists.' [2]

Martin protected important buildings, important ideas and he made people feel good about space and colour. After Martin's passing, many artists painted tribute pictures to their friend and mentor. South Hill Gallery's celebration of Martin in their 2014 *Art for Mart* exhibition was a flood of pictures from Martin's peers and admirers. Roger's lightbox creation *Abraxas Redux* and Philippe's portrait of Martin with Vincent certainly stood out.

Sitting in his lounge room where the walls feature five big Martin Sharp posters, Lex Marinos described his feelings when Martin died. Lex reminisced, 'I was writing to Richard Walsh at the time Martin died - I was working with Richard on a book – I wrote: "whatever it is you're feeling today, I'm sitting here writing this in what is the happiest room in the house". We've been in this house 30 or something years now. We've had deaths, weddings, births, anniversaries, all in there and it's just the happiest room in the house. Every morning I walk into it and I turn around and look at all these posters and think – WOW - I just feel good. I'm eternally in Martin's debt for that!' [3]

# NOTES

**CHAPTER 1**

(1) Inquiry into the fire and deaths at Luna Park, NSW Coroner's Court, 3 September 1979, p. 1082-1086.

(2) Tina Shakeshaft, Police statement, North Sydney Police Station, 10 June 1979.

(3) Trevor Dinsmore, Police statement, North Sydney Police Station, 10 June 1979.

(4) Robert Baikie, sworn statement to the Coroner, 21 August 1979.

(5) Leslie Dowd, statement given to John Bracey (private detective) and Grahame Gambie (journalist).

(6) Robert Tilley, Funhouse: Luna Park and the Ghost Train Fire: A Secret History, unpublished, see end of Chapter 3.

(7) Martin Sharp, interview 3 March 1984.

(8) Peter Kingston, interview 24 October 2114.

(9) Martin Sharp, interview 3 March 1984.

(10) Martin Sharp, interview 18 August 1983.

(11) Duncan McNab, pp. 1-20, 77, The Usual Suspect, the Life of Abe Saffron, Pan Macmillan Australia, 2005.

(12) Ibid, pp. 82-84.

(13) Roger Foley-Fogg, interview 23 October 2014.

(14) Sam Everingham, Madam Lash, p. 71, Allen & Unwin, 2010, 288 pp.

(15) Jonny Lewis and Roger Foley, interview 26 July 2014.

(16) Duncan McNab, pp. 137-139.

(17) Martin Sharp, interview 3 March 1984.

(18) Sam Marshall, Luna Park, Just for Fun, p. 117-120, Luna Park Reserve Trust 1995.

(19) Report on Luna Park Sydney, Australia, 1980. Section titled, 'History of the Friends of Luna Park'.

(20) Registration of the company Harbourside Amusement Park Pty under the NSW Companies Act.

(21) Martin Sharp, interview 3 March 1984.

(22) Martin Sharp, interview 3 March 1984.

(23) Maurice Spatt, taped statement to Russell Sharp, 31 May 1981.

(24) Sam Marshall, Luna Park, Just for Fun, p. 125.

(25) Auction Catalog, called 'Auction Souvenir, Sun/Mon May 31/June 1', 28 pages, printed on a duplicating machine by Geoff K Gray Pty Ltd, 1981.

(26) Martin Sharp, interview 11 December 1983.

(27) Martin Sharp, interview 7 November 1983.

(28) Peter Kingston, interview 24 October 2114.

(29) Jon Lewis, Facebook message, 28 July 2015.

(30) Martin Sharp, interview 7 March 1984.

(31) John Barker, Facebook message, 5 May 2115.

(32) Mal Ramage, interview 8 February 2116.

(33) Susan Jensen, Facebook message June 2115.

(34) Ian Reid, interview 13 February 2116.

(35) Martin Sharp, interview 27 May 2005.

(36) Richard Neville, article, 'An Enfant Terrible Turns 20', Sydney Morning Herald, Good Weekend, 9 April 1983.

(37) Martin Sharp, interview 7 November 1983.

(38) Martin Sharp, interview 7 March 1984.

(39) Street of Dreams, film (as screened by ABC Television).

(40) Martin Sharp, interview 1 February 1983.

(41) These are the full credits for contributors to Street of Dreams, the Brighton Cut (1988). Produced and directed by Martin Sharp. Executive Producer: Jo Sharp. Co-Producer: Deanne Judson. Supervising Editor: Paul Healy. Assistant Editor: Marilyn Karet. Musical Director: Nathan Waks. Associate Producers: Elizabeth Knight, Hadyn Keenan, Marilyn Karet. Assistant to the Producers: Marsha Bennett, Russell Sharp. Camera: Geoff Burton, Russell Boyd, Tom Cowan, George Gittoes, Mike Edols, Mike Molloy, Simon Smith, Peter Levy, David Sanderson, Michael Glasheen. Camera Assistants: Marsha Ansara, Fergus Lindsay, Jan Kenny, John Brock. Lighting Directors: Brian Bansgrove, Roger Foley, Paul Moyes. Extra Special Lighting: Michael Glasheen, David Lourie, James Ricketson, George Greenough. Recording Engineers: Jeff Doring, Bill Hicks, Rob Hicks, Mark Lewis, Laurie Fitzgerald, David Glasser, Richard Merryman, Nick Swift, Barry Wolfison, Ted Robinson, Grant Roberts, Peter Hammond. Editors: Michael Balson, John Scott, Chris Cordeaux. Editing Assistants: Pam Barnetta, Mitzi Goldman, Helen Martin, Claire O'Brien. Sound Editors: Sally Fitzpatrick, Ashley Grenville, Malcolm B Smith, Jodi Rose, Sarah-Jane Campbell. Sound Mixing: Peter Fenton, Martin Oswin. Palais Design at Luna Park: Richard Liney, Tim Lewis. Wardrobe: Melody Cooper, Les Bean. Tailor: Tony Bonnici. Make-Up Artists: Edwina Archer, Melody Cooper, David Lucas, Richard Lucas. Research: Alison Lockwood, Chris Connolly, Amy Wells. Marathon Musicians: John Harding (violin), Dave Donovan (electric guitar), Dave Ellis (bass), Jeff Oakes (sax), Doug Gallagher (drums),

Tony Ansell (electric piano), Peter Haslem (trombone). Additional Musicians: Tommy and Phil Emmanuel (guitars), Nathan Waks (piano, cello), Alistair Jones (piano), Mike Kenny (electric piano), Eric Thompson (trumpet), David Gulpilil (didgeridoo). Song Marathon Continuity: Linda Ray, Still Photographers: William Yang, Jon Lewis, Robert McFarlane. Production Assistants: Albert Peck, Doris Ricona, Andrew Sharp, Jannie Higginson. Production Secretaries: Wilma Schinella, Alison Gentle. American Crew: Director Mike Edols. Associate Producers: Sussan Ray, Raymond Brazil. Gaffers: Karl Shumann, Mark Peterson. Sound Recordists: Helen Kaplan, Silvi Thomrad, Larry Hoff. Title Animation: Michael Glasheen.

(42) Martin Sharp interview 13 April 1983.

(43) In 2006 (approx.) Dave Rowe transferred the Marathon to CD format but it has never been commercially available to the public.

(44) Mic Conway, interview 24 January 2015.

(45) Lex Marinos, interview 27 May 2115.

(46) Jeannie Lewis, interview 7 May 2115.

(47) The picture Couples (created in 1979) was purchased by Patrick White, a bequest to the Art Gallery of New South Wales.

(48) Sam Marshall, Luna Park, Just for Fun, p. 130-131.

## CHAPTER 2

(1) Martin Sharp, interview 6 September 1982.

(2) Ken Done, interview 23 May 1990.

(3) Richie Walsh, author's diary notes, 19 December 2005.

(4) Richard Neville and Julie Clarke, The Life and Crimes of Charles Sobhraj, Jonathon Cape 1979.

(5) For a sample of his wide-ranging subject matter see Richard Neville, Out of my Mind, Penguin Books, 1996.

(6) Max Skeen, interview 24 February 2016.

(7) Jim Anderson, 12 May 2115.

(8) Philippe Mora, email 1 September 2016.

(9) For Albie Thoms see, Polemics for a New Cinema, 427p, Wild & Woolley, 1978. For Roger Foley-Fogg see, Maggie Tabberer, Maggie, pp. 160-161, 164-165, 209, 275. Allen and Unwin 1998.

(10) Amber Tarling, interview 20 February 2016. Zoë Lake, 23 February 2016.

(11) Electra Foley, Ginger in Japan, Sceggs Darlinghurst Year 9 Visual Arts Assignment, 2001.

(12) Roslyn Sharp, email 28 September 2016. Also see, William Yang, Sydney Diary, pp. 24-27, James Fraser Publishers, 1984.

(13) Martin Sharp, interview 29 November 2009.

(14) See: www.environment.nsw.gov.au

(15) Martin Sharp, interview 29 December 1990.

(16) Martin Sharp, interview 16 October 2003.

(17) Martin Sharp, interview 27 May, 2005.

(18) Born in 1960, to Ruth and Ross Campbell, Cressida Campbell studied at East Sydney Technical College in 1978-1979. Having developed an interest in woodblock printing, in 1980 she left Australia to study at the Yoshida Hanga Academy in Tokyo. Cressida is Little Nell's the youngest sister.

(19) Kathy Lette, quoted in Living in the 70s by Alison Pressley, p.123, Random House Australia, 2002.

(20) John Dale, Huckstepp – A Dangerous Life, pp. 135-136, Allen & Unwin, 2000.

(21) William Yang, interview 5 August 1983.

(22) Martin Sharp, interview 5 August 1983.

(23) William Yang, interview 5 August 1983.

(24) Martin Sharp, interview 5 August 1983.

(25) Melody Cooper, email 5 July 2115.

(26) William Yang, interview 5 August 1983.

(27) Martin Sharp, interview 5 August 1983.

(28) Melody Cooper, email 5 July 2115.

(29) Russell Sharp, interview 5 June, 2115. And Stephen Lawson, interview 10 June 2115.

(30) Roslyn Sharp, interview 1 April 2016.

(31) Russell Sharp, interview 5 June, 2115. Russell assisted Martin in creating the finished artwork for the Chameleon cover using a photograph of Tiny Tim taken by William Yang.

(32) The Chameleon sessions were released on LP record in 1982. Rereleased to CD in 2006, the tracks St Louis Blues, Dancing in the Street and Tiny Bubbles were included on the CD, and Stayin' Alive was remixed to include David Gulpilil on didgeridoo.

(33) Martin Sharp, interview 13 April 1983.

(34) William Yang and Martin Sharp, interview 5 August 1983.

(35) Tiny Tim, interview 24 August 1982.

(36) Martin Sharp, interview 5 August 1983.

(37) Mal Ramage, interview 8 February 2016.

## CHAPTER 3

(1) Martin Sharp, interview 6 September 1982.

(2) Stephen Lawson, interview 10 June 2015.

(3) Martin Sharp, interview 6 January 2006.

(4) 'William Sharp (Australian politician)' see Wikipedia, and Martin Sharp, interview 1 February 1983.

(5) Dave Rowe, interview 8 May 2015.

(6) Martin Sharp, interview 1 February 1983.

(7) Dingo is the title song on the 1974 album released on the Charisma label. We Want Freedom (The Charter of Aboriginal Rights) appears on the 1964 album Songs of Our Time. See also Gary Shearston, interview 1 November 2001.

(8) Martin Sharp, interview 6 January 1991.

(9) Tiny Tim, Live at the Royal Albert Hall was released to CD by Rhino Records (a division of Warner) in 2000.

(10) Albert Goldman, Elvis, Viking Books, 1981. See also, New York Times, 28 April 1968.

(11) Albert Goldman, letter to Martin Sharp dated 7 February 1982.

(12) Albert Goldman, letter to Martin Sharp dated 20 April 1982. See also, Albert Goldman, Ladies and Gentlemen – Lenny Bruce!! pp. 448, 457, 498, Random House, 1974.

(13) Martin Sharp, interview 6 September 1982.

(14) Lowell Tarling, diary notes, 27 August 1982.

(15) Tiny Tim, interview 24 August 1982.

(16) Lowell Tarling, 'The Great Pretender', Southern Flyer, September 1982.

(17) Martin Sharp, interview 1 February 1983.

(18) Martin Sharp, interview 25 February 2002.

(19) Martin Sharp, interview 6 September 1982.

(20) Martin Sharp, interview 1 February 1983.

(21) Mic Conway, interview 24 January 2115.

(22) John Singleton, Martin Sharp and Tiny Tim, taped conversation at Eliza's Restaurant Double Bay, 26 August 1982.

(23) Roslyn Sharp, interview 1 April 2116.

(24) Tiny Tim, interview 24 August 1982.

(25) Martin Sharp and Tiny Tim, interviewed on ABC Radio by Tony Bowral, 1982.

(26) The Olcott Hotel is located in New York City's Upper West Side, close to the Dakota Hotel. It was Tiny's home for the next 12 years. His mother Tillie lived with him until her passing in 1986.

(27) Bucks Burnett, Facebook 2016.

(28) Michael Duffy, 'At Home with Clive Evatt', Sydney Morning Herald, 15 April 2012.

(29) Peter Kingston, interview 7 October 2010. Kingo did the Marquette and a tradesperson from Lithgow took the design and created the sculptures.

(30) Martin Sharp interview 7 July 1984.

(31) Russell Sharp, interview 5 June 2115.

(32) Roslyn Sharp, interview 1 April 2116.

(33) Martin Sharp, interview 13 May 1983.

(34) Letter from Martin Sharp to Lowell Tarling, 30 July 1984.

(35) Martin Sharp, Cartoons, p. 40, 47, Scripts Pty Ltd, 1966.

## CHAPTER 4

(1) Martin Sharp interview 5 July 1984.

(2) Martin Sharp interview 18 August 1983.

(3) Martin Sharp interview 6 September 1982.

(4) Martin Sharp interview 1 February 1983.

(5) Tiny Tim, Keeping My Troubles to Myself, 45 rpm mini-album. A Noive and Voive Production for Street of Dreams 1983. Kinselas poster, see James Anfuso, Rockin Australia – 50 Years of Concert Posters 1957-2007, Volume 3, page 1916, Starman Books, Tuart Hill WA, 2014.

(6) Martin Sharp interview 14 November 1984.

(7) Toto Renshaw and Peter Royles at Wirian, 16 April 1983.

(8) Martin Sharp interview 13 April 1983.

(9) Martin Sharp interview 5 August 1983.

(10) Peter Royles, statement recorded by Martin Sharp, 27 July 1983.

(11) William Yang, Sydney Diary, James Fraser Publishing, 1984, page 129.

(12) Martin Sharp interview 5 August 1983.

(13) Martin Sharp letter to Lowell Tarling, 30 July 1984.

(14) Ludvig Nordstrom, William Kopson's Diary, 144 pages, translation by GM Lindergren, published by Alb Boniers Boktryckeri, Stockholm, 1933. See also, Martin Sharp interview 11 April 1993.

(15) Stephen Lawson interview 10 June 2015. See also, Stephen Lawson, Martin Sharp Works on Paper, 38 pages, published by Stephen Lawson 2010.

(16) Roslyn Sharp, interview 23 April 2011.

(17) Tiny Tim, Peter Royles and guests ('room' tape), 21 August 1983.

(18) Les Bean, interview 3 September 1983.

(19) Neil Hollander expelling Les Bean from the Wentworthville Leagues Club, (taped) 3 September 1983.

(20) Tiny Tim plays the Castanet Club, Newcastle, (tape) 4 September 1983. See also, Joyce Morgan, 'Tiny on Love, Sex and Sin', Newcastle Herald, 5 September 1983.

(21) Tiny Tim plays Kinselas Sydney (tape), 1 September 1983.

(22) The musicians were: Denny Burgess (bass), Di Pritchard (guitar), Mac Lancaster (keyboards), Colin Burgess (drums). Musical producer: Al Jones. Recorded at Sun Studios Sydney, 7 October 1983.

(23) Denny Burgess interview 28 July 2115.

(24) Kate Fitzpatrick, 'Tiny Tim, What's That Secret You're Keeping?', The Good Weekend, Sydney Morning Herald, 3 September 1983.

(25) Justin Martell and Alanna Wray McDonald, pp. 258-260, Eternal Troubadour, the Improbably Life of Tiny Tim, Jawbone Press, 2116. See also, Truth, 14 September 1985.

(26) Martin Sharp interview 7 November 1983.

(27) Gary Shearston, Dingo from the album of the same name, Charisma Records, 1977.

(28) Robert Wolfgramm and Lowell Tarling, Persecution Games LP, Galilee Records 1985.

## CHAPTER 5

(1) Martin's 'Syd Fest '84' colour poster was also the cover of the festival's program and their A4 handbill. The second poster resembled Martin's Catalog. It was a full page in Sydney Morning Herald, 7 December 1983.

(2) POL magazine, January 1984, for sale on p.42 for $20. This issue featured a 'summary' collage of Martin's past two years. Pages 57-58 were a double-page Jonny Lewis collage of Martin, Albie, Toto, Cressida, Jo, Brett, Kingo, William, Richard, Yensoon – and Jonny himself.

(3) See Michael Organ, University of Wollongong online. 'Martin Sharp posters 1982-1983': (1) Adelaide Festival, (2) The Arias, (3) Art Sale for Land Rights, (4) Festival of Sydney, (5) Circus OZ, (6) Tiny Paddo Masquerade, (7-8) Cold Chisel Circus Animals – two posters, (9) Tiny Tim – The Chameleon, (10) Tiny Tim Eternal Troubadour Opera House, (11) Jeannie Lewis, So You Want Blood, (12) Sydney Opera House is Ten, (13) Music Week, (14) Maureen Turquoise, Sydney Textile Fashion Show, (15) Tiny Tim Kinselas.

(4) Stephen Lawson interview 10 June 2115.

(5) Martin Sharp interview 11 December 1983.

(6) Martin Sharp interview 12 February 2011.

(7) Roslyn Sharp interview 1 April 2016.

(8) Martin Sharp interview 3 March 1984.

(9) Allan Broadhurst interview 25 May 2014.

(10) Martin Sharp, letter to Lowell Tarling, 30 July 1984.

(11) Phil Ward, Azaria! What the Jury Were Not Told, 192 pp, published by PCW 1984. See also Lowell Tarling, Azaria's Rock, Rolling Stone magazine (Aust), April 1984 pages 70-77, 87-88. In October, Martin bought the John Bryson book Evil Angels, on which the film was based.

(12) Michael Chamberlain, telephone conversation with author, 15 May 1984.

(13) Martin Sharp, letter to Lowell Tarling, 4-7 May 1984.

(14) Tape of Dr Des Ford's sermon at Macquarie University, 25 February 1984.

(15) Martin Sharp interview 23 August 1983. Exhibition catalog, The Face of Sydney, 24p, Sydney College of Advanced Education, 1984.

(16) Patrick White quoted by Martin Sharp, 23 August 1983.

(17) Martin Sharp interview 23 August 1983.

(18) Sam Marshall, Luna Park: Just for Fun p. 131.

(19) Strange Days comic, written by written by Peter Milligan, art by Brendan McCarthy and Brett Ewins, Eclipse Comics, California, 1984. Also, Outcast pages 17-18, Vol 1 No 1, Angus & Robertson, North Ryde, 1980.

(20) Jeannie Lewis interview 7 May 2015.

(21) Roslyn Sharp interview 1 April 2116.

(22) Garry Shead and Judit Englert-Shead, The Mural, The Meaning, NSW TAFE Information Services Division, 47pp, April 1985.

(23) Garry Shead interview 13 February 2115.

(24) Lowell Tarling diary notes, 13 January 1985.

(25) Malcolm Mead, statement 1 June 1985.

(26) Patrick Howard, 'The Case of the Unexplained Fires', The National Times, 28 June-4 July 1985. The six properties are: The Creole Disco – Bondi Beach, 148 Brighton Boulvarde – Bondi, 194 Victoria Street – Kings Cross, The Peak Restaurant – Bondi Junction, The Venus Room – Kings Cross and Fonzies Amusement Arcade – Darlinghurst.

(27) 'The Good Shepard Dumped', Sunday Telegraph 1 September 1985.

(28) Sun Herald, Sunday 13 October, Luna Park Enquiry re-opened.

(29) John Barker, statement 31 May 1985.

(30) John Barker, Facebook message, September 12, 2012.

(31) Martin Sharp, statement 1 June 1985.

(32) Lowell Tarling, diary notes.

(33) Duncan McNab, The Usual Suspect, the Life of Abe Saffron, pp. 245-248.

## CHAPTER 6

(1) Laurie Duggan, The New Australian Poetry p. 277. Also, Martin Sharp interview 29 January 1985.

(2) Bernard O'Dowd, 'Australia' p.187, Poetry in Australia Volume 1, From the Ballads to Brennan, Angus & Robertson 1964. Martin Sharp, interview 11 April 1993.

(3) Thomas Moore, The Meeting of the Waters.

(4) Amber Mackenzie, interview 20 February 2016.

(5) Martin Sharp, interview 5 July 1984.

(6) Albie Thoms, Polemics for a New Cinema, 426pp, Wild & Woolley 1978.

(7) Philippe Mora, films 1976-1987 – Mad Dog Morgan (1976), The Beast Within (1982), The Return of Captain Invincible (1983), A Breed Apart (1984), Howling II (1985), Death of a Soldier (1986), Howling III (1987).

(8) William Yang, Starting Again, 122pp, William Heinemann, 1989.

(9) Tiny Tim, interview 6 September 1983.

(10) Tiny Tim, interview 30 August 1983.

(11) Linda Langton, interview 9 October 1987.

(12) Ken Done, interview 23 May 1990.

(13) Dare Jennings, interview 17 December 1991.

(14) Peewee and Carla Wilson, interview 14 February 1984. See also, Timothy Leary, The Politics of Ecstasy, 302pp, Paladin 1970.

(15) Jonny Lewis, interview 8 June 2016.

(16) Martin Sharp, interview 11 November 1992.

(17) Jonny Lewis, interview 8 June 2016.

(18) Gillian Armstrong, concert video of Bob Dylan's True Confessions tour. Screened as an HBO special.

(19) Jonny Lewis, interview 8 June 2016.

(20) Martin Sharp, interview 11 November 1992.

(21) Dave Rowe, interview 8 May 2015.

(22) Arthur McIntyre, 'Man-Child Sharp - a force for good', The Age, 13 September 1986.

(23) Roslyn Oxley9 catalogue for 'Sharp Art Show'.

(24) Martin Sharp, Art Book, p. 31, Mathews Miller Dunbar, 1972. Martin incorporates 'Red Room' by Matisse, 'Bird in Flight' by Magritte and Vincent van Gogh's 'Chair with Pipe'.

(25) Stephen Lawson, interview 10 June 2015.

(26) Louis Whitely Strieber, Transformation: The Breakthrough, Beech Tree Books, New York, 1988. Strieber uses Jo Sharp as a case study about the shattering effects of an assault from the unknown. He quotes directly from Martin and Yensoon's written notes.

(27) Martin Sharp, interview 3 March 2011.

(28) Martin Sharp and Robbie Tarling, diary notes (Lowell Tarling) 26 March 1987.

(29) William Yang and Martin Sharp, interview 5 August 1983.

(30) Tom Thompson, interview 8 July 2015. See also, Tom Thompson, Growing Up in the 60s, 88pp, Kangaroo Press, 1986. And, Lowell Tarling, 1967, This Is It! 214pp, Generation Books 1990.

(31) Peter Royles, 7 November 2014. And, Lowell Tarling, 1987 diary notes.

(32) Martin Sharp, diary notes (Lowell Tarling) January-February 1987.

(33) Martin Sharp, diary notes (Lowell Tarling) 22 May 1987.

(34) James Cockington and Caroline Taylor, 'A Collective Obsession', Sydney Morning Herald, 4 June 1987.

(35) Martin Sharp, letter to Lowell Tarling, 14 July 1987.

(36) Hugh Anderson, Australia to OZ? The making of the tapestry, 24 pp, Red Rooster Press 1996.

(37) Russell Sharp, Facebook 26 September 2015.

## CHAPTER 7

(1) Lowell Tarling, diary notes 10 March 1988.

(2) Peter Draffin, interview Peter Draffin, 20 March 2015.

(3) Peter Draffin, letter to Lowell Tarling 12 January 1989.

(4) Street of Dreams, film, see in its entirety on youtube.

(5) Martin Sharp, letter to Lowell Tarling, 7 August 1988.

(6) Martin Sharp, interview 29 November 2004.

(7) Roslyn Sharp, interview 1 April 2016.

(8) Martin Sharp, interview 29 November 2004.

(9) Susan Young, 'World Beater!' Evening Argus, 28 May 1988.

(10) Bucks Burnett, liner notes Girl CD, Rounder Records 1996.

(11) Sue Khaury, interview 1 April 2002.

(12) Susan Young, 'World Beater!' Evening Argus, 28 May 1988.

(13) Martin Sharp, interview 29 November 2004.

(14) Martin Sharp, letter to Lowell Tarling, 8 October 1988.

(15) Steven Puchalski, ShockCin@aol.com.

(16) Martin Sharp, interview 29 November 2004.

(17) Justin Martell & Alanna Wray McDonald, Eternal Troubadour, the Improbable Life of Tiny Tim, p. 381, Jawbone Press, 2016.

(18) Dave Rowe, interview 8 May 2015. See also, Martin Sharp, 'Notes from the River Caves, p. 34, Quadrant magazine, February 1977. And, Mark St Leon, Circus in Australia, p.112,

Greenhouse Publications 1983. Lilian Roxon, 'Sawdust, Greasepaint , Sideshows & Spruikers', Australia Album, 96p, Sungravure Sydney, 1974.

(19) Tiny Tim, World Non-Stop Singing Record, Brighton 1988, Street of Dreams, 1989.

(20) Dave Rowe, interview 8 May 2015.

(21) Dave Rowe, interview 21 August 1992.

(22) Martin Sharp, letter to Lowell Tarling, 7 August 1988.

(23) Martin Sharp, letter to Lowell Tarling, 8 October 1988.

(24) Dave Rowe, interview 8 May 2015.

(25) Denny and Clare Burgess, interview 28 July 2115.

(26) Martin Sharp, interview 24 January 1994.

(27) 'The Luna Park Fire Tragedy…a link with the occult?' New Idea, 11 February 1989.

(28) Tiny Tim, Highway to Hell/I Love Rock and Roll, cassingle, Regular Records 1989.

(29) Tiny Tim, Highway to Hell, youtube. Production: Martin Sharp and Michael Glasheen.

(30) Regular Records 1979-1989, the Boxed Set, two LP records and one DVD, four variations of Martin's Boofhead Band as cover images for each of the two LPs, the video and the box itself.

(31) Lowell Tarling, diary notes 1989.

(32) Martin Sharp, letter to Lowell Tarling, 8 October 1988.

## CHAPTER 8

(1) Joanna Mendelsshon, 'The Yellow House, A Brief History', Art and Australia, Winter 1990, page 568-575.

(2) Nic Lyon, interview 16 August 2015.

(3) Tony Bond, interview 12 June 2015.

(4) Sam Marshall, Luna Park – Just for Fun, p. 132-143.

(5) Martin Sharp, interview 29 December 1990. See Vincent van Gogh letter to Emile Bernard, 27 June 1888.

(6) Tony Bond, interview 12 June 2015.

(7) Letter dated 31 October 1988, from Albie Thoms to Roger Foley.

(8) Tony Bond, interview 12 June 2015.

(9) Martin Sharp, interview 29 December 1990.

(10) Berwyn Lewis, 'Viva Vincent', The Australian magazine, 14-15 July 1990 p 42. FMG magazine, June-July 1990.

(11) Lowell Tarling, diary notes 24 January 1990.

(12) Tony Bond, interview 12 June 2015.

(13) Albie Thoms Productions, circular letter dated 6 February 1989. To Yellow House artists.

(14) Greg Weight, a series of 18 b/w postcards published by Aggie Read, printed by Southwood Press Sydney, 1971.

(15) The Yellow House 1970-1972 catalogue, 56pp, Art Gallery of New South Wales.

(16) Tony Bond, interview 12 June 2015.

(17) Martin Sharp, interview 14 October 2006.

(18) Tony Bond, interview 12 June 2015.
(19) Martin Sharp, interview 29 December 1990.
(20) Roger Foley, interview 11 February 2014.
(21) Martin Sharp, interview 29 December 1990.
(22) Tim Lewis, interview 2 June 2013.
(23) Martin Sharp, quoted by Nikki Barraclough in 'Curious Yellow', Good Weekend 30 June 1990.
(24) Joanna Mendelsshon, 'The Yellow House, A Brief History', Art and Australia, Winter 1990, page 568-575.
(25) Albie Thoms, quoted in FMG magazine, June-July 1990.
(26) Nikki Barraclough, 'Curious Yellow', Good Weekend, 30 June 1990.
(27) Jonny Lewis, quoted by Berwyn Lewis, 'Viva Vincent', The Australian magazine, 14-15 July 1990.
(28) Collectibles, The Yellow House, Australian Business, 3 October 1990.
(29) Roger Foley, interview 11 February 2014.
(30) Tony Bond, interview 12 June 2015.
(31) Martin Sharp, interview 25 July 1990. The song 'Emmaus' appears on Robert Wolfgramm's CD titled Refugee, Galilee Records 1979.
(32) Albie Thoms Productions, circular letter dated 6 February 1989. To Yellow House artists.
(33) Yellow House Film Program July 25-September 21 1990. 8p. Published by the Public Programmes Department of the Art Gallery of New South Wales.
(34) The Yellow House 1970-1974, pp. 48-49, published by the Art Gallery of New South Wales.
(35) Adrian Rawlins, filmed by Roger Foley inside the reconstructed Stone Room, 1990.
(36) Jason Whalley, Facebook statement, 10 March 2015.
(37) Josef Lebovic, interview 23 July 1991. See also Brett Whiteley, Graphics, 72pp, (38) The Ginger Meggs School of Arts (The Yellow House) flyer, 8pp, Josef Lebovic Gallery, 1990. Art Gallery of Western Australia 1986.
(39) Martin Sharp, interview 29 December 1990.
(40) Greg Weight, interview 24 November 2014.
(41) Tony Bond, interview 12 June 2015.

## CHAPTER 9

(1) Martin Sharp, interview 16 January 1991.
(2) http://remogiuffre.com/post/100398132342/general-thinker
(3) Tim Lewis, interview 2 June 2013.
(4) Martin Sharp, interview 15 November 1991.
(5) Martin Sharp, interview 15 November 1991.
(6) Martin Sharp, police statement, 9 November 1991.
(7) Gria Shead, interview 19 January 2017.

(8) Property of Robbie Tarling, purchased from Josef Lebovic Gallery. The three versions of Courage My Friend are on p.32, 'Martin Sharp, Work on Paper', by Stephen Lawson, 2005.

(9) Gria Shead, interview 19 January 2017.

(10) Tim Lewis, interview 2 June 2013.

(11) Martin Sharp, interview 5 January 1991.

(12) Joel Tarling, interview 11 June 2016.

(13) Martin Sharp, interview 16 January 1991.

(14) Gordon Stintson, interview 21 October 1991. See also Tiny Tim, 45 rpm single, Leave Me Satisfied/I Wanna Get Crazy With You, released on NGT Records, 1993.

(15) Sam Marshall, Luna Park, Just for Fun, was first published in 1995 and well received as a concise history that summarised its creation, the artists and the highlights, 152pp, Luna Park Reserve Trust. In 2004 it was condensed into an attractive (40p) volume, again, well received.

(16) Tom Thompson, interview 8 July 2015. Letter to Martin Sharp from Tom Thompson, ETT Imprint, 8 June 1995.

(17) Martin Sharp, interview 5 January 1991.

(18) Martin Sharp, interview 11 November 1992.

(19) Martin Sharp, interview 6 January 1992.

(20) Amber Mackenzie, interview 20 February 2016.

(21) Ian Reid, interview 13 February 2016.

(22) Martin Sharp, interview 15 November 1991.

(23) Mark Riley, 'Jilted Lover Ends Mother's Dream of Seeing her Son', Sydney Morning Herald, 11 November 1991. Also, John McNamee, 'Woman Dies in Blaze', Sunday Telegraph 10 November 1991.

(24) Catalogue, Luna Park, Fragments of a Funfair, 8p, Historic Houses Trust of New South Wales.

(25) Tim Lewis, interview 2 June 2013.

(26) Martin Sharp, interview 11 November 1992.

(27) Dave Rowe, interview 15 April 1992.

(28) Denny Burgess, interview 11 July 2015.

(29) Tiny Tim's 60th Birthday Party produced by Martin Sharp
https://youtu.be/pW1404dWLZ0)

(30) Denny Burgess, interview 11 July 2015.

(31) Chris Löfvén, interview 25 June 2005.

(32) Allan Broadhurst, interview 25 May 2014.

(33) Dave Rowe, interview 15 April 1992.

(34) John Botica, Facebook, 11 March 2017.

(35) Dave Rowe, interview 15 April 1992.

(36) Robert Adamson, 'Creon's Dream' pp.69-77, Black Water, Brandl & Schlesinger, 1999. Whiteley, An Unauthorised Life, by Margot Hilton and Graeme Blundell, p.265, Macmillan, 1996. Martin Sharp, 'Thirroul' drawing 1992.

(37) Martin Sharp, interview 18 January 1994.

(38) 'Moronic Genius', pp. 339-341, Encyclopaedia of Aberrations, 1920.

(39) Dierdre O'Connoll, The Ballad of Blind Tom, p.10, Overlook Duckworth, 2009.

(40) Martin Sharp, interview 2 November 1992.

## CHAPTER 10

(1) Martin Sharp, interview 11 November 1992.

(2) Martin Sharp, interview 11 November 1992.

(3) Dave Rowe, phone 29 January 1992.

(4) Lowell Tarling, diary notes 24 January 1992.

(5) Martin Sharp, interview 16 January 1991.

(6) Ludvig Nordstrom, William Kopson's Diary, 144 pages, translation by GM Lindergren, published by Alb Boniers Boktryckeri, Stockholm, 1933.

(7) Stephen Lawson, interview June 2015.

(8) Martin Sharp, letter to the Luna Park Reserve Trust, 18 June 1993. General manager Chris Mangin, letter to Martin Sharp, 25 June 1993.

(9) Jenny Poidevin, letter to Luna Park Reserve Trust, read by Martin Sharp, interview 11 November 1992.

(10) Tiny Tim, Bob Dylan and the Band, Down In The Basement, released to CD in 1996. And, the Beatles 1968 Christmas Record.

(11) James 'Bucks' Burnett, cover lines, Tiny Tim with Brave Combo, Girl CD, 1996.

(12) Justin Martell and Alanna Wray McDonald, Eternal Troubadour, the Improbably Life of Tiny Tim, p. 447.

(13) Martin Sharp, interview 2 November 1993.

(14) Dave Rowe, interview 8 May 2015.

(15) Lowell Tarling, diary notes 2 November 1993.

(16) Martin Sharp, interview, 2 November 1993.

(17) Vivien Kooper and Stephen Plym, Tiny Tim and Mr Plym, p.27, Edee Rose Publishing 2004.

(18) Martin Sharp, interview, 2 November 1993.

(19) Dave Rowe, interview, 8 May 2015.

(20) Tiny Tim, Rock, Regular Records 1993.

(21) Dave Rowe, interview 8 May 2015.

(22) John Botica, Facebook message 30 August 2016.

(23) Dave Rowe, interview, 8 May 2015.

(24) Martin Sharp, interview 18 January 1994.

(25) Dave Rowe, interview, 8 May 2015.

(26) Tiny Tim, Tiny Tim's Christmas Album, released from England on the Durtro label, 1995. Also Tiny Tim's Pop Album, which has never been released. Tracks are: Satisfaction, St Louis Blues, Rainbow On the River, Caravan, Mission Bell, My Girl, House of the Rising Sun, People R Strange, Those Were the Days, I Am I Said, Without You, Egotesticle (with Nitocris).

(27) Angelica Tremblay, interview 23 April 2013.

(28) Joyce Morgan, The Life and Times of Martin Sharp, Allen & Unwin 2017. Also Philip Drew, The Masterpiece, Jorn Utzon – A Secret Life, 574pp, Hardie Grant Books, 1999.

(29) Martin Sharp, Tiny Tim Times, front page, January 1994.

(30) Sue Khaury, interview 30 March 2002.

(31) Sue Khaury, Memories of My Husband, Tiny Tim, p. 3, unpublished 1998.

(32) Tiny Tim, Prisoner of Love, Ponk Media 1995.

(33) Clare Burgess, interview 11 July 2015.

(34) Tiny Tim, Songs of an Impotent Troubadour, Durtro label 1995.

(35) Tiny Tim, I Love Me, Ponk Media 1995.

(36) Tiny Tim, Live in Chicago, Bughouse Records 1995.

(37) Tiny Tim, Tiny's Musical History Tour, unreleased 5 CDs, transferred from three VHS vidoes by Ernie Clark, USA.

(38) Tiny Tim, Live in London, Durtro, 1997.

(39) David Tibet, interview 7 April 2002.

(40) Mark Mitchell, interview 30 March 2002.

(41) Nicole Siverman & Jim Nelson, 'Tiny Tim's Desperate Plea to Daughter: Please Forgive Me', National Enquirer.

(42) Sue Khaury, interview 30 March 2002.

(43) Martin Sharp, 'My Friend Tiny Tim', Daily Telegraph, 3 December 1996.

(44) Martin Sharp, interview 3 December 1996.

## CHAPTER 11

(1) James 'Big Bucks' Burnett, Facebook message, 12 March 2015.

(2) Martin Sharp, interview 24 January 1997.

(3) Martin Sharp, 'Bound for Heaven – My Amazing Friend', Sydney Morning Herald, 3 December 1996.

(4) Martin Sharp, interview 24 January 1997.

(5) Joel Tarling, interview 11 June 2016.

(6) Sydney Morning Herald, 4 June 1996. See also Richard Neville, Out Of My Mind, 216pp, Penguin Books 1995.

(7) Canon Jim Glennon founded the St Andrews Cathedral's Healing Ministry in 1960.

(8) One book that strongly influenced Garry 60s-70s was Authoritative Occultism by HA Wallis, a 40-page book published by Garry Shead. See Garry Shead, interview, 13 February 2015.

(9) George Gittoes, Blood Mystic, 400pp, Pan Macmillan Australia, 2016.

(10) Roger Foley, email 11 May 2017.

(11) Susan Jensen, email, 11 July 2015.

(12) Ian Reid, interview 13 February 2016.

(13) Mic Conway, interview 24 January 2015.

(14) Martin Sharp, interview 3 March 1984.

(15) Jeannie Lewis, interview, 7 May 2015.

(16) Lowell Tarling, diary notes.

(17) David Tibet, interview 7 April 2002.
(18) Martin Sharp, interview 29 December 1990.
(19) Martin Sharp, interview 1 February 1983.
(20) Martin Sharp, interview 17 April 2002.
(21) Robert Wolfgramm, Refugee CD, Galilee Records, 1979.
(22) Robert Wolfgramm, 'The King's King of Kings', a sermon preached in Frankston Seventh-day Adventist Church. A transcript was sent to Martin.
(23) Gary Shearston, interview 1 November 2001.
(24) Gary Shearston, Baiame (The Greatest Stone on Earth), Anthology, Rouseabout Records, 2007.
(25) Frances Greening (Angelica Tremblay), Straight Over the Moon CD, 1997.
(26) Martin Sharp, interview 3 March 1984.
(27) Martin Sharp, interview, 5 January 1991.
(28) Robert Tilley, Funhouse, an unpublished manuscript.
(29) Robert Tilley, email 3 February 2015.
(30) Robert Tilley, email 16 March 2017.
(31) Robert Tilley, email 2 July 2015.
(32) Lowell Tarling, diary notes, 24 January 1997.
(33) Martin Sharp, telephone conversation, Lowell Tarling, diary notes, 16 May 1997.
(34) Martin Sharp interview with William Yang and Lowell Tarling, 5 August 1983.
(35) Richard Neville, Playing Around, Arrow Books, 1991.
(36) Geoffrey Robertson, The Trials of OZ, a video-taped BBC television drama shown in the UK, 9 November 1991.
(37) Richard Neville, Hippie Hippie Shake, 376pp, William Heinemann 1995.
(38) Martin Sharp, interview 16 May 1995.
(39) Martin Sharp, interview 22 October 2003.
(40) David Leitch, Obituary: Jill Neville, The Independent, 12 June 1997.
(41) Martin Sharp interview, 30 January 2003.
(42) Martin Sharp, interview 17 April 2002.
(43) Lowell Tarling, diary notes 8 November 1997.
(44) Street of Dreams, see www.youtube.com/watch?v=pzvbDL-ilZQ
(45) Susan Khaury, Memories of My Husband, Tiny Tim, an unpublished manuscript, 1998.
(46) Joyce Morgan, Martin Sharp: His Life and Times, p. 254-256, Allen & Unwin 2017.
(47) Jim Anderson, interview 12 May 2015. Also Jim Anderson, email, 19 May 2017.
(48) Catalogue, 'Yellow House Now', Michael Nagy Fine Art, 1999.
(49) Mic Conway's National Junk Band, Diagonally Parked in a Parallel Universe CD, 2014.
(50) The Backsliders, Poverty Deluxe CD, Shock Records, 1999.

## CHAPTER 12

(1) Keith Dunstan, Ratbags, p. 177-183, Golden Press 1979.
(2) Martin Sharp, interview 5 January 1991.

(3) Douglas Stewart, poem, Arthur Stace.

(4) Martin Sharp, interview 5 January 1991.

(5) Maggie Hamilton, Mister Eternity, 234pp, Scholastic Press, 1997.

(6) Eternity, produced with the assistance of the Australian Film Commission, the NSW Film and Television Office and Film Victoria, 1994.

(7) The Eternity Man, a film by Julien Temple, made for Channel 4 and the Australian Broadcasting Commission, Madman 2008.

(8) Marion Stell (editor), Eternity, Stories from the emotional heart of Australia, 124pp, National Museum of Australia, 2001.

(9) Mark Skelsey, Daily Telegraph, 6 January 2000.

(10) Martin Sharp, interview 7 January 2004.

(11) Roslyn Sharp, interview 1 April 2016.

(12) Martin Sharp, interview 17 April 2002.

(13) Basquali, Catherine, Intimate Portrait of a Champion, Pan Macmillan 2000.

(14) Martin Sharp, interview 17 April 2002.

(15) Jeannie Lewis, interview 7 May 2015. Gary Shearston, interview 1 November 2001.

(16) Martin Sharp, interview 16 October 2003.

(17) Jimmy Little, interview 1 November 1999.

(18) Martin Sharp, interview 17 April 2002.

(19) Lowell Tarling, diary notes.

(20) Dave Rowe, interview 1 August 2002.

(21) Martin Sharp, letter to Lowell Tarling, 2 August 2000.

(22) Dave Rowe, interview 8 May 2015.

(23) Electra Foley, Ginger in Japan, SCEGGS Darlinghurst Year 9 Visual Arts Assignment, 2001.

(24) Martin Sharp, letter to Electra Foley, 31 December 2001/1 January 2002.

(25) Greg Weight, May 1993, 'George Gittoes' Industrial Revolution', Australian Artist. Also, 'Kangaroo! Garry Shead's Tribute to DH Lawrence', August 1993.

(26) Gria Shead, interview 19 January 2017.

(27) Gria Shead, interview 19 January 2017.

(28) Janet Hawley, Arkie Whiteley, Obituaries Australia.

(29) Sunday Telegraph, 3 December 2000.

## CHAPTER 13

(1) NECA Head Knockers figurine, *Susan Khaury, under license.

(2) Roslyn Sharp, interview 1 April 2016.

(3) Richard Macey, 'Back to the wall in fight to rescue artist's salvation; Sydney Morning Herald, 6 March 2002.

(4) Michael Wilkinson, 'Tim's Just a Tiny Bit Broke, The Melbourne Sun, 26 June 1976.

(5) Michael Chamberlain with Lowell Tarling, Beyond Azariah, 214pp, Information Australia, 1999.

(6) Martin Sharp, interview 25 February 2002.
(7) Martin Sharp, interview 25 February 2002.
(8) Mic Conway, 6 May 2002.
(9) Mic Conway, 6 May 2002.
(10) Songs: Welcome To My Dream (God Bless Tiny Tim), Legend In My Time (3 May 1976), Tiptoe Through The Tulips (God Bless), Stay Down Here Where You Belong (God Bless), Mr Phonograph (Luna Park Marathon 1979), O Gee I'm Glad I'm A Boy (Live at the Albert Hall), Original song: mother expressing disgust, People Are Strange (Stardust), Satisfaction (Stardust), The Great Pretender (Chameleon), Street of Dreams (Chameleon), Deep Tongue (… in a vault somewhere), Original song: The Tightrope of Desire, On The Old Front Porch (God Bless), Great Balls of Fire (Tiny Tim's 2nd Album), Religious Medley (Christmas Album), That Wonderful Mother of Mine (Wonderful World of Romance) Daddy Daddy, What Is Heaven Like (God Bless), The Other Side (God Bless), Beautiful Dreamer (3 May 1975), She's Just Laughing At Me (Tiny Tim's 2nd Album), Have You Seen My Little Sue (Tiny Tim's 2nd Album), I Got You Babe (Live at the Royal Albert Hall), Beautiful Dreamer (3 May 1975), Tiptoe Through The Tulips (God Bless), Stayin' Alive (Chameleon).
(11) Tulip Stewart (Miss Tulip), interview 2 April 2002.
(12) Martin Sharp, interview 6 May 2002.
(13) Martin Sharp, Memories of Telford, a special interest publication, 2002.
(14) Gary Shearston, interview 1 November 2001.
(15) The concert was held at Almost Acoustic, Rozelle, 14 August 2004.
(16) Dave Rowe, interview 8 May 2015.
(17) Martin Sharp, interview 19 March 2005.
(18) Dave Rowe, interview 1 August 2002.
(19) Domain, Sydney Morning Herald, 2-3 August 2003.
(20) Dave Rowe, interview 8 May 2015.
(21) Roslyn Sharp, interview 1 April 2016.
(22) Dave Rowe, interview 8 May 2015.
(23) Richard Neville, interview 21 February 2003.
(24) Lowell Tarling, diary notes, 24 February 2003.
(25) Richard Neville, Footprints of the Future, p. 55, Richmond Ventures, 2002.
(26) Dave Rowe, interview 23 July 2017.
(27) Martin Sharp, interview 5 April 2011.
(28) Susan Wyndham, 'Family Hang-Ups', Sydney Morning Herald, 1-2 March 2003.
(29) Arthur Rackman, Cinderella, p.82, Exeter Books, 1987.
(30) Dave Rowe, interview 8 May 2015.
(31) Jeannie Lewis, Southheart, 2 CD, Sole Music, 2002.
(32) Philippe Mora, Art Monthly, p 8-12, Dec-Feb 2003.
(33) John Lennon, Wonsaponatime CD, track 8 - God Save OZ.
(34) Larrikins in London, curator Nick Waterlow, 120pp, CFOA-UNSW, 2003.

# CHAPTER 14

(1) John Platt, 161pp, Schirmer Trade Books; Disraeli Gears CD; Cream, Those Were The Days 4-CD boxed set; Classic Albums DVD.

(2) Disraeli Gears, Classic Albums DVD, Rajon Vision, 2006.

(3) Martin Sharp interview, Johann Rai, 19 March 2005.

(4) Lowell Tarling, diary notes 28 September 2005.

(5) Martin Sharp, interview 8 June 2005.

(6) Jonathon Pearlman, 'The Building that is really a Smokestack', Sydney Morning Herald, 2 January 2004.

(7) Martin Sharp, interview 30 January 2003.

(8) Martin Sharp, interview 7 January 2004.

(9) Eric Wilmott, Pemulwuy – The Rainbow Warrior, 310pp, Weldon, 1987.

(10) Martin Sharp, interview 31 July 2003.

(11) Roslyn Sharp, interview 1 April 2016.

(12) Martin Sharp, interview 18 June 2005.

(13) Roslyn Sharp, interview 1 April 2016.

(14) Allan Broadhurst, interview 25 May 2014.

(15) Martin Sharp, interview 18 June 2005.

(16) Martin Sharp, interview 18 June 2005.

(17) Roslyn Sharp, interview 1 April 2016. Professor Tom Borody suggests this was probably TPA (Tissue Plasminogen Activator) with a trade name of Alteplase.

(18) Martin Sharp, interview 18 June 2005.

(19) Robert Tilley, email 16 March 2017.

(20) Martin Sharp, interview 19 March 2005.

(21) Eric Clapton, The Autobiography, p. 324-325, Century London 2007.

(22) Martin Sharp, interview 19 March 2005.

(23) Dave Thompson, Cream, The World's First Supergroup, p. 256-257, Virgin 2005.

(24) Martin Sharp and Eric Clapton, Disraeli Gears, Classic Albums DVD, Rajon Vision, 2006.

(25) Lowell Tarling, diary notes 17 July 2005.

(26) The Illustrated Ape, Issue 21, Dennis Publishing, 2005.

(27) Felix Dennis, Lives and Rhymes poetry CD, Dennis Publishing, 2005.

(28) Robert Hughes, The Guardian, 7 March 2005.

(29) Matthew Thompson, 'Pop Art Master Accepts Postie's Advice', Sydney Morning Herald, 13 June 2005.

(30) Martin Sharp, interview 18 June 2005.

(31) Lowell Tarling, diary notes, 7 October 2005.

(32) Lowell Tarling, diary notes, 12 November 2005.

(33) The Everlasting World of Martin Sharp, p. 25, Ivan Dougherty Gallery 2006.

(34) Martin Sharp, interview 16 January 2011.

(35) 'Eternity finds its home in Redfern', South Sydney Herald, front page, November 2005.

(36) Jim Beloff, The Ukulele, A Visual History, 'Tiny Tim', pp. 70-72, Miller Freeman Books, 1997.

(37) Lowell Tarling, diary notes, 1 January 2006.

(38) Martin Sharp presents "Eternal Troubadour" Tiny Tim, the tracks were: Street of Dreams, Song Without a Name, Wonderful World of Romance, Love You Funny Thing, Memories of France, Satisfaction, I Am I Said. Zero 2006.

(39) Roger Foley, interview 11 February 2014.

(40) David Braithwaite, Sydney Morning Herald, 13 March 2006.

(41) James Phelps, 'Historic Church is lost for all Eternity', Daily Telegraph 10 May 2006.

(42) Geraldine Harris, 'Favourite Things', The Good Weekend, 6 October 2007.

(43) Roslyn Sharp, interview 1 April 2016.

(44) Art & About, 28pp, City of Sydney.

(45) Marianne Faithfull, 'Marianne Faithfull makes full recovery from breast cancer', Daily Mail, 6 November 2006.

(46) Bob Dylan, Chronicles Volume One, pp.11-15, Simon & Schuster, 2004.

(47) Martin Sharp, interview 8 November 2006. Elizabeth Fortescue, 'Now the Truth Behind Oz's Standing Joke', Daily Telegraph, 3 November 2006.

(48) John MacDonald, 'A The Sharp End of Satire', Sydney Morning Herald, 16-17 December 2006. The Everlasting World of Martin Sharp, 30p, Ivan Dougherty Gallery 2006.

## CHAPTER 15

(1) Martin Sharp, interview 6 January 2006.

(2) Spectrum (cover), Sydney Morning Herald, 24-25 October 2009.

(3) See Tiny Tim, Wonderful World of Romance CD and Cinderella illustrated by Arthur Rackman.

(4) The three CDs are: Chameleon, Wonderful World of Romance and Stardust, Zero Communications 2006. Martin Sharp, inside cover lines.

(5) Dave Rowe, interview 8 May 2015.

(6) Gria Shead, interview 19 January 2017.

(7) Luke Scriberras, quoted by Peter Adams, Ore What! p 163, Lettuce Spray Productions 2010.

(8) Gria Shead, interview 19 January 2017.

(9) Roslyn Sharp, interview 1 April 2016.

(10) Judit and Garry Shead, A Creative Collaboration, 48pp, Australian Galleries, 2007.

(11) Kate McClymont, 'Niece Links Saffron to seven deaths', Sydney Morning Herald, 26-27 May 2007.

(12) Kate McClymont, 'King of the X', Sydney Morning Herald, pp. 46-49, The (Sydney) Magazine, June 2007.

(13) Alan Saffron, Gentle Satan, 166pp, Penguin 2008.

(14) Martin Sharp, interview 11 November 1992.

(15) Roslyn Sharp, interview 1 April 2016.

(16) Jenny Diski, 'Whatever happened to Ed Victor', London Review of Books, Vol 17 No 13, 6 July 1995.

(17) Paola Totaro, 'Hippie Hippie Shock: Hollywood deflowers the pioneers of Oz', Sydney Morning Herald, 17-18 November 2007.

(18) Lowell Tarling, diary notes, 20 September 2007.

(19) Barbara McMahon, 'Film to lay bare Greer's hippy days', The Guardian, 1 July 2007.

(20) Paola Totaro, 'Hippie Horror! The wizards of OZ face trial by film', The Age, 17 November 2007.

(21) Philippe Mora, quoted in Paola Totaro, 'Hippie Hippie Shock: Hollywood deflowers the pioneers of Oz', Sydney Morning Herald, 17-18 November 2007.

(22) Martin Sharp, interview 19 March 2005.

(23) Lowell Tarling, diary notes, 2 December 2006.

(24) Helen McGrath and Cris Parker, The Art of Fun, a 45-minute documentary, the Stanton Library and North Sydney Heritage Centre, 2009.

(25) Robert Tilley, Benedict XVI and the Search for Truth, Sydney: St Pauls Pr, 2007.

(26) Nai Vola Tabu Salavata, NFT Parallel Bible, commissioned by Ambassador Sir James Michael Ah Koy, 2009.

(27) Robert Wolfgramm, email 20 May 2017.

(28) Lowell Tarling, diary notes, 8 December 2007.

(29) Street of Dreams, film (as screened by ABC Television).

(30) Lowell Tarling, diary notes, 21 December 2007.

(31) Perry Keyes, interview 9 May 2015.

(32) Clare Burgess, interview 11 July 2015.

(33) Lowell Tarling, diary notes, Thursday 28 October 2008.

(34) Denny Burgess, interview 11 July 2015.

(35) Tony Bond, interview 12 June 2015.

## CHAPTER 16

(1) Martin Sharp, interview 18 May 2013.

(2) Roslyn Sharp, interview 1 April 2016.

(3) Roslyn Sharp, interview 1 April 2016.

(4) Martin Sharp, interview 8 November 2006.

(5) Sharp family document, 423 pp, unpublished 2013.

(6) Martin Sharp, interview 12 February 2011.

(7) Martin Sharp, interview 12 February 2011.

(8) Nigel Featherstone, 'An Icon Reborn', Canberra Times, 5 March 2011. Also, Leigh Bottrell, 'Their Home is where the Art is', Goulburn Post, 29 June 2011.

(9) Jon Lewis, email 14 July 2016.

(10) Martin Sharp, interview 16 January 2011.

(11) Justin Martell and Alanna Wray McDonald, Eternal Troubadour, the Improbable Life of Tiny Tim, pp. 478.

(12) Martin Sharp, interview 16 January 2011.

(13) The Eternity Man, a film by Julien Temple, made for Channel 4 and the Australian Broadcasting Commission, Madman 2008.

(14) Martin Sharp, interview 16 January 2011.

(15) John MacDonald, 'Sydney's Master of Familiarities', Sydney Morning Herald, 6-7 February 2010.

(16) Martin Sharp, interview 8 November 2006.

(17) Footnote.

(18) Lowell Tarling, diary notes, 3 March 2011.

(19) Martin Sharp, interview 8 November 2006.

(20) Michaela Boland, 'Gallery Owner courts new incarnation for his treasures', The Australian, 14 December 2010.

(21) Rachel Kohn, 'The Spiritual Vision of Martin Sharp', 26 December 2010, ABC Radio National.

(22) Tiny Tim, I've Never Seen a Straight Banana CD.

(23) Roslyn Sharp, interview 1 April 2016.

(24) Jim Anderson, interview 12 May 2015.

(25) Dave Rowe, interview 8 May 2115.

(26) Lowell Tarling, diary notes, 2 April 2003.

(27) Lowell Tarling, diary notes, 19 July 2011.

(28) Marius Benson, A Conversation with Margaret Olley, The World Today, ABC Radio, 27 July 2011.

(29) John McDonald, 'The 60th Blake Prize Exhibition', Sydney Morning Herald, 1 October 2011.

(30) Angelica Tremblay, Facebook message, 8 February 2-17.

(31) Lowell Tarling, diary notes, 24 December 2011.

## CHAPTER 17

(1) See Myeloma, Wikipedia.

(2) Roslyn Sharp, email 12 January 2012.

(3) Tim Lewis, interview 2 June 2014.

(4) Roslyn Sharp, 12 January 2012 and interview 1 April 2016.

(5) Mal Ramage, interview 8 February 2016.

(6) Roslyn Sharp, interview 1 April 2016.

(7) Martin Sharp, interview 8 November 2006.

(8) Martin Sharp, interview 18 May 2013.

(9) Honorary Awards, the University of Sydney, http://sydney.edu.au/arms/archives/history/HonSharp.

(10) Roslyn Sharp, email 12 January 2012.

(11) Martin Sharp, notebook entry, February 2012.

(12) Garry Shead, interview 13 February 2015.

(13) Lowell Tarling, diary notes 23 February 2012.
(14) Roslyn Sharp, interview 1 April 2016.
(15) Lowell Tarling, diary notes, 18 May 2012.
(16) Dave Rowe, interview 8 May 2015.
(17) Roslyn Sharp, interview 1 April 2016.
(18) Martin Sharp, interview 18 May 2013.
(19) 'Robert Hughes Made High Art Accessible', The Australian, 7 August 2012.
(20) Tim Lewis, interview 2 June 2014.
(21) Albie Thoms, Foreword, My Generation, 480pp, Media21 Publishing, 2012.
(22) Jeannie Lewis, interview 7 May 2015. James A Michener, The Hokusai Sketchbooks, Charles E. Tuttle, 1959.
(23) 'OZ – Fifty Years Ago, a maverick magazine changed the way we see the world'. Helen Trinca, 'The Sum of OZ', Weekend Australian, 23-24 March 2013. Richard Walsh, 'Wizards of Satire put OZ on the map', The Australian 25 March 2013. 'OZ era's feminist offspring', Helen Trinca, The Australian, 26 March 2013.
(24) Lowell Tarling, diary notes 17 March 2013.
(25) Lowell Tarling, diary notes, 17 April 2013.
(26) Angelica Tremblay, interview 23 April 2013.
(27) Bobbie Hardy, Their Work was Australian, The Story of the Hudson Family, Hudson Family, 1970.
(28) Angelica Tremblay, Lowell Tarling, diary notes July 2013.
(29) Garry Shead, interview 13 February 2015.
(30) Peter Royles, Yellow House Reunion film, 28 July 2013.
(31) The Everlasting World of Martin Sharp, p 15, Ivan Dougherty Gallery 2006.
(32) Roslyn Sharp, interview 1 April 2016.
(33) Damien Minton, May 2013, an invitation to artists to contribute to the Gracelands exhibition.
(34) Denny and Clare Burgess, interview 11 July 2015.
(35) Mic Conway, interview 24 January 2015.
(36) Jeannie Lewis, interview 7 May 2015.
(37) Roslyn Sharp, interview 1 April 2016.
(38) Angelica Tremblay, FB 30 October 2014.
(39) Joni Rush, FB 18 January 2017.
(40) Roslyn Sharp, interview 1 April 2016.
(41) Angelica Tremblay, FB 21 February 2016.
(42) Garry Shead, interview 13 February 2015.

## CHAPTER 18

(1) John Walker, Cross-Overs – Art into Pop, Pop into Art, p.12, Comedia Methuen, 1987.
(2) Louise Hall and Lucy Macken, 'Artist tells school hands off my estate', Sydney Morning Herald, 31 October 2015.

(3) Lex Marinos, interview 25 May 2015.

## BIBLIOGRAPHY

Aiton, Doug & Lane, Terry, The First Century, Information Australia 2000.

Anderson, Jim, Lampoon, Dennis Publishing, 2011.

Anfuso, James, Rockin Australia – 50 Years of Concert Posters 1957-2007, Starman Books, Tuart Hill WA, 2014.

Auction Catalog, called 'Auction Souvenir, Sun/Mon May 31/June 1', 28 pages, printed on a duplicating machine by Geoff K Gray Pty Ltd, 1981.

Baker, Ginger, Hellraiser, John Blake Publishing 2010.

Baker, Glenn A, The Beatles Down Under, Magnum Imprint 1996.

Baldwin, Neil, Man Ray – American Artist, Da Capo Press 2001.

Basquali, M, Catherine: Intimate Portrait of a Champion, Pan Macmillan 2000.

Beloff, Jim, The Ukulele, A Visual History, Miller Freeman Books, 1997.

Bonython, Kym, Modern Australian Painting 1975-1980, Rigby Ltd 1980.

Bourke, Antony, and Rendell, John, A Lion Called Christian, Bantam Press 1971, expanded and updated 2009.

Bruce, Jack, Composing Himself, Jawbone Press, 2010.

Buck, Paul, Performance, A biography of the classic sixties film, Omnibus Press 2012.

Bungey, Darlene, John Olsen, An Artist's Life, ABC Books, 2014.

Catalogue, Luna Park - Fragments of a Funfair, 8p, Historic Houses Trust of New South Wales.

Chamberlain, Michael, with Lowell Tarling, Beyond Azariah, 214pp, Information Australia, 1999.

Child, AC, Cranbrook – The First Fifty Years (1918-1968), Waite & Bull, 1968.

Clapton, Eric, The Autobiography, Century London, 2007.

Coombs, Anne, Sex and Anarchy, The Life and Death of the Sydney Push, Penguin Books 1996.

Dale, John, Huckstepp – A Dangerous Life, Allen & Unwin, 2000.

Dennis, Felix, Lives and Rhymes, Dennis Publishing, 2005.a

De Saint-Exupéry, Antoine, The Little Prince p. 82, Harcourt Inc, 1941.

Draffin, Peter, Pop, Scripts Pty Ltd, 1967.

Drew, Philip, The Masterpiece, Jorn Utzon – A Secret Life, 574pp, Hardie Grant Books, 1999.

Dunstan, Keith, Ratbags, Golden Press 1979.

Dutton, Geoffrey, The Innovators, MacMillan 1986.

Dylan, Bob, Chronicles Volume One, pp.11-15, Simon & Schuster, 2004.

Errico, Angie, author of Rock Album Covers, Octopus 1979.

Everingham, Sam, Madam Lash, Allen & Unwin, 2010, 288 pp.

Foley, Electra, Ginger in Japan, Sceggs Darlinghurst, Year 9 Visual Arts Assignment, 2001.

Fountain, Nigel, Underground – the London Alternative Press 1966-1974, Routledge, 1988.

Goldman, Albert, Elvis, Viking Books, 1981.

Graham, Bill, My Life Inside Rock and Out, Da Capo Press, 1992.

Jonathon Green, Days in the Life – Voices from the English Underground 1961-1971, Heinemann, 1988.

Greer, Germaine, The Female Eunuch, Granada Publishing, 1970.

Hamilton, Maggie, Mister Eternity, 234pp, Scholastic Press, 1997.

Hardy, Bobbie, Their Work Was Australian, The Story of the Hudson Family, Hudson Family, 1970.

Hewison, Robert, Too Much, Art and Society in the Sixties, Oxford University Press, 1987.

J Hillier, Hokusai, Phaidon Press, 1955.

Hilton, Margot and Graeme Blundell, Whiteley, An Unauthorised Life, Pan MacMillan, 1996.

Howell, Georgina, In Vogue, Sixty years of celebrities and fashion from British Vogue, Penguin Books 1975.

Hughes, Robert, Heaven and Hell in Western Art, Weidenfeld & Nicolson, 1968.

Humphries, Barry, Neglected Poems and Other Creatures, Angus & Robertson, 1991.

Carl Jung, Synchronicity – An Acausal Connecting Principle, Routledge and Kegan Paul, 1972.

Kee, Jenny, A Big Life, Penguin 2006.

Kennedy, Brian, A Passion to Oppose, John Anderson, Philosopher, Melbourne University Press 1995.

Khaury, Susan, Memories of My Husband, Tiny Tim, an unpublished manuscript, 1998.

Lanceley, Colin, Colin Lanceley, Craftsman House 1987.

Lawson, Stephen, Martin Sharp Works on Paper, 38 pages, published by Stephen Lawson 2010.

Leary, Timothy, The Politics of Ecstasy, Paladin 1970.

Lewisohn, Mark, The Complete Beatles Recording Sessions, Hamlyn 1988.

Litvinoff, Emmanuel, Journey Through a Small Planet, Penguin, 1972.

Marinos, Lex, Blood and Circuses, An Irresponsible Memoir, Allen & Unwin, 2014.

Marshall, Sam, Luna Park – Just for Fun, Luna Park Reserve Trust, 1995.

Martell Justin, with Alanna Wray McDonald, Eternal Troubadour, the Improbable Life of Tiny Tim, Jawbone Press 2016.

McGregor, Craig, People, Politics and Pop, Ure Smith, 1968.

McNab, Duncan, The Usual Suspect, the Life of Abe Saffron, MacMillan 2005.

Mendelsshon, Joanna, 'The Yellow House, A Brief History', Art and Australia, Winter 1990.

Meyrick, Julian, See How It Runs, Nimrod and the New Wave, Currency Press, 2002.

Michener, James A, The Hokusai Sketchbooks, Charles E. Tuttle, 1959.

Milligan, Peter, Strange Days comic, Eclipse Comics, California, 1984.

Mora, Mirka, Wicked But Virtuous, My Life, Viking, 2000.

Morgan, Joyce, The Life and Times of Martin Sharp, Allen & Unwin 2017.

Muybridge, Eadweard, The Human Figure in Motion, Bonanza Books NY, 1989.

Neville, Richard, Hippie Hippie Shake, Wm Heinemann Australia 1995.

Neville, Richard and Clarke, Julie, The Life and Crimes of Charles Sobhraj, Jonathon Cape Ltd, 1979.

Neville, Richard, Out of my Mind, Penguin Books, 1996.

Neville, Richard, Playing Around, Arrow Books, 1991.

Neville, Richard, Playpower, Jonathon Cape, 1970.

Nordstrom, Ludvig, William Kopson's Diary, 144 pages, translation by GM Lindergren, published by Alb Boniers Boktryckeri, Stockholm, 1933.

O'Connell, Dierdre, The Ballad of Blind Tom, Overlook Duckworth, 2009.

Organ, Michael, Sixties Sharp - the pop & psychedelic art of Martin Sharp, online.

Palmer, Tony, The Trials of Oz, Blond & Briggs, 1971.

Pressley, Alison, Living in the 70s, Random House Australia, 2002.

Rackman, Arthur, Cinderella, p.82, Exeter Books, 1987.

Report on Luna Park Sydney, Australia, 1980.

Rhodes, Zandra, The Art of Zandra Rhodes, Jonathon Cape, 1984.

Rice, Brian & Evans, Tony, The English Sunrise, 80pp, Mathews Miller & Dunbar, 1972.

Roland, Betty, The Eye of the Beholder, Hale & Ironmonger 1984.

Roxon, Lilian, 'Sawdust, Greasepaint , Sideshows & Spruikers', Australia Album, 96p, Sungravure Sydney, 1974.

Scaduto, Anthony, Bob Dylan, Abacus, 1972, p.236, 239.

Sharp, Martin, Art Book, Mathews Miller Dunbar, London 1972.

Sharp, Martin, Cartoons, Scripts Pty Ltd 1966.

Sharp, Martin, Catalog, Reid Books, 1971.

Sharp, Martin, exhibition catalog, The Face of Sydney, 24p, 1984.

Sharp, Martin, 'Notes from the River Caves', Quadrant magazine, February 1977.

Sharp, Martin, Twice Upon A Time, unpublished, 1966.

Shead, Garry and Englert-Shead, Judit, The Mural, The Meaning, NSW TAFE Information Services Division, 47pp, 1985.

Shead, Garry and Englert-Shead, Judit, A Creative Collaboration, 48pp, Australian Galleries, 2007.

Stell, Marion, (editor), Eternity, Stories from the emotional heart of Australia, 124pp, National Museum of Australia, 2001.

Strieber, Louis Whitely, Transformation: The Breakthrough, Beech Tree Books, New York, 1988.

St Leon, Mark, Circus in Australia, Greenhouse Publications 1983.

Stewart, Meg, Margaret Olley, Far From a Still Life, Random House, 2005.

Tabberer, Maggie, Maggie, Allen & Unwin, 1998.

Tarling, Lowell, 1967, This Is It! 214pp, Generation Books 1990.

Thompson, Tom, Growing Up in the 60s, 88pp, Kangaroo Press, 1986.

Thoms, Albie, My Generation, Media21 Publishing, 2012.

Thoms, Albie, Polemics for a New Cinema, 427p, Wild & Woolley, 1978.

Tilley, Robert, Benedict XVI and the Search for Truth, Sydney: St Pauls Pr, 2007.

Tilley, Robert, Funhouse: Luna Park and the Ghost Train Fire: A Secret History, unpublished.

Tiny Tim, Beautiful Thoughts, 1969 JP Torcher.

Townshend, Pete, Who I Am, Harper Collins 2012.

Van Gogh, Vincent, The Complete Letters of Vincent van Gogh, in 3 volumes, Thames & Hudson, 1958.

John Walker, Art Since Pop, Thames and Hudson, 1975.

John Walker, Cross-Overs – Art into Pop, Pop into Art, p.12, Comedia Menthuen, 1987.

Wallace, Christine, Greer – Untamed Shrew, Macmillan 1997.

Ward, Phil, Azaria! What the Jury Were Not Told, 192 pp, published by PCW 1984.

Waterlow, Nick, The Everlasting World of Martin Sharp, 30p, Ivan Dougherty Gallery 2006.

Waterlow, Nick, Larrikins in London, 120pp, CFOA-University of New South Wales, 2003.

Bob Whitaker, Bob, The Unseen Beatles, Conran Octopus 1991.

Whiteley, Brett, Another Way of Looking at Vincent Van Gogh, Richard Griffin Publisher, 1983.

Weight, Greg, a series of 18 b/w Yellow House postcards published by Aggie Read, printed by Southwood Press Sydney, 1971.

Wilmott, Eric, Pemulwuy – The Rainbow Warrior, 310pp, Weldon, 1987.

Yang, William, Starting Again, 122pp, William Heinemann, 1989.

Yang, William, Sydney Diary, James Fraser Publishing, 1984.

The Yellow House 1970-1972, published by Art Gallery of New South Wales, 1990.

# INDEX

## A

*Abalone Diver* – 28, 87, 89, 92, 97, 143, 150-151.
AC/DC – 43, 74.
Acme Framing – 46.
Adams, Phillip – 82, 139, 174.
Adamson, Robert – 97.
Ashton, Will – 73.
Ashton, Wilfreda – 73.
Aims, Pleasure – 13.
Alchemy – 60.
Alice in Wonderland – 33, 57.
Alice Springs – 34, 149.
All My Lovin' – 69.
Allan, Richard – 59.
Allen, Peter – 19.
Alweiss, Jan (Miss Jan) – 47, 69-72.
Anderson, Jim – 18, 119, 129-130, 139, 149, 157, 171.
Anderson, 'Big' Jim – 7, 55.
Anderson, Kevin – 5.
*Anyone for Tennis* – 120.
*Apmira, Art Sale for Land Rights* – 28.
Aquarius Festival – 82.
Arcadia Amusements & Vending – 10, *Are You Lonesome Tonight* – 40, 42, 107.
Armstrong, Gillian – 60.
Alan Arkin – 57.
Art Galaxy – 119-120, 184.
Art Gallery of New South Wales – 20, 55.
*Artoons* – 16, 83.
Attenborough, Richard – 68-69.
*Aussie Blue* – 58, 75, 83, 114.
Australian Amusements – 10, 50.
Australian Film Commission – 16, 24, 32, 46.
*Azaria, What the Jury Wasn't Told* – 47, 50.

## B

Backsliders – 120.
Baffsky, David – 10, 55.
Baikie, Robert – 5.
Baker, Ginger – 138, 145-146, 187.
Barbie (doll) – 33.
Barker, John – 12, 54-55, 68, 161.
Barker, Michael – 11-13.
Barnes, Jimmy – 19.
Barraclough, Nikki – 82.
Barrett, Denis – 34.
Barton, Arthur – 10, 19, 37, 49-50, 89, 94, 141, 158, 188.
Bashir, Marie – 176, 178.
Bass, Tom – 150-151.
*The Beast Within* – 18.
Bechini, Tony – 30, 95.
Belafonte, Harry – 7, 126.
Bell, Cheery – 56.
Bell, John – 18.
Beresford, Bruce – 57, 139.
Best, Blazey – 95-97.
Bianchi, Vittorio – 16.

# B

*The Bible My Mother Left For Me* – 31, 36.
Big O Posters – 135, 138, 140,
Billings, Jonathon – 52, 141, 158.
*Billy Blue* – 16.
Black Room – 83.
Blaxland, Gregory – 33.
Blind Tom – 98.
*Blood Harvest* – 59, 70.
Blush, Edwina – 129.
Bohm, Stephanie – 102.
Bond, Antony (Tony) – 77-81, 83, 86, 161.
Boofhead – 33, 75, 119, 123, 153.
*Bop Til Ya Drop* – 40, 56, 60.
Botica, John – 96-97.
Botticelli, Sandro – 90, 92, 188.
Bourke, Anthony (Ace) – 139, 167.
Boy George – 32.
Boyd, Arthur – 33.
Boyd, Pattie – 50.
Bonzai Room – 83, 98.
Braund, Michael – 18,
Briebauer, Magdalene (Marie) – 84.
*Brighton Cut* (Street of Dreams film) – 67-68. 70, 72, 83, 118, 160.
Brighton International Festival – 66-72, 75, 95.
Broadhurst, Allan – 46, 97, 143.
Broadhurst, Kate – 46.
Brooks, Donnie – 70, 74.
Brown, Peter (Charlie) – 41.
Brown, Rupert – 49.
Browne, Clem – 139.
Bruce, Jack – 138, 145-146.
Bruce, Lenny – 29.
Bryce, Quentin - 176.
Budinger, Vicki (Miss Vicki) – 26.
*The Building of Loona Park* – 19, 37, 89.
Burgess, Clare – 47, 107, 161, 183.
Burgess, Col – 43, 96.
Burgess, Denny – 43, 47, 73-74, 95-96, 105, 107, 161, 183.
Burnett, James 'Bucks' – 32, 69-70, 102, 106-107, 110, 166.
Burns, Tim – 83-84.
Burr, Henry – 116.
Burrows, Sally – 32.
Butel, Elizabeth – 63, 90.

# C

Cammell, Donald – 125.
Campbell, Cressida – 21-23, 57, 75, 97, 128, 131.
Campbell, Laura (Little Nell) – 18, 20,
Capon, Edmund – 77, 86.
Capsis, Paul – 132.
Captain Beefheart – 28.
Captain Matchbox Whoopee Band – 14.
Carey, Gabrielle – 21.
Carroll, Richard – 52, 141, 158.
*Cartoons* – 35.
Cash, Johnny – 7.
Cassab, Judy – 92.
Cassidy, David – 101.
Castanet Club – 42, 78.
*Catalog* – 63, 83, 172.
Cawood, Ian – 47-48.
Cawood, Val – 47-48.
Ceberano, Kate – 71, 144.
Chamberlain, Azaria – 34-35, 44, 46-50, 58, 117, 131, 134, 145.
Chamberlain, Lindy – 34-35, 47-50, 58, 63, 111, 145.
Chamberlain, Michael – 47-49, 58, 88, 111, 131, 178.
*Chameleon* – 23-24, 27, 30, 32, 42, 71, 104, 106, 125-126, 132, 148, 153-154, 160, 166, 172.
Charles, Ray – 28, 65.
Checker, Chubby – 7.
*Circus Animals* – 14.
Circus OZ – 14, 27-28.
Clapton, Conor – 91.
Clapton, Eric – 19, 31, 50, 57, 72, 75, 91, 98, 102, 127, 135, 138-140, 145-146, 148, 154, 186-187.
Clark, Ernie – 106, 110, 132, 148, 166.
Clarke, Julie – 17-18, 21, 37, 47, 94, 182.
Clarke, Rolley – 17-18.
Cloud Room – 83.
Clune, Terry – 183.
Clune, Thelma – 58, 183.
Cobden, Victoria – 12, 21, 35, 75, 91, 111, 178.
Coburn, John – 183.
Coburn, Kristin – 28.
Coburn, Steve – 97.
Cold Chisel – 14, 27-28, 38, 136, 174.
Coleman, Jonathon – 7, 30.

Colombo, Russ – 106.
Comedy Theatre (Melbourne) – 131-133.
*The Complete Letters of Vincent Van Gogh* – 56, 82, 113, 166.
Conway, Janie – 134.
Conway, Jim – 28, 30-31, 134, 138, 184.
Conway, Mic – 14, 27-28, 30-31, 112, 130, 132, 134, 144, 184.
Conway, Tango – 184.
Conyngham, Peter – 29-30.
Cook, Kay – 136, 141, 145.
Coon, Caroline – 139.
Cooper, Melody – 21-23.
Cordeaux, Chris – 18, 31.
Cosmopolitan Hotel – 29-30.
*Country Queen* – 24.
*Couples* – 14.
*Courage My Friend* (painting) – 87, 92, 98.
*Courage My Friend* (song) - 87, 97.
Cowan, Tom – 139.
Cox, Paul – 83.
Craddock, Crash – 7.
*Crafty Old Captain* – 83.
Cramphorn, Rex – 22.
Cranbrook School – 19-20, 40, 56, 65, 89, 102, 141, 144-145, 154, 163, 167, 176, 184-185, 190.
Crittle, John -139.
Crumb, Robert – 89, 171.
Cream – 102, 120, 138-140, 145-146, 154, 186-187.
Crosthwaite, Roger – 30.
Crowe, Russell – 19.

# D

Dale, John – 21.
Dalton, Gabrielle – 18,
*Daily Telegraph* – 30, 54, 122, 150.
Damien Minton Gallery – 181, 183.
*Dancing in the Street* – 24.
Darmody, Stephen – 111, 145, 148, 166, 170, 176.
De Chirico, Giorgio – 116, 151, 183, 188.
De La Vega, Willy – 37, 88, 92-93, 100, 111, 169-170.
*Dead Poets Society* – 57.
Dean, William – 124-125.
*Deep Night* – 24.
Delltones – 40-42, 56, 60.

Dean-Butcher, Peter – 31.
Dennis, Felix – 139, 146-147, 158, 171.
*Diagonally Parked in a Parallel Universe* – 120.
*Dietetic Baby* – 24.
*Dingo* (song) – 28, 44, 134.
Dinsmore, Trevor – 5.
Dire Straits – 60.
*Disraeli Gears* – 120, 140, 146, 170, 172-173, 186-187.
*Do the OZ* – 139.
Dog Trumpet – 103.
*Doll's House* – 70.
Done, Judy – 17.
Done, Ken – 16-17, 88.
Dowd, Leslie – 5, 55.
*Down Under* – 42.
Downes, Harmonie – 115-116, 118, 136, 170.
Draffin, Christabel – 19, 72.
Draffin, Peter – 58, 65, 68, 72.
Dream Museum – 19-21, 33, 41, 51, 57, 72, 89-91, 114, 184, 188-189.
Driscoll, Michael – 60.
*Dr Gachet* – 82, 178.
Droga, Hal – 50.
Drysdale, Russell – 182.
Duggan, Laurie – 56.
Dundas, Kerry – 139.
Dunlop, Weary – 92.
Dunn, Donald (Duck) – 50.
Dunstan, Keith – 122-123.
Dusty, Slim – 14.
Dylan, Bob – 9, 39, 60-61, 92, 102, 137, 150, 162, 186.

# E

Easybeats – 139.
Edols, Mike – 13.
Edgley, Michael – 10,
Elgar, Frank – 79.
Elstrom, Peter – 48.
*Elvis Calling from Heaven* – 39-40.
Emerson, Francesca – 149.
*Emmaus* – 83, 113.
Englert-Shead, Judit – 18, 52, 58, 61, 74, 100, 131, 155.
*Eternity* – 87-88, 91, 107, 118-119, 121-124, 130, 141, 148, 153, 166, 169, 183, 188-189.
Evans, Wendy – 72-73, 111, 116, 131, 138, 145, 160-161, 166.

Evatt, Clive – 22, 32-33, 169.
Evatt, Elizabeth – 32-33, 169.
Evatt, Herbert Vere – 32.
*Eve of Destruction* – 97.
*Extra Dimensions* – 57.

## F

Fabinyi, Martin – 71, 91.
Faithfull, Marianne – 19, 91, 135, 137, 150, 169.
Fasan, Steve – 95.
Fawkner, Dave – 96, 103-104.
Ferrier, Louise – 117, 139, 149, 157, 170.
Ferrier, Noel – 176,
Fields WC – 37.
Fink, Leon – 5.
Fink, Margaret – 37, 47, 130.
*Finks Circus* – 14.
*First No Pinky* – 123.
Firth-Smith, John – 18.
Fisher, Andrew – 139.
Fitzgerald, Sally – 18.
Fitzpatrick, Kate – 43.
Fix-It Bob – 47, 53.
Flamer-Caldera, Nico – 31, 43.
Flamingo Park – 16.
Fogg Capsule – 83.
Foley, Electra – 19, 127.
Foley, Roger (Ellis D Fogg) – 7-8, 19, 45, 58, 79, 81-84, 100, 111, 119, 127, 130, 149, 165.
Ford, Desmond – 49.
Ford, Harrison – 57.
*Forever Miss Dixie* – 31, 36, 74.
*Fragments of a Funfair* – 94-95.
*Free Fall Through Featherless Flight* – 83.
Freels, Larry – 10.
Freeman, Cathy – 124-125.
Freeman, Oliver – 117.
Friends of Luna Park – 9, 10-11, 14, 50, 54, 78, 188.
*Fringe Dwellers* – 57.
*Funhouse* – 114.

## G

Garland, Nicholas – 139.
Gassman, Pierre – 79.
Geldof, Bob – 19.
Gemes, Judy (Juno) – 84, 139.
Geoff K Gray Auctioneer – 10.

George, Sir Arthur – 10, 23.
Geyer, Renee – 50.
Ghost Train – 5, 11-13, 16, 21, 34, 39, 43-44, 46, 48, 51-54, 65, 73, 78, 92, 98, 114, 141, 155, 158, 161, 188.
Giffen, Robyn – 33, 47, 52-53, 105, 130.
Ginger Meggs – 123, 128, 133, 178.
*Ginger Meggs in Japan* – 14, 127.
Ginger Meggs Memorial School of Arts – 82, 183.
*Ginge's Last Stand* – 27.
Girl – 69-70, 102.
Gittoes, Gabrielle (Dalton) – 18, 57.
Gittoes, George – 18-19, 57, 59, 67, 72, 74, 76-79, 82-85, 100, 111, 118, 120, 1128, 133-135, 139, 143, 183.
Gittoes, Joyce – 84.
Gittoes, Naomi – 19.
Giuffré, Remo – 87, 123-124, 189.
Glasheen, Michael (Mick) – 18, 58, 74-75, 79, 83-84, 120, 165.
Glennon, Jim – 111, 145.
Glover, John – 73.
*God Bless Tiny Tim* – 14.
*God Save OZ* – 139.
Godson, Craig – 73, 101, 141.
Godson, Damien – 73, 101, 141.
Godson, Jenny (Poidevin) – 48, 73, 98, 101, 178, 188.
Godson, John – 101, 141.
*Goin' Down* – 41.
Goldman, Albert – 29.
Golding, John Ivor – 38.
Goldstein, Colman – 10, 55.
Goldstein, Harold – 10, 55.
Goofy – 37.
Goold, Bruce – 58, 79, 83-85, 120. 144.
Gordon, Lee – 7.
Grant, Hugh – 98.
Greenough, George – 83.
Greer, Germaine – 17-18, 57, 139.
Gregory-Roberts, John – 63, 176.
Greiner, Nick – 78.
*Growing Up in the 60s* – 64.
Gulpilil, David – 19, 24, 125, 131, 141, 146, 150, 152-153, 159, 165, 173.
Gumbert, Linda – 164-165.
Gumbert, Roland – 164-165.
Gutman, Sandy (Austen Tayshus) – 35, 59, 71, 105, 129, 165.
Gypsy Fire (Emelia) – 92.

# H

Halligan & Wilton (architects) – 19.
Hanrahan, Peter – 139.
Happy Daze – 17-18, 21, 100, 171, 181.
Harbourside Amusements P/L – 10, 26.
Haring, Keith – 19, 47, 162.
Harris, Rolf – 139.
Harrison, George – 136.
Healy, Paul -18, 68, 92.
*Heaven Is My Home* – 13.
Hedges, Noni – 34.
Henderson, Gavin – 66-68.
Hero of Waterloo – 57, 79, 82, 89.
*Highway to Hell* – 43, 59, 72-75, 95-96, 103-104.
Hillier, Joseph – 28.
*Hippie Hippie Shake* (book) – 117, 137, 156.
*Hippy Hippy Shake* (film) – 137, 157-158.
Hobbs, Leigh – 158.
Hockney, David – 139, 146, 162.
Hogarth Galleries – 16, 18, 32, 169.
Hokusai – 28, 87, 89, 92, 97, 119, 153, 177, 181, 189.
*The Hokusai Sketchbooks* – 177, 181.
*Hokusai's Wave* – 119, 153, 189.
Hollander, Bill – 30.
Hollander, Neil – 41-42.
Holman, Jason – 158, 172.
Holmes, Darryl – 14.
Hoodoo Gurus – 96, 102-104.
Hope, Laurence – 139.
Hopkins, Ted – 11, 50, 94.
Howard, Patrick – 53.
*How Great Thou Art* – 38.
Huckstepp, Sallie-Anne – 18, 21, 58.
Hudson, Andrew – 133.
Hughes, Danne Emerson – 139.
Hughes, Danton – 99.
Hughes, David – 101.
Hughes, Robert (Bob) – 18, 57, 99, 139, 147, 180.
Hummingbirds – 77.
Humphries, Barry – 18, 57, 132, 139, 147.

# I

*I Got You Babe* – 28.
*I Saw Mr Presley Tip-toeing Through the Tulips* – 73, 107.
*Ignatz Paints His World* – 14.
*The Illustrated Ape* – 146.
*In The Garden* – 60.
*Incredible Shrinking Exhibition* – 83.
Infinity Room – 83.
Ink Group – 59.
INXS – 32.
International Socialist Congress – 27-28.
Ivan Dougherty Gallery – 44, 46, 49, 139, 151, 183.
*I've Got a Tiger by the Tail* – 90.
*I Wanna Get Crazy With You* – 90.

# J

Jackson, Michael - 32.
Jagger, Mick – 72, 91, 170.
James, Clive – 139.
Jennings, Dare – 59.
Jensen, Peter – 37, 105.
Jensen, Susan – 12, 21, 112.
Jessop, Clytie – 139.
Jesus Adam – 111.
Jesus Christ – 13, 52, 73, 78, 112-115, 127, 138.
Jimmy & the Boys – 16, 37.
John, Elton – 16.
Johnson, Franklin – 83-85.
Johnson, Michael – 52, 141, 158.
Johnson, Stephen – 14.
Jones, Alistair (Al) – 14, 18, 23, 21, 27, 36, 43, 47, 51, 68, 74-75, 88, 129.
Jones, Ignatius – 78, 124, 189.
Judson, Deanne – 68.
Juillet's Restaurant – 8.
*Just For Love* (also the Flower King) – 34, 51.

# K

*Kangaroo* – 97.
Kannis, John -102.
Karet, Marilyn – 13, 18, 21, 38, 43, 47, 51, 56, 58, 62, 68, 98, 100-101, 118, 135, 145, 159, 170, 176.
Karvan, Arthur – 79.
Karvan, Claudia – 19.
Kaspar – 27.
Kazaz, Tom – 105.
Keating, Paul – 101, 124-125.
Kee, Jenny – 17, 99, 111, 124, 139, 157, 180.
Keenan, Haydn – 8, 24, 41, 48, 98.
*Keeping My Troubles to Myself* – 31, 36, 41, 48-49, 132.

Keyes, Perry – 161.
Khaury-Gardner, Sue (Miss Sue) – 106-108, 118, 130, 132.
Khaury, Tillie – 13, 47, 159.
Khaury, Tulip (Stewart) – 108, 132-133, 178.
Kidron, Beeban – 157.
Kincaid, Hilton – 6.
Kinoshita, Satoshi – 104, 106, 126, 148, 153, 166.
Kinselas – 16, 37, 41-42, 132.
Kiss – 12.
Kissler, Anou – 118.
Kingston, Fairlie – 174, 176,
Kingston, Peter (Kingo) – 5, 9, 11, 18, 33, 37, 40, 50, 52, 59, 61, 64, 78-79, 83-85, 92, 94, 100, 120, 128-129, 133, 141, 144, 149, 154-158, 160, 178, 181-183, 186, 188.
*Knockin' On Heaven's Door* – 60.
Kohn, Rachel – 163, 169.
*Kold Komfort Kaffee* – 27, 61.
Kopson, William (great-grandfather) – 40, 100, 182.
*Krazy 4 You* – 14.
Kung, Hans – 114.

# L

Lanceley, Colin – 139.
Lanceley, Kay – 139.
Langton, Linda – 59.
Lascaris, Manoly – 16.
*The Last Mile of the Way* – 31, 33, 36, 74,
Lawrence, DH – 97.
Lawson, Henry – 180.
Lawson, Stephen – 23, 40, 45, 62, 66, 101.
Lawson, William – 33.
*Leave Me Satisfied* – 90.
Lebovic, Josef – 84-85, 171.
Ledeboer, Peter – 135.
Lee, Christopher – 57.
Lennon, John – 32, 136, 139.
Leonard, Roma (Nursy) – 176
Les Bean – 37, 41, 43, 47, 51, 58, 65, 142.
Lette, Kathy – 21, 57.
Leunig, Michael – 67, 97, 99, 141.
Leurella – 32-33, 189.
Lewis, Berwyn – 82.
Lewis, Jeannie – 14, 28, 37, 44, 47, 51, 57, 83, 85, 112, 124, 129, 138, 149, 181, 184.
Lewis, Jon (Jonny) – 8, 11, 18, 22-23, 40, 43, 47, 58-60, 63, 79, 82, 84, 94, 120, 125, 133, 139, 165, 176, 180.
Lewis, Marvin – 69.

Lewis, Tilly – 19, 72, 98.
Lewis, Tim – 9, 14, 18, 20, 40, 47, 58-59, 79, 82, 84-85, 87-89, 93-95, 98, 116, 120, 127, 149, 183, 188.
*The Life and Crimes of Charles Sobhraj* – 17.
Lindsay, Fergus – 43, 46-47, 49, 51.
Liney, Richard – 9, 20-21, 33, 41, 83, 189.
Liney, Sharon – 20-21.
Little, Jimmy – 124-125.
Little Richard – 112.
Litvinoff, David – 8.
Liverpool Biennial Festival of Contemporary Art – 138, 140-142.
Löfvén, Chris – 95, 97.
London, Laurie – 142.
Lowe Chica – 92.
Lourie, David – 83.
Lucas, Bill – 38.
*Luna Images* – 46, 49.
Luna Park – 5-6, 8-14, 18, 22-23, 26-27, 29, 32-35, 37, 39, 42, 44, 46, 49-56, 61, 63, 65-66, 68, 72-73, 78-79. 88, 90-95, 98-99, 101, 105, 114-116, 127, 141, 149, 153, 155, 158, 160, 167-169, 177-179, 182, 185, 188.
Luna Park Amusements – 99.
Luna Park Report – 9-12.
Luna Park Song – 14, 27.
Lydon, John – 101.
Lyon, Nic – 77, 83, 129.

# M

Mabo, Eddie – 124-125.
*Mad Dog Morgan* – 18.
Mad Hatter – 33.
*Mad Max* – 16, 38.
Madonna – 32.
Magritte, René – 62, 79, 82-83, 188.
Mambo – 23, 58-60, 123.
Marinos, Lex – 14, 30, 124, 190.
Marriner Group – 133.
Marshall, Sam – 9-10, 14, 50, 59, 78, 188.
Martell, Justin – 166, 172.
Martin, Charlotte – 146.
Master's Apprentices – 43, 139.
Matthews, Freja – 139.
May, Phil – 126.
McCarthy, Brendan – 51.
McCartney, Paul – 106, 135, 179.
McClean, Don – 39.
McCullough, Chris – 83.

McCreadie, Sky – 19, 47.
McGregor, Craig – 64, 74.
McGregor Screenprints – 23, 40.
McKenzie, Steve – 47.
McNab, Duncan – 6-7.
McPherson, Lennie – 7-8.
Mead, Mal – 53, 55.
Melody Burlesque – 13.
*Memories of My Husband* –118.
Men at Work – 42.
Mendelsson, Joanna – 76, 80, 82.
Mental As Anything – 9, 60, 71, 103.
Michael Nagy Gallery – 84, 119.
Mickey Mouse – 37, 49, 63, 74, 116, 178.
*Mike Walsh Show* – 17.
Miller, Sienna – 157.
Mingella, Max – 157.
Miningerie, Nui – 48.
*Mission Bell* – 70, 105.
Mitchell, Mark – 108, 132.
Modigliani, Amadeo – 92.
Molloy, Mike – 139.
Mombassa, Reg – 19, 103, 144, 165, 184.
Moore, Thomas – 56.
Moorehouse, Frank – 46.
Mora, Philippe – 18, 37, 47, 57, 67, 125, 136, 139, 157-158, 190.
Mora, William – 67.
Morgan, Joyce – 118-119.
Morley, Lewis – 139.
Morse, Isabelle – 47.
Mortimer, John – 139.
Mr Ed – 32, 69.
Murawalla, Black Allen – 124.
Murphy, Cillian – 159.
*My Song* – 24.
*My Way* – 29.
Myriad, Carrl – 134, 142.

# N

*Nation Review* – 17.
Nelson, Joni – 184.
Nelson, Sandra – 8,
Neville, Jill – 117, 139.
Neville, Richard – 13, 17-18, 21-22, 37, 57, 64-65, 91-92, 94, 98, 111-112, 117, 119, 130, 136, 139, 147, 149, 156, 167, 178, 181-182, 187.
New Ensemble Circus – 14.
Nimrod (posters) – 16, 23, 27, 61, 127.

*Nimrod 10* – 27.
Noddy – 33.
*Noive & Voive Records* – 23.
Nolan, Sidney – 139.
North Sydney Swimming Pool – 12.
Nowra, Louis – 14.
Noyce, Phillip – 57.
Nuclear Disarmament Party – 27.

# O

O'Brien, Justin – 40, 58, 61, 100, 145, 173, 180.
O'Dowd, Bernard – 56, 66.
O'Keefe, Johnny – 40.
Olcott Hotel – 32, 47, 103.
Olley, Margaret – 147, 173.
*On the Road to Tarascon* – 88, 92, 98,188.
Ono, Yoko – 139.
Orbison, Roy – 7.
Organ, Michael – 85.
*Outcast* – 51.
Owens, Buck – 90.
Oxley, Ros – 61-62, 65, 70, 74.
*OZ* – 16-17.
*OZ?* (tapestry) – 12, 66, 72, 188.

# P

*Pandemonium* – 48, 98.
Paolozzi, Eduardo – 83.
Parnell, Jim – 31.
Peck, Albert – 18, 21-23, 26, 29.
Pengally, Vivienne – 84.
*Pentecost* – 62, 65, 75, 101, 120, 177, 188.
*Performance* – 92.
Perry, David – 83.
Perry, Richard – 28, 31, 132-133, 190.
*Persecution Games* – 40, 44, 49.
Petty, Bruce – 83, 99.
Phongsittisak, Paiwan – 88-96, 98,
*Piaf* – 14.
Piccolo Bar – 16, 23.
*Picnic at Hanging Rock* – 34, 138.
Pineapple, Johnny – 107.
Pink Bob – 107.
Pinniger, Gretel (Madam Lash) – 8, 16.
Pinter, Harold – 38.
*Playing Around* – 117.
Plym, Stephen – 103, 105-107.
Prince Charles – 37, 117.

Princess Diana – 37, 117.
*Polemics for a New Cinema* – 57.
*The Politics of Ecstasy* – 60.
Pointer Sisters – 28.
Popov, Alex – 47.
Powditch, Peter – 84, 180.
*Poverty Deluxe* – 120.
Pratt, Natalie – 178, 180, 185.
Presley, Elvis – 24, 29, 35, 38-40, 61, 73, 95, 107, 113-114, 138, 151, 179, 183-184, 186.
Prickles – 95-97.
Princess Eugenie – 19.
*Prisoner of Love* – 106.
Prome Investments P/L – 68.
Puppet Theatre – 82-83.
Purves, Stuart – 131.

# R

Rai, Jonathon – 140.
Rahilly, Seamus – 52, 141, 158.
Ramage, Mal – 12,
Ramsden, Michael – 139.
Rawlins, Adrian – 30, 37, 70, 84, 129.
Read, Aggy – 83.
Rebane, Bill – 70.
*Rebel Yell* – 96.
*Refugee* – 40, 183.
Regular Records – 16, 60, 71, 74-75, 103.
Reid, Catherine (Katie), née Sharp – 12.
Reid, Ian – 12, 92, 112.
Reid, Kate – 12, 38, 99, 137-138.
Reid, Rupert – 180.
Reid, Sam – 145.
Reller, Paul – 106.
Renshaw, Anthony (Toto) – 22-23, 38, 47, 50, 52, 58, 74, 111.
Renshaw, Jack – 22.
Rhodes, Zandra – 19, 70, 72.
Rich, Andrew – 59.
Ricketson, James – 58.
Ritchie, Henry Lucas St George – 46.
Ritchie, Stuart (maternal grandfather) – 19-21, 23, 34, 46, 147.
Ritchie, Vega (Vee) née Kopson (maternal grandmother) – 19-20, 40, 57.
Ritchie, William – 46.
Robertson, Geoffrey – 98, 117, 139, 170.
Robson, Karen – 91.
*Rock* – 102, 104,
*Rock Around the Clock* – 42.

*Rocky Horror Show* – 14, 57.
Roeg, Nick – 72, 125.
*Rosemary's Baby* – 32.
Rosen, Robert – 103.
Roslyn Oxley Gallery – 61-62, 65, 70.
Rowe, Alfred (The Great Onzalo) – 70-71.
Rowe, Dave – 27, 61, 70-71, 88-89, 100. 103-104, 106, 126, 139, 175, 179.
Rowe, Marsha – 139.
Royal Albert Hall – 26, 28-29, 31, 135, 142, 145-146, 153.
Royles, Peter – 22, 38-39, 41-43, 47, 50, 55, 57-58, 64-65, 105, 130, 154, 165, 183.
Rubin, Victor – 21, 31.
Ruff, Carol – 149, 185.
Rushdie, Salmon – 18.
Rydell, Bobby – 7.

# S

Saffron, Abe – 6-9, 22, 49, 53, 55, 78, 91, 113, 147, 150, 155-156, 163. 188.
Saffron, Doreen – 7.
Sale, Julia – 83.
Samson, Nicholas – 184.
Sanderson, David – 48, 52, 58, 64, 130.
*Save Luna Park* (poster) -14.
Sciberras, Luke – 92, 119, 128-129, 131, 135, 143, 145, 147, 149, 154, 176, 178.
Seidler, Polly – 91.
*Self Portrait* (painting/Tim) – 94.
Serio, Terry – 77.
*Sgt Pepper's Lonely Hearts Club Band* – 14.
Shakeshaft, Tina – 5.
Sharman, Jimmy – 49, 83.
Sharman, Jim – 49, 83.
Sharp, Alexander (Sandy) – 137-138, 176.
Sharp, Andrew – 23, 57, 156.
Sharp, Dorothy, née Muller (stepmother) – 45, 130-131, 136, 150, 154-155, 163-164, 176.
Sharp, Elizabeth (Bessie) – 45.
Sharp, Henry Ritchie (father) – 20, 37, 45, 56-57, 100, 138, 163.
Sharp, Joan (Jo) née Ritchie (mother) – 20, 24, 37, 43, 45, 51, 62-63, 75, 92, 100, 133, 180.
Sharp, Marcello (Cello) – 118.
Sharp, Phillip – 143.
Sharp, Roslyn – 23, 32, 34, 38, 41, 45, 52, 61, 67-69, 74, 118, 124, 133, 136-138, 142-143, 150, 155-156, 163-164, 170, 173-179, 183-185.

Sharp, Russell – 10, 18-19, 23, 27, 30, 34, 38, 51, 66, 133, 170, 173.
Sharp, William Henry (great-grandfather) – 27, 153.
Shead Garry – 18, 47, 52, 58, 61, 67, 74, 83, 85, 97, 100, 111, 120, 122, 128, 131, 139, 143-144, 155, 165, 170, 178-180, 182.
Shead, Gria – 19, 74, 88, 90, 92-93, 128-129, 154, 174, 176, 178.
Shead, Meryl – 128.
Shearston, Gary – 28, 44, 47-48, 58, 75, 78, 83, 111, 114, 134, 142, 165, 182.
Shepard, Ernie – 53-54.
Shepherd Brad – 96.
*Sideshow in Burlesco* – 27.
*Signal Driver* – 14.
Simmonds, Anita – 34.
Simmonds, Peter – 34.
Simms, Clayton – 47, 53, 74.
Sinatra, Frank – 7.
Singleton, John (Singo) – 16, 26, 30-31, 93, 113.
Skeen, Max – 18.
Skrzynski, Joe – 118-119.
*Slow Train Coming* – 9, 60.
Smart, Geoffrey – 33.
Smedley, David – 88, 93-94.
Smith, Mona – 55.
*Snow Job* – 35, 150.
*So You Want Blood* – 28, 181.
Soapbox Circus – 14.
Solanas, Valerie – 20.
*Song Without A Name* – 24.
*Songs of a Impotent Troubadour* – 106-107, 110, 113.
South Hill Gallery – 165.
Spatt, Maurice – 10.
Speakeasy Club – 146.
Spookyland – 83, 129.
St Barnabas Church – 122, 149.
*St Louis Blues* – 24.
St Mary Magdalene Church – 53, 168.
Stables Theatre – 14.
Stace, Arthur – 87, 121-123, 149, 166, 189.
Stanton, Terry – 94-96, 100, 128, 166.
Starkiewicz, Antionette – 83-85, 120.
Starr, Ringo – 28.
*Stayin' Alive* – 24, 153.
Stein, Hal – 19, 99, 160.
Stein, Sherry – 19, 160.
Stewart, Rod – 28, 133.
Stinson, Gordon – 90.
*Straight Over the Moon* – 114.
*Street of Dreams* (film) – 14, 24, 41, 46, 70, 83, 118.
*Street of Dreams* (song) – 30, 184.
Street of Dreams Productions – 14, 23, 27, 30, 46, 72.
Stone Room – 80, 83-84.
Storrier, Tim – 33.
*Strange Days* – 51, 53.
Strauss, Lucinda – 41.
Stewart, Douglas – 122.
Suitch, Max – 53.
Sweeten, Jimmy – 8.
Sweet Art – 96.
*Sydney Diary* – 39.
Sydney Festival – 17.
Sydney Opera House – 9, 29-31, 44, 49, 61, 66, 101, 105, 118-119, 132, 145, 149, 160, 189.
Sydney Textile Museum – 40.
Sylvia & the Synthetics – 16.

# T

Tabberer, Maggie – 19.
*Tales of Brave Ulysses* – 30, 84, 95, 102, 118, 120, 127, 146, 153-154, 161.
Tarling, Amber (McKenzie) – 19, 92, 95.
Tarling, Joel – 87, 89, 111.
Tarling, Zoë (Lake) – 19.
*Tears of Steel & the Clowning Calaveras* – 44.
Teather, Steven – 21-22.
Telford – 133-134.
Temple, Julien – 123, 166.
Thiering, Barbara – 73.
Thompson, Jack – 19, 125, 159, 166.
Thompson, Peter (Pilot Pete) – 47, 52-53, 105, 130.
Thompson, Tom – 40, 63-64, 90, 97, 100.
Thoms, Albie – 18, 57-58, 74, 79-80.
Thornton, Harold (the Kangaroo) – 47, 51, 59, 81, 142.
*Those Were the Days* – 120.
*Thriller* – 32.
*Throb* – 43.
Tibet, David – 106-107, 110, 113, 132.
Tilley, Robert – 110, 114-115, 131, 135, 145, 154, 158, 160, 170.
Tintin – 33.
*Tiny Bubbles* – 24.

Tiny Tim (Herbert Khaury) – 9, 13-14, 16, 19-20, 23-33, 36-38, 40-44, 47-50, 59-61, 64, 66-75, 79, 84, 88-91, 94-99, 102-116, 118, 122, 125-127, 130-127, 130-133, 135, 138, 142-145, 147-148, 150-151, 153-154, 159-161, 165-167, 169-170, 172, 175, 177-179, 183-185, 188-190.
*Tiny Tim's Christmas Album* – 104-105, 108, 110, 112-114, 132,
*Tiny Tim's Second Album* – 28, 184.
*Tiny Tim Times* – 101.
*Tiptoe Through the Tulips* – 26, 43, 69, 74, 102-103, 106, 108, 150.
Togima Leasing P/L – 8.
Toohey, Brian – 53.
Tom Petty & the Heartbreakers – 60.
Townshend, Pete – 58.
Treasure, Brian – 10.
Trella, Bernadette – 98, 133.
Tremblay, Angelica (Frances Greening) – 105, 107, 111, 114, 154, 161, 173-178, 180-182, 184-185.
Tsai, Yensoon – 39, 41, 43, 47, 50-52, 58, 62, 64, 72, 75, 111.
Tunnicliffe, Wayne – 161-162.
Turquoise, Maureen – 40.

# U

Uluru (Ayers Rock) – 34, 66, 117.
Utzon, Jan – 118, 149.
Utzon, Jorn – 44, 49, 101, 105, 118-119, 149, 189.
Utzon, Lin – 19, 44, 57, 59, 101, 105, 118, 130, 135, 145, 149, 175, 178-179.
Utzon, Mika – 130, 178.

# V

Vallee, Rudy – 14.
Van Gogh, Vincent – 35, 37, 44, 56, 62, 64, 78, 82-85, 98, 113, 118-119, 148, 166, 178, 185, 188, 190.
*Vaude Villians* – 28.
Vehka Aho, Eija – 75, 135.
*Venetian Twins* – 27.
*Vincent van Gogh* (collage) – 35, 37, 44, 82.
*Visions* – 14.
*Vizard* – 78, 95.
The Volares – 110.

# W

Waks, Candice – 68.
Waks, Nathan – 18, 30, 68-69, 133.
Walker, Kath (Oodgeroo Nunnuccal) – 28.
Walken, Christopher – 57.
Walsh, Maggie – 152-153, 178, 181.
Walsh, Richard (Richie) – 17, 51, 57, 112, 139, 147, 181, 187.
Ward, Phil – 47-50, 63.
Warhol, Andy – 20, 61, 162.
Waterlow, Nick – 139, 151, 167.
Waverley College – 52, 158.
Weekes, Trevor – 51.
Weight, Alex – 19.
Weight, Greg – 11, 18-19, 58, 74, 77-80, 82-85, 88, 94, 98, 111, 116, 120, 128, 133, 138, 143-144, 149, 165, 173, 178, 184-185.
Weight, Minyo – 19, 92, 95.
Weight, Osha – 19.
Weight, Richard (Dicky) – 79, 98, 120, 165.
Weight, Suzie (née Cuthbert) – 19, 58, 88.
Weir, Peter – 57, 83.
*We'll Meet Again* – 69.
Wentworth, William Charles – 33.
Whalley, Jason – 84.
Whitaker, Robert (Bob) – 139, 173, 186-187.
White, Patrick – 14, 16, 49-50, 88.
Whiteley, Arkie – 19,129.
Whiteley, Brett – 16, 18, 26, 31, 33, 50, 58, 60-61, 67, 77, 79, 82-85, 94, 97-98, 116, 119-120, 139.
Whiteley, Wendy – 50, 97, 139.
Whitlam, Gough – 27, 181.
Whittingslow Amusement Group – 99.
Wilkinson, Michael – 131-133.
Williams, Robin – 57.
Wilson, Carla – 47, 60.
Wilson, Peewee – 40, 47, 56, 60.
*Wind in the Willows* – 14.
Winmatti, Nipper – 48.
Wirian, 3 Victoria Road, Bellevue Hill – 8, 10-12, 16, 18-21, 23-24, 29, 31-32, 38-44, 46-54, 57-59, 61, 64-66, 68, 71-72, 74-75, 79, 82, 88-95, 97-98, 100-102, 104, 110-111, 114-116, 118-119, 124-125, 127-128, 130-131, 133-134, 136-138, 143-144, 152-155, 158-160, 170-171, 173, 176-178, 180, 184-185, 190.
Wolfgramm, Robert – 40, 44, 47, 49, 111, 113-114, 158-159.

*Wonderful World of Romance* – 27, 42, 132, 153, 166.
Woodward, Claude – 96.
World Non-Stop Singing Marathon – 69.
Wran, Jill (Hickson) – 44, 167.
Wran, Neville – 10, 112, 167.
Wran Marcia, Wran – 10.
Wright, Mandy – 154.
Wright, Peter – 8, 77, 83-85, 119-120, 129, 154, 183.

# Y

Yang, William – 18, 21, 23-24, 28, 32, 36, 38-39, 43, 50-52, 58, 63, 75, 160, 165.
Yellow House – 7-8, 12, 16-18, 30, 33, 41, 50, 63, 67, 91-92, 98, 112, 119, 129, 134-136, 141, 147, 165, 170, 172, 180, 182-183, 189.
Yellow House Retrospective (AGNSW) – 72, 74, 76-88.
*Young Mo* – 27.

# Z

Zappa, Frank - 104.
Zero Communications – 126, 148, 153, 166.

www.ingramcontent.com/pod-product-compliance
Lightning Source LLC
Chambersburg PA
CBHW032040150426
43194CB00006B/357